Olympiodorus

Life of Plato

and

On Plato
First Alcibiades 1–9

Ancient Commentators on Aristotle

GENERAL EDITORS: Richard Sorabji, Honorary Fellow, Wolfson College, University of Oxford, and Emeritus Professor, King's College London, UK; and Michael Griffin, Assistant Professor, Department of Philosophy, University of British Columbia, Canada.

This prestigious series translates the extant ancient Greek philosophical commentaries on Aristotle. Written mostly between 200 and 600 AD, the works represent the classroom teaching of the Aristotelian and Neoplatonic schools in a crucial period during which pagan and Christian thought were reacting to each other. The translation in each volume is accompanied by an introduction, comprehensive commentary notes, bibliography, glossary of translated terms and a subject index. Making these key philosophical works accessible to the modern scholar, this series fills an important gap in the history of European thought.

Olympiodorus

Life of Plato

and

On Plato
First Alcibiades 1–9

Translated by Michael Griffin

Bloomsbury Academic
An imprint of Bloomsbury Publishing Plc

B L O O M S B U R Y
LONDON · OXFORD · NEW YORK · NEW DELHI · SYDNEY

Bloomsbury Academic

An imprint of Bloomsbury Publishing Plc

50 Bedford Square
London
WC1B 3DP
UK

1385 Broadway
New York
NY 10018
USA

www.bloomsbury.com

BLOOMSBURY and the Diana logo are trademarks of Bloomsbury Publishing Plc

First published 2015
Paperback edition first published 2016

British Library Cataloguing-in-Publication Data
A catalogue record for this book is available from the British Library.

ISBN: HB: 978-1-47258-830-2
PB: 978-1-47429-564-2
ePDF: 978-1-47258-832-6
ePub: 978-1-47258-831-9

Library of Congress Cataloging-in-Publication Data
A catalog record for this book is available from the Library of Congress.

Acknowledgements
The present translations have been made possible by generous and imaginative funding from
the following sources: the National Endowment for the Humanities, Division of Research
Programs, an independent federal agency of the USA; the Leverhulme Trust; the British
Academy; the Jowett Copyright Trustees; the Royal Society (UK); Centro Internazionale A.
Beltrame di Storia dello Spazio e del Tempo (Padua); Mario Mignucci; Liverpool University; the
Leventis Foundation; the Arts and Humanities Research Council; Gresham College; the
Esmée Fairbairn Charitable Trust; the Henry Brown Trust; Mr and Mrs N. Egon; the
Netherlands Organisation for Scientific Research (NWO/GW); the Ashdown Trust; the Lorne
Thyssen Research Fund for Ancient World Topics at Wolfson College, Oxford; Dr Victoria
Solomonides, the Cultural Attaché of the Greek Embassy in London; and the Social Sciences
and Humanities Research Council of Canada. The editors wish to thank Harry Edinger, Anne
Hewitt, Mossman Roueché, Michael Share and Carlos Steel for their comments; Alice Reid,
Commissioning Editor at Bloomsbury Academic, for her diligence in seeing each volume of
the series to press; and Deborah Blake, who has carefully read every volume since the first.

Series: Ancient Commentators on Aristotle

Typeset by RefineCatch Limited, Bungay, Suffolk

Contents

Preface

This translation has been long in the making. Alongside the generous funders and editors acknowledged above, I would like to extend my gratitude to Richard Sorabji for his encouragement to proceed with the project and his tireless and constructive criticism along the way; to the project's readers for their remarkably careful commentary and creative suggestions, and for saving me from many errors; to Mossman Roueché and Gyburg Uhlmann for valuable comments on the Introduction; to Harold Tarrant and François Renaud for thoughtful remarks and suggestions that improved the text in several places; and to Annie Hewitt for her characteristically diligent editing of the Introduction, First Lecture and Bibliography. I am also grateful to Ryan Fowler and de Gruyter Press for permission to reprint, in the Introduction, portions of my chapter 'Pliable Platonism? Olympiodorus and the Profession of Philosophy in Sixth-Century Alexandria', in R.C. Fowler (ed.), *Plato in the Third Sophistic* (Berlin: de Gruyter, 2014), 73–101. Finally, I am glad to register a special debt of gratitude to Robert Todd, under whose kind and patient supervision I ventured to translate my first pages of Olympiodorus during my last undergraduate year at the University of British Columbia, and to Tobias Reinhardt and Michael Frede, under whose guidance at the University of Oxford I developed early drafts of the first lectures and Introduction. The volume's remaining defects, of course, remain entirely my own responsibility.

I am grateful to George Boys-Stones and Topher Kurfess for suggesting a number of helpful corrections, several of which I have been able to introduce in the Print on Demand edition.

M.J.G.

Conventions

[. . .] Square brackets enclose words or phrases that have been added to the translation for purposes of clarity.

<. . .> Angle brackets enclose conjectures to the Greek and Latin text, i.e. additions to the transmitted text deriving from parallel sources and editorial conjecture, and transposition of words and phrases. Accompanying notes provide further details.

(. . .) Round brackets, besides being used for ordinary parentheses, contain transliterated Greek words.

Abbreviations

Alc. = Plato *First Alcibiades*

Anon. Prol. = L.G. Westerink, *Anonymous Prolegomena to Platonic Philosophy*. Amsterdam: North-Holland Publishing Co., 1962; reprinted Westbury: Prometheus Trust, 2010

DL = Diogenes Laertius

El. Theol. = E.R. Dodds, *Proclus: The Elements of Theology*, 2nd edn. Oxford: Clarendon Press, 1963

Enn. = Plotinus *Enneads*

Herm. = Hermias

in Alc. = *Commentary on the Alcibiades*

in Gorg. = *Commentary on the Gorgias*

LS = A.A. Long and D.N. Sedley, *The Hellenistic Philosophers*, 2 vols. Cambridge: Cambridge University Press, 1987

LSJ = H.G. Liddell and R. Scott, *A Greek-English Lexicon*, 9th edn. Oxford: Clarendon Press, 1966

Olymp. = Olympiodorus

Plot. = Plotinus

Proleg. Log. = Olympiodorus, *Prolegomena to Aristotelian Logic*

Sorabji 2005 = R.R.K. Sorabji, *The Philosophy of the Commentators 200–600 AD. A Sourcebook*, vol. 1: *Psychology (With Ethics and Religion)*; vol. 2: *Physics*; vol. 3: *Logic and Metaphysics*. Ithaca: Cornell University Press, 2005 [first published London: Duckworth, 2004]

SVF = H.F.A. von Arnim, *Stoicorum Veterum Fragmenta*, 4 vols. Stuttgart: Teubner, 1964

For all other ancient works standard abbreviations are used.

The chapter and line number references for Olympiodorus *On the Gorgias* follow the edition of Westerink (1970). Those for Olympiodorus *On the Phaedo* follow the edition of Westerink (1976).

Introduction

1. Olympiodorus in his world

1.1. Overview

> By the beginning of the sixth century, no philosopher of the old religion could have any illusions about the world in which he now lived. Plato's meditations on the role of the philosopher in a 'corrupt city' seemed to speak, only too well, of the non-Christian philosopher's role in his own times.
>
> (Peter Brown, *Power and Persuasion*)[1]

> So too if they accuse me, asking why I am teaching the youth, will they ever be persuaded that I do this in their interests, in order that they may become men of true quality (*kaloi k'agathoi*)? So under such a constitution, one must create a fortress (*teikhion*) for oneself, and live quietly (*hêsukhazein*) within it all the time.
>
> (Olympiodorus, *Lectures on Plato's Gorgias* 45.2,32–6)[2]

Olympiodorus the Younger (c. 500–570 AD),[3] perhaps the last pagan to profess philosophy from the public chair at Alexandria, offered this autobiographical reflection to his students early in his career, during a series of lectures on Plato's *Gorgias*.[4] He caught his own reflection in the character of Socrates, a philosophical educator who risked being haled into court and put to death by a hostile state (*Gorgias* 522C–D; cf. Olymp. *in Gorg.* 1.6, 45.2). Socrates was unfazed by this danger, 'for no one with even a little reason and courage is afraid to die; doing what's unjust is what he fears' (522E), and a good man cannot really be harmed by injustice, a Socratic paradox that Olympiodorus himself warmly endorses (*in Gorg.* 45.2).[5] But in his own life, perhaps bearing in mind the violent unrest of the past century, Olympiodorus does not advocate ideological martyrdom.[6] He favours the quiet pragmatism of *Republic* 6

(496C–E): under a hostile constitution, the philosopher's best choice is to build a 'fortress' or wall (*dei . . . teikhion heautôi poiein*) and to dwell in peace behind it, drawing little attention and causing less trouble.[7]

The context of the *Republic* passage, also uttered by Socrates, draws out the force of Olympiodorus' allusion:[8]

> The members of this small group have tasted how sweet and blessed a possession philosophy is, and at the same time they've also seen the madness of the majority (*tôn pollôn*) and realised . . . that there is no ally with whom they might go to the aid of justice and survive, that instead they'd perish before they could profit either their city or their friends and be useless both to themselves and to others, just like a man who has fallen among wild animals and is neither willing to join them in doing injustice nor sufficiently strong to oppose the general savagery alone. . . . Taking all this into account, they lead a quiet life (*hêsukhian ekhôn*) and do their own work. Thus, like someone who takes refuge under a little wall (*teikhion*) from a storm of dust or hail driven by the wind, the philosopher . . . is satisfied if he can somehow lead his present life free from injustice and impious acts and depart from it with good hope, blameless and content.
>
> (*Republic* 6, 496C–E, tr. Grube, rev. Reeve, in Cooper and Hutchinson 1997)

The juxtaposition of Olympiodorus' unconcealed paganism with his flourishing teaching career marks him out as an interesting figure for study at the intersection of traditional *paideia* and Christianity in the twilight of late antiquity. Who are 'they', the counterparts of Socrates' hypothesised accusers (*emou ean katêgorêsôsi*, in *Gorg.* 45.2,32–3), on account of whose suspicions he saw fit to emulate the philosophers of *Republic* 6 and retreat to a *teikhion*? The turbulent social and political backdrop of his career offers some context: as a public intellectual committed to the value of Platonic philosophy and traditional Hellenic piety,[9] the young Olympiodorus lived to see the closure of the Platonic Academy in Athens, the exile of his Athenian peers Simplicius (*c.* 490–560 AD) and Damascius (*c.* 462–after 532 AD)[10] and the confiscation of their property (cf. *in Alc.* 141,1–3), and the implementation of 'a machinery . . . to wipe out paganism on a broad scale' across the empire (cf. *Codex Justinianus* 1.11.9–10), including legislation under which pagans could be tried and executed (cf. Wildberg 2005, 332). (In late antiquity, the atmosphere of the Neoplatonic academic communities combined intellectual and religious traits; on this atmosphere, see for example Hoffman 2012, esp. 597–601, Festugière 1966, and Saffrey 1984.)

Olympiodorus' 'fortress', perhaps, rested on the honour of his profession[11] and the uneasy foundations of the agreement, whatever it had been, that his predecessor Ammonius (*c*. 435/45–517/26) had struck with the Bishop of Alexandria.[12] Nevertheless, the surviving records from Olympiodorus' lifetime of lecturing suggest no hostility or frustration.[13] He did not withdraw from the philosophical positions that typified later ancient Platonism, nor did he target Christian doctrines for refutation. Instead, his (predominantly Christian) students encountered a wholesale defender of the webwork of Hellenic *paideia*,[14] who professed traditionally pagan views about contentious philosophical topics including the eternity of the natural world, the reverence of stone images, the transmigration of souls, the nature of *daimônes*, and even the virtue of ritual theurgy,[15] while carefully making room for the confessional comforts of his classroom.

1.2. Olympiodorus and Christianity[16]

Olympiodorus is careful to strike a conciliatory tone where the 'popular doctrine' (*sunêtheia*) of Christianity is concerned. One often-cited example occurs in his lectures on the *First Alcibiades* (hereafter *Alcibiades* or *Alc.*).[17] Here, Olympiodorus usually follows the magisterial commentary of Proclus of Athens (412–485 AD).[18] Proclus had remarked (*in Alc.* 264,5–6) that general social consensus is not always a guide to truth, and he had cited as evidence the fact that people 'in the present age' agree that the gods do not exist (an apparent reference to the prevalence of Christianity). Olympiodorus' commentary adopts the remark, but substitutes 'Democriteans' for the offending party (92,4–9).

But it was especially Olympiodorus' *manner* of accommodating Christianity that led Westerink to attribute to him 'a pliability so extreme indeed that it might be more correct to speak of a teaching routine than a philosophy'.[19] It has appeared to some commentators that his willingness to accommodate other viewpoints might lead to an impossibly pliant and so incoherent philosophy, a 'toothless Platonism' (for discussion, see Wildberg 2005, 321).

Several passages from the lectures on Plato's *Gorgias* and *Alcibiades* have been cited to illustrate Olympiodorus' 'pliable' approach to Christianity:

- When Olympiodorus comments on Socrates' oath 'by Hera' at *Gorgias* 449D, he excuses Plato's reference to the pagan god with the remark that 'we should not understand things spoken in mythical mode in their surface meaning', stressing that the name 'Hera' really signifies the rational soul (*in Gorg.* 4.3). 'We too know', Olympiodorus continues, 'that there is the one first cause, namely God, and not many . . . '. The group with which Olympiodorus identifies himself in the first person plural are evidently monotheists.

- The same thought is elaborated in a later lecture, as Olympiodorus begins to comment on the *Gorgias* myth (*in Gorg.* Lecture 47, beginning at 523A). The poets speak of many gods in a 'mythical mode', concealing the consensus of 'the philosophers' that there is a 'single starting-point of all things and a single transcendent cause that is first of all' (*in Gorg.* 47.1; thus the subject of the first person plural in 4.3 above was presumably also 'the philosophers' cited here). Further, Olympiodorus enjoins his students not to be 'disturbed by names', hearing talk of a Power of Cronus or a Power of Zeus (47.2): the mythical use of names for many gods can be said to answer in reality to the powers or capacities of one God. For example, Kronos is really *koros-nous*, the power of pure veridical awareness or 'intellect' (*nous*) (47.3; cf. *Cratylus* 395E), and *Zên* and *Zeus* can refer to the power of life (47.5).

- Continuing with this theme, Olympiodorus asks his students not to believe that 'philosophers honour representations in stone as divine' (47.5). Much as mythical and poetic names for gods (which may appear to be at odds with Christian doctrine) represent deeper philosophical truths (which turn out to be in keeping with Christian doctrine), representations of gods in stone serve 'as a reminder' of bodiless and immaterial 'powers', reflecting Olympiodorus' earlier comment that different gods could be viewed as 'powers' of the one God.

- In commenting on Socrates' discussion of the 'daimon'[20] that has prevented him from conversing with Alcibiades (*Alcibiades* 103A5), Olympiodorus embarks on a detailed excursus into the theory of daimons and their ranks and functions (translated in this volume). This may look like thin ice, given the contemporary pejorative view of daimons in Christianity, but he handles it deftly, announcing that the individual's allotted daimon really means an individual's conscience or *suneidos* (23).[21] He then explicitly tackles the challenge by stressing that in 'the common custom' (*sunêtheia*) – a familiar way of talking about the prevailing Christian usage[22] – daimons are spoken of as 'angels' and experienced by priests (21): in fact, *Plato* would have called them 'angels' if he had adopted a different (Chaldaean) division of the realm in between gods and the sublunar realm. Thus, once again, we are dealing here simply with a superficial difference of names that conceals a substantial agreement.

As Harold Tarrant has pointed out,[23] the 'pliability' that has been attributed to Olympiodorus in his relationship to Christianity should be viewed in the broader light of his philosophy as a whole. In all these cases, Olympiodorus' treatment of names and myths is not confined to a response to Christianity. In Olympiodorus' view, all myths are falsehoods picturing the truth, as we will see below.[24] His contemporary society, however, 'respects only what is apparent, and does not search at all for what is concealed in the depths of the myth' (*in Gorg.* 46.4). In general, his entire treatment of the dialogue form is indebted to the exegetical principle that the characters are symbolic (*in Gorg.*, Proem; *in Alc.*); as he puts it elsewhere (34.4) the 'actual truth' which the philosophers pursue in a myth is the *epimuthion*, the moral of the story. It is highly characteristic of Olympiodorus to suggest that superficial disagreement on the level of 'names' overlies deeper and genuine agreement on the level of reality.

I argue below (§2.1) that Olympiodorus strives to construct a distinctive identity for himself as a 'philosopher' distinguished both from the uneducated majority (*hoi polloi*) and from the diverse pedagogues and skilled experts who share his goal of improving the young (especially poets, grammarians, and rhetoricians). He frames all non-philosophers as engaged in the study of 'appearances' (*phainomena*) or myths, and thereby liable to doctrinal disagreement and dispute, whereas genuine philosophers drill down to the real, psychological meaning of myth and doctrine, and therefore rarely disagree. The opinions of the majority (*hoi polloi*) and other craft experts can be reconciled with each other by philosophers, who are mediators *par excellence*. Within this framework, Christian doctrine is generally synonymous with the view of the majority, and is treated by Olympiodorus as a myth that will agree with Homeric or Platonic myths *as long as it is not taken literally*. It is not because it is Christian doctrine that Olympiodorus 'accommodates' Christian language, but because it is the view of the majority, and therefore where he must begin his instruction. From this point of view, there is nothing fundamentally *new* in Olympiodorus' approach to Christianity, in that (on his view) philosophers have *always* needed to adopt this conciliatory approach toward the majority. Olympiodorus can still regard himself as operating within a timeless tradition of Hellenism.

Olympiodorus treats the language of Christian doctrine, when it is mentioned, as if it belongs to the exegetical 'level' of myth or *phantasia*. Like any myth, however, it is not simply false: it refers to real facts within the human soul or psyche (*psukhê*). We may speak of Hera, or a certain 'power' of the Christian God, but in either case the philosopher will recognise that what is *meant* is a certain capacity of the soul. We may speak of daimons or angels, but in both cases we are genuinely referring to human conscience. The overt language used, whether pagan or Christian, lies at the level of *phainomena* or appearances. Thus Olympiodorus is able to represent 'philosophy' as a more fundamental framework that can accommodate various mythological systems and worldviews and facilitate their agreement.[25]

Olympiodorus' treatment raises the interesting question of whether he would regard the Christian 'myths' as poetic or philosophical. Would the Christian 'myth' be acceptable and harmless at the 'exoteric' or literal layer (like Plato's philosophical myths), or socially dangerous? Olympidorus may have leaned toward the former view, at least where morality is concerned: Olympiodorus appears to treat Christian doctrine as harmonious with the 'common notions' (as Tarrant 1997, 189–91 points out): that 'God is good' and worthy of honour or that parents are worthy of respect (*in Gorg.* 41.2), for example, appear to be points of common ground between Christianity and traditional Hellenic piety. On the other hand, Olympiodorus clearly rejects certain ideas that were popular in the Christianity of his day (such as the idea of eternal punishment, as well as the temporal beginning and end of the world).

Olympiodorus' impression of 'extreme pliability' arises from his manner of accommodating nearly every non-philosophical sphere of expertise at the level of 'imagination'. Only genuine philosophers *could* disagree about the facts, since other experts debate only *representations* of the facts. But genuine philosophers, by merit of their access to the facts, are unlikely to disagree. When they appear to disagree it is the exegete's task to determine whether the disagreement is on the level of appearance (*phainomena*) or of reality (*pragmata*).[26]

Olympiodorus assumes that his students are familiar with the general curriculum of the later Mediterranean educated gentleman, including the oeuvre of Homer and Attic poetry and the schools of the grammarian and the rhetorician; he also assumes that true education (*paideia*) necessarily leads to virtue or excellence of character (*aretê*), and regards the function of *paideia* in the Hellenic tradition as the instillation of such excellence. He regards his project as contiguous with the truly 'philosophical' movements of the past, and able to give explanatory continuity to the 'sophistics' of the past and the present. He makes special claims for his own discipline of philosophy as able to bestow the fundamentals of the 'good life' in a way that other areas of expertise cannot.

2. Human excellence and the *First Alcibiades* in later Neoplatonism

2.1. The excellences (*aretai*) of the ideal philosopher

Olympiodorus, then, refers to himself as a philosopher (*philosophos*) and occasionally as an interpreter or commentator (*exêgêtês*). He begins lectures by praising the power of philosophy to improve the life of his students:

> Since we wish to enjoy the fountain of goods, we hurry to lay hold of Aristotle's philosophy, which furnishes life with the source of good things . . .
>
> (*Proleg. Log.* 1,3–4)

> [A]ll human beings reach out for Plato's philosophy, because all people wish to draw benefit from it; they are eager to be enchanted by its fountain, and to quench their thirst with Plato's inspirations.
>
> (*in Alc.* 1,6–7)[27]

The philosopher's profession is 'to make good people': again, for Olympiodorus, the philosopher is the only expert who can validly make this claim, and so philosophy is set apart from rhetoric, medicine, and other skills that merely reproduce themselves (*in Alc.* 140,18–22). Philosophy targets the young, who may be 'turned' or 'reverted' toward a happier way of life (*in Gorg.* 1.6), as Olympiodorus hopes for his own students to become excellent human beings (*kaloi k'agathoi*,[28] *in Gorg.* 45.2). To live well – to be *spoudaios* (*in Alc.* 229,5–6) or *khrêstos* – just is to live the 'philosophic life' (*emphilosophôs zôntas, in Gorg.* 0.1). Like ancient rhetoricians and purveyors of *paideia*, Olympiodorus promises that the study of his subject will cultivate and realise individual excellence (*aretê*).[29]

We have found Olympiodorus envisaging himself as a philosopher operating in an environment comprised of two broad groups: ordinary people (*hoi polloi*), and the educated class (*pepaideumenoi*) that includes teachers and practitioners of grammar, rhetoric, medicine, and poetry (cf. *in Alc.* 95,17). Following traditional definitions, Olympiodorus envisages philosophy as the master craft (*tekhnê tekhnôn*) among these areas of expertise (*in Alc.* 87,10 and 65,8). Here, I begin by exploring Olympiodorus' construction of 'philosophy' as a category, and then look into his methods of differentiating himself, and his discipline, both from the majority of ordinary people (*hoi polloi*) and from other arenas of intellectual activity and *paideia*; this will help us to contextualise the function that he would assign to his lectures on the *Alcibiades*.

Olympiodorus builds on definitions of philosophy that had become standard by Ammonius' time. Philosophy, like any craft, might be defined by its *subject* and its *goal* (Ammonius *in Isag.* 2,22–9,7). Philosophy addresses itself to the well-being of persons, who are, in the strictest sense, their soul or psyche (*psukhê*) alone. The subject of philosophy is the soul, and its goal is to achieve the Good of the soul (Olymp. *Proleg. Log.* 1,4–20; *in Alc.* 1,6–7, 2,13), which is 'likeness to God, as far as human ability allows' (*Proleg. Log.* 16,25, echoing the famous phrase of Plato's *Theaetetus* 176B).

How does Olympiodorus' craft strive for this goal? Olympiodorus suggests that the philosopher is an imitator of God (*in Phaed.* 1.2,6). First, he resembles God as a contemplator of the truth (cf. *in Gorg.* 25.1), one who knows beings in themselves (*onta hêi onta: in Alc.* 25,2, 175,17–178,6) and nature as a whole (*phusis, in Cat.* 138,15, *in Alc.* 2,94). This knowledge resembles divine pleasure (*in Gorg.* 26,15). Second, as a statesman or civic agent (*politikos*), he acts providentially for the best organisation of his inner, psychological 'city' (the 'polity' of reason, spirit, and appetite, adopting the model of Plato's *Republic*), and he strives for the analogous improvement of his fellow citizens wherever he can (*in Gorg.* 8.1, etc.), healing souls or preventing their injury (*in Gorg.* 49.6, *in Alc.* 6,5–7). This philosophy has two indispensable phases: one looks 'upward' or 'inward' (in terms shared by Olympiodorus and Damascius), and the other looks 'outward' or 'downward':

> The contemplative [philosopher's] gaze always flies toward the divine, whereas the [philosopher-]statesman's, if he has worthy citizens, remains

and shapes them. If they are not worthy, then in truth he retreats and makes a fortress (*teikhion*) for himself. . . . This is what Plato and Socrates did.

(in Gorg. 26.18, tr. Jackson et al. 1998)

During a lifetime, we might develop from the latter, statesmanly kind of philosopher into the former, contemplative kind:

> Understand that we should always pursue philosophy, when we are young for the sake of soothing the passions, and especially when we are old, for then the passions begin to subside, and reason flourishes. We should always have philosophy as our patron, since it is she who performs the task of Homer's Athena, scattering mist.

(in Gorg. 26.13, tr. Jackson et al. 1998)

In fact, Olympiodorus develops a ladder of philosophical 'grades' of human excellence or virtue (*aretê*) that we might climb, coinciding with the reading curriculum in Platonic philosophy:[30] for source texts and a helpful overview, see Sorabji 2005.1, 15(a). The ascent, sometimes described as a *scala virtutum* ('ladder of virtues'), has roots in the work of the Neoplatonic movement's founder, Plotinus (204/5–270 AD), and his pupil Porphyry (*c.* 234–*c.* 305 AD),[31] but as with so much else in later Neoplatonism, its core was laid down by Iamblichus of Chalcis (*c.* 240–325 AD), and further systematised by Proclus and Damascius. There are seven 'rungs' on the ladder elaborated by Damascius, which is virtually identical to Olympiodorus' own system: human excellence can be ranked, in ascending order, as (1) natural, (2) habituative, (3) civic, (4) purificatory, (5) contemplative, (6) exemplary, and (7) hieratic (Damascius *in Phaed.* 1.138–51). It will be useful to sketch the whole progression briefly, since Olympiodorus uses this framework to situate his lectures on the *Alcibiades*. As I argue below (§5), Olympiodorus presents both Plato and Alcibiades – through the *Life of Plato* and the *Alcibiades* respectively – as exemplars. Alcibiades serves as a model for his students to turn from (1–2) the 'pre-philosophical' grades of excellence to (3) civic excellence (*politikê aretê*), the first degree of philosophical achievement; the biography of Plato presents a model for the entire cycle of human excellence.

The seven grades of excellence

Following Damascius, Olympiodorus envisages 'pre-philosophical' forms of excellence that belong to us either (1) by our natural constitution (*phusikê aretê*, over which we have little control, as a lion is bound to be courageous and an ox temperate),[32] or (2) by habituation and upbringing (*êthikê aretê*),[33] which might be fostered by myths and stories and rhetoric (such as the Pythagorean *Golden Verses* or the *Handbook* of Epictetus, although the moralising interpretation of classical myths, learned in schools of rhetoric,[34] could also serve this function).

Next, when we embark on philosophical training, we begin to foster rational virtues (*logôi khrônto . . . aretai*, Olymp. *in Phaed.* 8.2,9). By contrast to the pre-philosophical forms of excellence, these philosophical forms require conscious, reasoned action (*praxis*). The first is (3) civic or social excellence (*politikê aretê*),[35] which cultivates the right inward organisation of our own soul and the souls of our fellow citizens. Civic excellence places reason (*logos*) in charge over spirited emotion or pride (*thumos*) and appetitive desires (*epithumia*). It still looks primarily to the outer world and our actions in it (cf. Olymp. *in Phaed.* 20.4). In the Platonic reading curriculum, it is cultivated by studying the *Alcibiades* and the *Gorgias*. Next, (4) we get to work on 'purifying' the soul (*kathartikê aretê*),[36] recognising what distinguishes it from the body, and learning to identify with those psychological functions that are independent of the body, especially reason (*logos*) and our intuitive grasp of eternal principles, the faculty called 'intellect' (*nous*). In the Platonic curriculum, this stage of excellence is fostered by reading the *Phaedo*. Philosophical, rational excellence culminates in the achievement of (5) contemplative excellence (*theôrêtikê aretê*). The contemplative philosopher studies names, human knowledge, nature, and first principles until he directly observes the eternal, intelligible realm of the Platonic Forms; to foster this excellence, he studies texts such as *Cratylus* (for names), *Theaetetus* (for knowledge), and *Philebus* (for reality). He also proceeds to a second cycle of 'perfect' or 'fulfilled' dialogues, namely *Timaeus* (for nature), and *Parmenides* (for first principles, or theology). In concluding this curriculum and becoming a person of 'contemplative' excellence, he arrives at the summit of philosophical achievement.

In fact, the contemplative philosopher has 'become' pure intellect (*nous*, Olymp. *in Phaed.* 8.2,19): in a sense, he has come to identify himself with his veridical awareness of the eternal realities and laws described by Plato as Forms, and commonly called 'intelligibles' (*noêta*) by the Neoplatonists. The classical Neoplatonist ontology describes three major grades of existence (*hupostaseis*): in ascending order, (a) soul (*psukhê*), (b) intellect (*nous*), and (c) the One (*to hen*).[37] In this framework, the contemplative philosopher has 'graduated', as it were, from the foggy and time-bound vision of (a) *psukhê* alone, to the veridical and timeless clarity of (b) intellect (*nous*), which sees real beings just as they are. In a certain sense, the contemplative philosopher has achieved 'likeness to God', insofar as intellect is regarded as divine, and as Porphyry argued (*Sent.* 32,63–70), here we also arrive at the highest exemplars of the traditional forms of excellence.

Beyond philosophy, however, lies a further sphere of achievement – at least for the later Neoplatonists, including Iamblichus, Proclus, Damascius, and Olympiodorus himself.[38] This sphere was the purview of the theurgic practitioner, who becomes authentically godlike (Olymp. *in Phaed.* 8.2,1–20) by engaging in 'divine practice' (*theourgia*).[39] Outwardly, the theurgist engaged in creative combinations of traditional religious symbols and practices from a variety of cultural backgrounds,[40] cultivating physical and mental images that 'resonated' with the gods. Through these activities, he strove to open a pathway for divine activity in the sublunar world, perhaps improving his community's material circumstances or his own.[41] But his essential goal was inward:[42] to heal his soul and to uncloud its inner sight (Iamblichus *De Mysteriis* 1.11–12). The unclouded mind became open to 'blessed visions' (*De Myst.* 1.12; cf. *Phaedrus* 247A), 'as the eye awaits the rising of the sun' (cf. Plotinus *Enn.* 5.5.8,1–5, introducing solar language that appeals to the later Neoplatonists): these visions are often portrayed as ascending grades of luminosity, culminating in clear light.[43] Following his preliminary cultivation of ritual symbols and practices and meditation on the visions that arise, the theurgist comes to *identify* with the clear light of divinity that he beholds, and so achieves likeness to divinity without separation (Olymp. *in Phaed.* 8.2,112–20).

> [F]or in the contemplation of the 'blessed visions' the soul exchanges one life for another and exerts a different activity, and considers itself to be no longer human – and quite rightly so; for often, having abandoned its own life, it has gained in exchange the most blessed activity of the gods. . . . Such activity . . . renders us . . . pure and immutable.
>
> (Iamblichus *De Myst.* 1.12, 41,9–42,3)

This marks the accomplishment of **(6)** 'exemplary' or 'archetypal' excellence (*paradeigmatikê aretê*),[44] cultivated through theurgy. Here, the practitioner has achieved union with the intelligible, exemplary reality that is the object of contemplation for intellect (*nous*). He has thereby gone beyond the contemplative philosopher, who, as pure intellect, simply *observed* intelligible reality without obstructions (Olymp. *in Phaed.* 8.2,19–20), but did not yet *identify* with his divine object. For Olympiodorus, we now arrive at the goal of theurgy (*in Phaed.* 8.2,20): our souls ascend to the eternal, intelligible realm 'beyond the cosmos', where they will remain either for good (as Iamblichus argued, ap. Damascium *in Phaed.* 1.548), or, as Olympiodorus maintained, will remain for a long time before descending again into genesis (Olymp. *in Phaed.* 10.14,8). At this stage, too, there are curricular readings to do: the *Chaldaean Oracles* or Orphic poems.[45]

But the intelligible divinity with whom the 'exemplary' theurgist identifies is perhaps not yet the One itself (*to hen*), the loftiest principle of unity and individuality, which is divinity in the strictest and fullest sense. Damascius preferred to break out a seventh, crowning stage of theurgical accomplishment, namely **(7)** 'hieratic excellence' (*hieratikê aretê*),[46] which transcends the intelligible altogether and arrives at the truly 'godlike part of the soul' (*to theoeides tês psukhês*, Damascius *in Phaed.* 1.144,1). Here the theurgist identifies himself with the One (*to hen*) or Good (*to agathon*), and realises all the previous six grades of excellence in a new way.[47] Olympiodorus omits this stage from his discussion at *in Phaed.* 8.2, and this may be because he regards union with the One as contained already at the 'exemplary' stage **(6)**, where on his view we already act 'as One' (*henoeidôs*, 8.2,18), or for another reason;[48] nonetheless, he certainly has a place for hieratic practice, which he portrays Plato as mastering from the Egyptian priests in his *Life of Plato* (*in Alc.* 2,134–5; see below, §5.4).

The full hierarchy according to Damascius and Olympiodorus might be sketched as shown in Table 1, bearing in mind that Olympiodorus may have collapsed stages **(6)** and **(7)** into a single stage of theurgy.

Philosophical excellence

In approaching the Platonic curriculum, Olympiodorus focused on the rational or 'philosophical' grades of human excellence, which fall in the middle of this broader hierarchy: **(3)** civic excellence, **(4)** purificatory excellence, and

Table 1. The seven grades of excellence

Excellence	(1) Natural (innate)	'Beneath' philosophy (innate or habituated)
	(2) Habituated	
	(3) Civic	Philosophical
	(4) Purificatory	
	(5) Contemplative	
	(6) Exemplary	'Beyond' philosophy (divine, inspired)
	(7) Hieratic	

Table 2. The philosophical grades of excellence

Excellence	(3) Civic			1. Introduction: *Alcibiades*
				2. *Gorgias* (civic)
	(4) Purificatory			3. *Phaedo* (purificatory)
	(5) Contemplative	On names		4. *Cratylus* (names)
		On concepts (*noêmata*)		5. *Theaetetus* (knowledge)
		On realities (*pragmata*)	Natural	6. *Sophist* (natural)
				7. *Statesman* (natural)
			Theological	8. *Phaedrus* (theological)
				9. *Symposium* (theological)
				10. Culmination: *Philebus* (Good)
	(5) Two 'complete' dialogues			11. *Timaeus* (Physics)
				12. *Parmenides* (Theology)

(5) contemplative excellence. Each could be inculcated by the close study, with a teacher, of one or more dialogues in the Platonic curriculum that had previously been advanced by Iamblichus. We might tabulate these as shown in Table 2 (above) (see Westerink 1962, XXXIX–XL).

What is achieved by philosophy?

For Olympiodorus, philosophy is distinguished from other practices by its exclusive focus on the soul (*psukhê*), where our true being resides (*in Gorg.* 1.1–2, 38.1). Poets and rhetoricians, by contrast, discuss the combination of body and soul, which suffers affections (*pathê*): to the philosopher, these are not really 'us', but merely 'ours' (*in Alc.* 200,8–9). To improve the psyche involves prevailing over irrational and unpredictable passions, or the 'many-headed' part of us (*in Gorg.* 34.3), which will facilitate a philosophical life of tranquillity and self-sufficiency (*in Gorg.* 36.3–5) and benefit to others.

This refers to the civic philosophical exercise of the statesman, which in traditional terms is 'practical'. It is perhaps not so difficult to see how civic excellence could create better human beings, and better communities. But what about the higher levels of philosophical excellence? How do contemplative philosophy and the understanding of reality help to create 'good people'?[49] Olympiodorus, following in a long tradition, argues that true happiness derives from these higher pursuits. Thus:

> The philosophers liken human life to the sea, because it is disturbed and concerned with begetting and salty and full of toil. Note that islands rise above the sea, being higher. So that constitution which rises above life and over becoming is what they call the Isles of the Blessed. The same thing applies to the Elysian plain. And this is also why Heracles performed his final labour in the western regions – he laboured against the dark and earthly life, and finally he lived in the daytime, i.e. in truth and in light.
>
> (*in Gorg.* 47.6, tr. Jackson et al. 1997)

Olympiodorus advances the following argument for the benefit of theoretical, contemplative knowledge in life. Anyone who knows her own soul (*psukhê*) also understands the basic formulae or rational principles (*logoi*) that it contains, because all human knowledge derives from such understanding.[50] Developing earlier ideas from Platonist, Aristotelian, and Stoic psychology, Olympiodorus maintains that each soul contains the rational principles of all things (a point also familiar from Plotinus, *Enn.* 4.3.10, 5.7.1, 6.2.5, and Proclus, *El. Theol.* 195); thus the person who knows the rational principles in the soul also knows all beings and thereby knows justice and the other virtues. By the principles of Socratic and Platonic rationalism (cf. Cooper 2012, 11–13), anyone who *knows* justice and virtue necessarily *is* just and virtuous (*in Alc.* 198,20–199,6).

The insight (*phronêsis*) that is achieved by philosophical excellence is not just a matter of detached investigation, but leads to better decisions in practical spheres of life, by way of a good understanding of what is to be pursued and avoided (Olymp. *in Phaed.* 4.1). Thus Olympiodorus remarks, following a lost passage of Proclus, that it is the particular individual human being 'for whom we care' (Olymp. *in Alc.* 210,13–16) in our quest for likeness to god. It is this care for our individual self, as well as our community (where we direct our activity as teachers), that drives us to philosophy. It is not sufficient to 'know ourselves' in general or abstract terms, for we must really know *us*, the unique person who acts in every particular instance:

> . . . the text says that if we are to ascertain what 'self itself' is, we must also learn what 'each self itself' is, since it is not enough simply to ascertain the human being, but we must know also what the individual (*atomon*) is, because the task in hand is to help Alcibiades find out who *he* is – namely, his soul: and actions are concerned with particular circumstances (*praxeis peri ta kath' hekasta katagignontai*).
>
> (Olymp. *in Alc.* 204,3–11)

The philosopher, then, is a person who achieves the godlike good for himself (by making his inner constitution just and whole, and becoming an accomplished observer of the realm of being), while striving to achieve the same good for his community, especially for the young (if the outward, collective constitution of his state permits: *in Gorg.* 45.2). His subject is the soul. He works on the soul using the tools of 'demonstration' (*apodeixis: Proleg.* 16,9; *in Gorg.* 10.7), not persuasiveness, or mythological tradition, or appeals to authority (even Plato's own authority: *in Gorg.* 41.9). He is fair-minded (*in Gorg.* 11.9), mild in temper (*in Gorg.* 18.6), not boastful (*in Phaed.* 8.17), adaptable to different situations and modes of argument (*in Gorg.* 14.4), and a swift learner, prone to offer a 'larger perspective' or more general vantage point on each challenge (*in Gorg.* 13.10). Because he has rightly identified his soul alone as the seat of his identity, and has no attachment to wealth or power or comfort (*in. Gorg.* 36.3–5), his life and his achievements are 'unmanifest' and 'invisible' (*in Phaed.* 8.1), but he is truly happy.

Olympiodorus often differentiates such an educated philosopher from 'the many' (e.g. *in Phaed.* 5.4), from the grammarian or rhetorician (*in Cat.* 42,8ff., *in Gorg.* 41.10), and from the poet or reciter of myths (*in Gorg.* 46.4, 46.6).[51] The distinctions of the philosopher are painted on the canvas of the scale of excellences described above. For example, Olympiodorus does not specifically attempt to frame 'the many' by contrast with the *Kulturwelt* of the educated class of the Roman world, but he tries to describe them by situating them on the ladder of excellence.

Non-philosophers are those who have not yet surpassed the first two grades of excellence, **(1)** natural (*phusikê aretê*) and **(2)** habituated (*êthikê aretê*) achievement. Such uneducated human beings may have natural (*phusikos*) talents, but these have not been realised; and perhaps those who have studied with grammarians or even rhetoricians have fostered good 'ethical' habits, but they have not learned actually to work on their souls or to begin the process of 'reversion' into their own souls, or transformation into a philosopher. Read with a knowledgeable teacher like Olympiodorus himself,[52] the Platonic *Alcibiades* plays a key role in the student's 'ascent' to philosophical excellence, as we can see in Table 2 above.

The following section attempts to show how the *Alcibiades* arrived at this pivotal position, and how Olympiodorus builds on his predecessors' commentaries in his use of the *Alcibiades* to introduce philosophy.

2.2. The role of the *First Alcibiades* in inculcating human excellence in later Neoplatonism

For the later Neoplatonists, the *Alcibiades* represents a crucial step on the 'ladder' of excellence's cultivation: it is literally the gateway to philosophical excellence (Olymp. *in Alc.* 11,3–6). Proclus, Damascius and Olympiodorus all wrote commentaries on the *Alcibiades*[53] and searched for a unifying 'purpose' or 'target' (*skopos*) of the work as a whole, unpacking Iamblichus' view that this dialogue contained all philosophy 'as if in a seed' (fr. 1 Dillon 1973). This style of reading represents the broader exegetical approach of later Neoplatonism, which sought to unify a complex intellectual and cultural heritage through allegory and interpretation.

But the *Alcibiades* was a particularly meaningful and sensitive case. As we notice in Proclus' commentary (discussed below, §4), its introductory and 'seminal' position demanded that the commentator provide complete and thorough coverage of his sources. Therefore, in interpreting the *Alcibiades*, Proclus will engage with the entire 'philosophical'[54] curriculum (*in Alc.* 11,4–15).[55]

In *Ennead* 1.1 [53], Plotinus took up the central argument of the *Alcibiades*: 'We' are the soul alone, which is regarded as separable, precisely because it is the separate 'user' of the body.[56] To recognise this truth is to begin our ascent to the divine, as philosophy draws our attention upward from the particular human person, with her inward affections (*pathê*), to the human person viewed as a whole, or universal, entity, who is able to rise to intellect (*nous*) and even to God, achieving the goal of likeness to divinity (*homoiôsis tôi theôi*).

Common to these readings of the *Alcibiades* is an exhortation to use philosophy in order to 'turn' inwards or upwards to the soul, to the true or authentic self. This idea grows in importance: such encouragement to privilege the mind (*nous*) as the true person is arguably already detectable in Stoicism, especially Roman Stoicism,[57] while Albinus already uses the *Alcibiades* to support this exhortation, and for Plotinus, the act of 'turning the eye of the soul upward' becomes crucial to the soul's ascent and salvation. The summit of Plato's Allegory of the Cave (*Republic* 7) provides a source for this talk of turning or reversion, together with the 'turn' to the Good at *Republic* 7, 518C.[58]

Superimposed on the Platonic allegory is the ideal relationship of the mature philosopher to the student. The philosopher of *Republic* 7, who has transcended the 'Cave' that represents mere material existence, glimpses and contemplates true, intelligible reality beyond. Afterwards, however, he descends again to the Cave to help others effect their own escape. That analogy holds for the philosophical teachers of the Neoplatonist schools. Many of these teachers have grasped the nature of reality: in Neoplatonic terms, they have vaulted to the summit of philosophical achievement, 'contemplative excellence', and cultivated a thorough understanding both of natural philosophy (physics) and first philosophy (theology) (see §2.1, Table 2, above); some have even obtained a kind of 'godlike' status. Yet they descend again from that height in order to help their students follow in their footsteps.

It was Iamblichus, as Proclus informs us at the outset of his commentary, who took up Albinus' suggestion to place the *Alcibiades* at the head of that formal curriculum, and ascribed a kind of seminal status to this dialogue. This claim might partly refer to the *Alcibiades'* tremendously wide range of quotation and allusion to many other Platonic dialogues, which lends it a 'handbook-like quality.'[59] Iamblichus, like Albinus, might also have placed value on the *Alcibiades'* treatment of the 'separable soul' as the self, and he may have shared Albinus' view that Alcibiades represented the ideal young recruit to philosophy.

Proclus makes it clear that Iamblichus treated the *Alcibiades* as 'seed-like' especially in the context of the Platonic curriculum. That curriculum was designed to inculcate philosophical excellence. When Iamblichus discussed the *Alcibiades* as containing philosophy in a seminal way, he might have meant that the *Alcibiades* anticipates the themes of the following ten dialogues, which together lead the way up the ladder of excellence.[60] In the *Anonymous Prolegomena to Platonic Philosophy*, we find a representation of the Iamblichean curriculum of dialogues as a succession of grades of excellence (*aretai*), which we have already discussed above (§2.1). As Blumenthal pointed out, Marinus' *Life of Proclus* reflects this same hierarchy expressed in the very life of the sage.[61] In fact, a narrative composed of a journey from 'natural' to 'civic' excellence, then an ascent to daimonic (semi-divine) and finally to divine status (*homoiôsis tôi theôi, Theaet.* 176B), comprising our completion or fulfilment (*teleiotês*), is already expressed in Plotinus 3.4 *On the Daimon*.[62]

The *Alcibiades* represents a process of 'turning upward' or 'reversion' from an exclusive focus on natural talent (*phusis*) – represented through Alcibiades' gymnastic training and natural advantages – to an understanding of (inner and outer) civic justice (*ta politika*). I would suggest that this 'turn upward' from pre-philosophical talent to civic excellence (*politikê aretê*) motivated Iamblichus to place the *Alcibiades* at the start of the 'philosophic' curriculum. For a single dialogue to contain Platonic *philosophy* in a seed-like or seminal way would require that it draw the reader out of natural and habituative excellence and advance him or her toward the first of the philosophical grades of excellence, namely the civic (*politikê*), and lead the reader toward the purificatory (*kathartikê*) and finally to the contemplative (*theôretikê*) grade of excellence. Iamblichus, as Olympiodorus explains in his commentary on the *Alcibiades*, used the image of a temple to describe his design: the *Alcibiades* would function as the forecourt, and the *Parmenides* as the *aduton* or holy of holies (11,3–6). (The Neoplatonists read the *Parmenides* as a dialogue concerning the nature of the One or Good, the highest of the three hypostases discussed above in §2.1: the One, intellect, and soul). Like the philosophical forms of excellence, the *Alcibiades* – on Iamblichus' reading – advances from a 'civic' starting point, concerning justice, to turn Alcibiades 'inward' to the 'purification' of the soul, and finally to the 'contemplation' of being, including even the divine. This progression mirrors the Iamblichean curriculum of ten dialogues.

If Iamblichus' commentary did follow this pattern, and he taught the other dialogues on a similar model, then the unique status of the *Alcibiades* at the head of the curriculum can be explained internally from the exegetical approach that Iamblichus applied. The *Alcibiades* pivots on the 'reversion' (*epistrophê*) of Alcibiades from obsession with natural gifts, by demonstrating that this advantage does not help him to address civic affairs (*politika*) with any competence. For this, he requires another degree of excellence, which is civic (*politikê*). This provides at least one plausible explanation for Iamblichus' choice to place this dialogue first. In pivoting from Alcibiades' natural gifts to the first properly 'philosophical' excellence, namely, civic excellence, it represents an ideal beginning for the 'philosophical' curriculum.

So far, we have aimed to situate Olympiodorus' commentary on the *Alcibiades* in its philosophical and social context. Next, we turn to a brief survey of the dialogue itself and its reception, culminating in a more detailed treatment of the commentaries by Proclus (§4) and Olympiodorus himself (§5).

3. The ancient tradition on the *First Alcibiades*

3.1. Overview

We need to find out in which dialogue especially Plato aims to reflect on our essence, in order that, starting from there, we may make our very first beginning upon the works of Plato. Now could we name any other prior to the *Alcibiades*, and the conversation of Socrates related in it?

(Proclus, *in Alc.* 6,4–9)[63]

So Proclus, writing in the fifth century AD, introduced the *Greater Alcibiades* as the cornerstone of the Platonic curriculum. Three centuries earlier, Albinus of Smyrna had already written in his *Prologue* that the Platonic curriculum should 'begin from the *Alcibiades*' (5.15–16), through which the young student will 'change direction, turn inwards, and recognise what he should be caring for'. This judgement on the dialogue was maintained throughout late antiquity and the Renaissance,[64] and prevailed well into the early modern period. But a radical change of perception came to the English-speaking world through William Dobson's 1836 translation of Schleiermacher's *Introductions to the Dialogues of Plato*.[65] Schleiermacher had described the *Alcibiades* as 'very insignificant and poor, and that to such a degree, that we cannot ascribe it to Plato', conceding 'a few very beautiful and genuinely Platonic passages floating sparsely scattered in a mass of inferior material'.[66] With this judgement, he inspired a lasting debate about the status of Socrates' dramatically inaugural conversation with his most controversial pupil, Alcibiades (c. 450–404 BC) – the precocious orator, general and statesman who would play an ambiguous role as one of Athens' greatest literary and historical heroes and antiheroes.[67]

Paul Friedländer, surveying the *Alcibiades*' scholarly fortunes from 1921 to 1955, defends his own sympathy for what he calls 'the strangest case in the Platonic corpus'.[68] Julia Annas' influential argument in favour of the dialogue's authenticity appeared in 1985, and several scholars, including for example Nicholas Denyer (2001, 14–26), have followed her, while others have pointed out unresolved challenges.[69] But detractors and defenders agree, as Denyer points out (2001, 14), that 'in ancient times, no one doubted that Plato wrote the *Alcibiades*'. In fact, this ancient tradition has become a tract of common ground in the otherwise wide-ranging debate about the provenance of the dialogue.

This is not the place to attempt a detailed treatment of the origins of the pervasive ancient tradition on the *Alcibiades*.[70] But we can see that the dialogue was well established by the second century AD. Galen directly cites 'Plato's *Alcibiades*' (*Inst. log.* 15.10, 2), and again, Albinus recommended this text as a propaedeutic to the Platonic curriculum (*Prologue* 5.15–16). Earlier, in the first century AD, Thrasyllus had included it in his monumental edition of Plato – not yet at the head of the list, but in the fourth tetralogy, firmly ensconced among the works which he regarded as authentic.[71] Friedländer argues that there are signs of the *Alcibiades'* influence earlier than this, and he cites testimonia that in his view answer artistically to the 'model' of the *Alcibiades*: Plutarch's biography of Alcibiades, Persius' fourth satire, and Polybius' first conversation with Scipio, as well as Aristotle's *Eroticus*, several scenes in Xenophon's *Memorabilia*, and the fragments of Aeschines' *Alcibiades*. Annas (1985, 113–14) finds some of these correspondences more persuasive than others, but in each case the argument rests on resemblances in the treatment of a common theme, rather than on a citation. It is at least possible that the composition of the *Alcibiades* could postdate some of these sources: as Friedländer puts it, 'if the reverse order of composition were true, then the author of the dialogue must have been the first to provide philosophical depth to the themes touched upon by Xenophon and Aischines' (1964, 231).

Annas and Denyer both draw attention to the testimony of Diogenes Laertius (3.56–62) that the *Alcibiades* already stood at the head of some curricula by the third century. Denyer (2001, 14) appeals to Carlini's *Index testimoniorum*[72] to claim that '[the *Alcibiades*] was frequently read, and frequently cited under Plato's name', which is undoubtedly true. But when we organise Carlini's index according to date (see Appendix)[73] it is clear that direct citations of the *Alcibiades* are not to be found before the second century AD. Apart from its relatively unostentatious introduction in Thrasyllus' fourth tetralogy, the few supposed allusions to the *Alcibiades* in the first century AD are oblique, and the only earlier possible references, namely several passages in Cicero and the probably pseudo-Aristotelian *Magna Moralia*, are even more allusive. If we want to make a persuasive case for the *Alcibiades'* authenticity, we might try to explain why it is not directly cited under Plato's name earlier than this (although it should be noted that many dialogues now beyond suspicion share that lack of direct citation in our surviving evidence prior to the first century).

In §3.2 below, I will review the contents of the *Alcibiades* itself. In §3.3, we briefly survey the Platonic and Aristotelian context of its basic claims about selfhood, and the terms of 'soul, body, and the combination', then review the evidence for the period before the first explicit citations, stretching from the fourth century BC to the second century AD, including brief remarks about Plotinus' treatise *What is the Living Being and What is the Human Person* (*Enn.* 1.1 [53]), which Olympiodorus describes as sharing 'the target (*skopos*)' of the *Alcibiades* (*in Alc.* 9,16). Finally, in §3.4, §4, and §5, I try to account for the function of the *Alcibiades* in the late Athenian and Alexandrian schools through a summary treatment of Proclus' commentary and the lectures of Olympiodorus that we have before us in this volume. I also try to support, in detail, my suggestion, briefly outlined above, that Iamblichus relocated the *Alcibiades* at the head of the curriculum because it depicts the 'pivot-point' between pre-philosophical and philosophical grades of excellence, particularly between natural excellence (*phusikê aretê*) and civic excellence (*politikê aretê*).

3.2. The *First Alcibiades*: from natural gifts to civic responsibility

The narrative arc of the *Alcibiades* traces the intellectual and moral journey of a young man – the famous future military leader and scoundrel Alcibiades – as Socrates 'reverts' or 'converts' him to philosophy on the verge of a public life of civic affairs (*ta politika*). Alcibiades is first made to recognise that his innate advantages and talents (*phusis*) do not make him a statesman (*politikos*), and that his upbringing thus far has relied on purely 'natural' traits (*phusikos,* 106E, cf. 119C), factors such as his birth and upbringing. (We might say today that Alcibiades has merely 'won the genetic lottery'). Having recognised this, Alcibiades turns next to investigate, with Socrates, what is 'better' in matters of public life (109C), and seeks a kind of *aretê* – excellence, betterness, or virtue (124E) – that is 'civic' (*politikos*), that is, entailing the just, healthy organisation of an individual civic society (*polis*) or soul (*psukhê*) (126D). This excellence (*aretê*) turns out to require an intentional, conscientious skill (*tekhnê*) that 'cares for' oneself in order to better oneself (127E), and this in turn demands self-knowledge, which amounts to the recognition that the 'human being is the soul alone' (129C–130A). Therefore, we should focus on discovering the excellence of the soul (133B; cf. Aristotle, *Nic. Eth.* 1.7, 1097b23–1098a16), which, on the analogy of the eye's own excellence (132B), is wisdom (*sophia*), and is also godlike. Should we succeed in securing this *aretê*, and turn from our trust in nature (*phusis*; cf. 122C) to the condition of the true statesman (*politikos*) and beyond, to 'wisdom' in the soul itself, we will have obtained a kind of 'likeness to god' (cf. *Theaet.* 176B), we will become pleasing to god, and we will be in a position to benefit the *polis* as a whole – provided that we have divine support (135D).

This discussion investigates self-knowledge and its benefits 'in practice'. It begins from Socrates' seemingly radical suggestion that Alcibiades cannot succeed in his search for civic power without the help that Socrates will give him (105D–E). Socrates' help, as it turns out, is delivered in the form of the dialectic which follows. He strives, through philosophical discussion, to turn Alcibiades from his focus on natural, innate gifts, toward a kind of civic excellence that comprises 'agreement' (*to homolegein*, 111B), between states, between citizens, or between the parts of an individual person (126C).[74] Action that is 'beneficial' (*sunoisi praxasin*, 113D4–5), whether to the individual or to the city-state, is said to depend upon such agreement.

The first two-thirds of the dialogue (106B–127E) establish that 'self-care' is a necessary prerequisite to this benefit. The final third of the dialogue (128A–135E) concludes that 'self-knowledge' must come first, for lacking this we may be deceived into caring for something which is not 'ourselves' (128A1), for instance, our 'belongings' (*ta hêmetera*). In fact, self-knowledge is identical with *sôphrosunê* (131B4, cf. *Charmides* 164D) and leads to knowledge of 'our own good and evil' (133C22–3) and of the soul's likeness to divinity (133C4–6). Possessing knowledge of ourselves and of our 'excellence' (*aretê*), we are able to 'take care' of ourselves, of our belongings, of the *polis*, and of its members; we can obtain the good life, and act in a manner which is 'loved by God' (133D2).

Thus the *Alcibiades* begins and ends with a practical problem, namely, how to gain power in the *polis* and exercise it well, and its resolution depends on reorienting Alcibiades himself towards a better understanding of civic excellence (*politikê aretê*). In the process of solving this problem, Socrates shows that a certain kind of individual excellence is necessary to attain any kind of useful power (124E3), and demonstrates that this excellence must be obtained through the knowledge of 'what we ourselves are'. Thus in general he encourages Alcibiades to recognise justice in himself before he looks outwards to the *polis*. Socrates' invocation of the Persian and Spartan kings as appropriate 'rivals' persuades Alcibiades to 'take care of himself' and to seek his natural excellence (123D). Once Alcibiades is committed to pursuing excellence through self-care (*epimeleia*), Socrates makes the case that self-care requires self-knowledge.

Here, then, around *Alc.* 128E–130C, the central arguments of the *Alcibiades* (as the Neoplatonic tradition interpreted it) are introduced. **(1)** In order to make anything better, Socrates contends, we must know *what it is* (128E). Therefore we must know 'what we ourselves are' (*ti pot' esmen autoi*, 129A) in order to know which skill (*tekhnê*) improves us (cf. 128D2–E3). The Delphic inscription confirms that self-knowledge lies in this, knowing what we are. Thus at 129B1 this aim is stated as discovering 'the self itself' (*auto to auto*). **(2)** At 130A, an influential tripartition is expressed. 'No one,' Socrates observes, 'would disagree with this: man is either soul (*psukhê*) or body (*sôma*) or the combination of both (*sunamphoteron to holon touto*).' Socrates will conclude that man is the soul. **(3)** In order to determine which of these options is correct, Socrates first introduces the distinction of the *user from the instrument* (*organon*). In any art, the user differs from the instrument (Socrates' preferred analogy is the instrument of speech, 129B). The entire body is the instrument of the human being, which rules and 'uses' it. Therefore 'we' cannot be identical with our body: the body cannot rule or use itself (130B2). For the same reason, 'we' cannot be the combination of soul and body (130C). Therefore the true human being (*anthrôpos*) must be the soul. As Sorabji (2006, 33) concisely summarises the dialogue's conclusion, the author of the *First Alcibiades* 'treats reason or intellect as if it constitutes the *essence* of the person'. More precisely, the objective of the human being lies in attaining the *aretê* of the soul, which may be described as 'alike to the divine' (133C4–6).

3.3. The *First Alcibiades* from the fourth century BC to Plotinus

Whether Plato or one of his followers wrote the *Alcibiades*, it is full of echoes and reminiscences from the other Platonic dialogues. Among these, the most thematically important for our purposes is the *Alcibiades'* treatment of the Socratic pursuit of self-knowledge (which can also be found, for example, at *Phaedrus* 229E and *Charmides* 164D). The *Alcibiades* reframes this inquiry into a classically Socratic, definitional question (cf. Aristotle, *Metaph.* 1.6): what are we, or what is the self (129A)? The *Alcibiades* offers three alternatives: the human person may be (1) soul, (2) body, or (3) a combination of the two

(130A). Socrates and Alcibiades conclude that the true self is the soul (*psukhê*) alone (130C). This answer is also classically Platonic (it may be found, for example, in Plato's *Phaedo* 115C–D and *Laws* 12, 959A–B), as is the accompanying injunction to value oneself beyond external goods (also in Plato, *Philebus* 48C). The *Alcibiades*, however, delivers the novel argument that the soul is the user of the body and therefore distinct from its instrument. The *Alcibiades* also seems to echo *Theaetetus* 176B when Socrates and Alcibiades agree that human excellence involves a kind of likeness to god (133C–D).

There are also relevant correspondences with Aristotle (384–322 BC), although they are less obvious than those in Plato, and would not become historically important in the ancient exegesis of the *Alcibiades* until Plotinus. Aristotle's 'hylemorphic' metaphysics analyses natural beings, such as animals, in terms of their form or structure (*eidos, morphê*) on the one hand, and their matter (*hulê*) on the other hand, which combine to generate a hylemorphic compound. A human animal can be analysed in the same way, into (1) the soul (which is form), (2) the body (which is, in this context, matter for the soul) and (3) the combination that arises from both (see for example *De Anima* 412a6–9, *Metaphysics* 7.11, 1037a5–11). The resemblance between this tripartition and the tripartition of *Alcibiades* 130A would not escape later Platonists, especially Plotinus, who in *Enn.* 1.1 would use Aristotelian resources to elaborate the *Alcibiades*' treatment of the self.

Evidence from the fourth and third centuries BC is inconclusive. There are intriguing parallels between the *Alc. I* and Xenophon's *Memorabilia*,[75] but it is impossible to know whether Xenophon and the author of our *Alcibiades* have a common source or have exercised some influence on each other. The *Alcibiades*' exhortation to pursue self-knowledge by beholding a loved one (132C–133B) is tantalisingly similar to a passage in the *Magna Moralia* attributed to Aristotle in antiquity (2.15.7–8, 1213a15–24), but again the echo is inconclusive. There are also interesting resonances between our *Alcibiades* and the fragments of the *Alcibiades* written by Aeschines (318–314 BC). Comments by other contemporary orators, like Demosthenes (*Eroticus* 45.6) and Isocrates (*Busiris* 11.5), demonstrate only that the relationship between Socrates and Alcibiades was a popular subject in the fourth century. There is even less to say about the third century, except that their relationship continued to be of interest.

Moving forward to the first century, there are a number of echoes in Cicero (106–43 BC) of the most (historically) influential themes of the *Alcibiades*, including the tripartition of possible answers to the question of self-knowledge (*Tusc. Disp.* 1.52), its answer in favour of the soul alone, its simile of the soul perceiving itself as the eye perceives itself (1.67), and its treatment of the godlikeness of the soul (1.65–70). After the publication of Thrasyllus' edition of Plato between 14–37 AD, however, references begin to become clearer. In Arrian's *Discourses*, the Stoic philosopher Epictetus (*c.* 55–*c.* 135 AD) may be paraphrasing the *Alcibiades* when he encourages his listeners to 'observe what Socrates says to Alcibiades' (3.1.42), although he does not quote the dialogue directly. The *Life of Alcibiades* in the *Lives* of Plutarch (46–120 AD) shares many themes with the *Alcibiades*, and I think there is a strong case that Plutarch read our dialogue: near the beginning of *Life of Alcibiades* (1.2), Plutarch claims that Plato names Zopyrus as Alcibiades' tutor. This must be a reference to *Alc.* 122B, as Zopyrus' name does not occur elsewhere in the Platonic corpus.

Albinus of Smyrna, writing in the second century AD, anticipates the later Neoplatonists in several respects. First, he brings the *Alcibiades* forward to the outset of the Platonic curriculum. He argues that this dialogue is tailored to the ideal young recruit to Platonic philosophy. He focuses on Alcibiades' natural aptitude, youth, and (following Plutarch and the *Alcibiades*) his public, civic aspirations eventually overcome by an inclination to philosophy. This dialogue, Albinus suggests, should therefore be the starting-point for the Platonic curriculum (*Prol.* 15–16). It will assist the young student to 'change direction, turn inwards, and recognise what he should be caring for', namely his soul (5.16–17). As we will see below, the later Neoplatonists also treat Alcibiades as an exemplar of the beginner philosophy student, and we can detect the first records of the Neoplatonic exegetical tradition on the dialogue here.

Finally, in the third century, Plotinus (204/5–270 AD) found resources in Aristotelian metaphysics to elaborate the *Alcibiades*' treatment of the self (see above). Aristotle had questioned whether the term 'living being' or 'animal' (*zôion*) referred to the embodied soul or the soul alone (*Metaph.* 8.3, 1043a35–1043b5); in the same passage, he asked whether the term 'human' (*anthrôpos*) should apply to soul alone. Plotinus' treatise on 'On What is the Living Being (*zôion*) and What is the Human Person' delivers an answer to these questions: the embodied soul is the 'living being' or animal, but the human person is truly soul alone, which, for Plotinus, means that the true human being is in fact identical with the essence of soul (*psukhêi einai*). In developing these claims, Plotinus works out a famously influential phenomenology of embodied human experience, aiming to demonstrate that 'we' (*hêmeis*) – the true self – are the rational soul, which naturally resides 'above' the affections of embodiment, but might 'turn' downward to the world of temporal multiplicity, or upward to the eternal world of intelligible being, and even beyond that, to divinity. Plotinus makes effective use of the *Alcibiades'* fundamental tripartition and recognition of the self and the soul alone, and lays the groundwork for the later Neoplatonist approach to the dialogue, especially the notion of the philosophical beginner as the rational soul on the verge of 'turning' upward or downward, which we will find in both Proclus and Olympiodorus.

3.4. Later Neoplatonist commentary

For reasons of space and focus, I will deal here only with the two extant commentaries by Proclus and Olympiodorus, and I will not deal directly with the evidence for Iamblichus', Syrianus' and Damascius' interpretations of the *Alcibiades*. Their interpretations – which are surveyed very helpfully by Segonds[76] – will naturally come into play as we review the extant commentaries. Proclus' commentary presents a particular challenge to the reader, as Proclus assumes some existing familiarity with Neoplatonic metaphysics and ethics. I will not explore these topics in any depth, but will try to provide a basic overview that will help readers of Olympiodorus to understand his intellectual background, and the more difficult material that Olympiodorus sets out to distil for his more elementary course. Olympiodorus' commentary, as we find below, is simplified and more accessible, to us as well as to his own students, who were not expected to bring any prior understanding of Neoplatonic philosophy to the classroom.[77]

4. Proclus on the *First Alcibiades*[78]

Proclus' commentary probably represents the mainstream teaching of the Platonic school in Athens, in mainland Greece. The contemporary school in

Alexandria in Egypt, where Olympiodorus taught, would begin teaching the *Alcibiades* immediately after completing the Aristotelian course with the work that they called *Theology (Metaphysics)*.[79] Proclus' commentary presents us with a deep, complicated stratigraphy: it incorporates content from Iamblichus' lost commentary, as Dillon (1973) points out in his comments on the first fragments of Iamblichus, and we can also assume that it represents what Proclus learned from his own teachers, Syrianus and Plutarch, and that many of Proclus' elaborations on Iamblichus are drawn from these sources.[80] In the present study, I shall attempt to draw out the main themes that Proclus tries to bring across, as well as his exegetical methodology. I shall try to do this with special regard for Proclus' treatment of the themes in the *Alcibiades* which have so far concerned us, and also with a view to those aspects of this commentary which shed light on the broader reading and teaching practice of later Neoplatonism.

The character of Alcibiades, on Proclus' view, stands for our soul's capacity for reason (*logos*), which is called 'rational soul' (*logikê psukhê*). This level of our being is balanced between, at its upper borders, the eternal intellect (*nous*), and, at its lower borders, the non-rational, embodied components of the tripartite soul such as spirited emotion (*thumos*) and appetite (*epithumia*). (Our discussion of the Neoplatonic ladder of excellence in §2.1 should provide some useful geography here: the soul consciously struggling to place reason (*logos*) in charge of spirited emotion and appetite is one and the same with the soul striving for civic excellence.) Spirited emotion and appetite are necessarily concerned with materiality and multiplicity,[81] and are limited to exist in one portion of time. The rational soul possesses the potential to turn either way, up or down: it may turn 'upward' by divesting itself of materiality and multiplicity, ultimately coming to contemplate the eternal intellect (*nous*) in achieving contemplative excellence, or it may turn 'downward' toward temporal partiality, becoming thoroughly identified with its material appetites and aversions. Alcibiades, then, stands for the rational soul in every human being: I would argue that, in Neoplatonist terms, a person who lives and acts at this 'level' is poised between the upper edge of habituative excellence (*êthikê aretê*) and, just above this, the lower edge of philosophical excellence (*politikê aretê*).

Proclus explains that 'we' (presumably, the teacher's 'we', meaning his readers) are in the same situation as Alcibiades (*in Alc.* 7,1–3), and that we stand in need of the 'same assistance' that Alcibiades receives from Socrates. This statement should be interpreted in light of the curricular position of the *Alcibiades*. The students whom Proclus is addressing are in Alcibiades' situation, beginning 'philosophy' in the proper sense, and the role of the school is to provide the same 'assistance' that Socrates had provided to Alcibiades. This is why the 'self' is here represented chiefly as the rational soul, whereas later in the curriculum, for instance in Proclus' *Parmenides* commentary or the summary *Elements of Theology*, 'we' may be regarded as a loftier kind of being, for example, intellect (*nous*) itself. We find reflected here the idea, already familiar from Albinus, that the ideal student will sympathise with Alcibiades, who is meant to represent the starting student; this notion has been retained with remarkable consistency throughout the commentary tradition, and well into later Neoplatonism.

Proclus' treatment begins with an account of where one ought to begin one's study of the dialogues of Plato and of philosophy as a whole (*pasês ... tês philosophou theôrias*). The firmest starting-point (*arkhê*), he suggests, is 'the recognition of our own being' (*tên tês heautôn ousias diagnôsin*, 1,4–5). Such self-knowledge is necessary for a practical purpose: 'having established this we shall in every way, I think, be able more accurately both to understand the good that is appropriate to us (*agathon to prosêkon hêmin*) and the evil that fights against it'. This particular argument in favour of self-knowledge also occurred in Cicero's *Tusculan Disputations* in the first century BC, which we briefly discussed above in §3.3: Cicero presents Antiochus of Ascalon's view that we must know 'what we are' in order to know what is good (*agathos*) or appropriate (*oikeios*) for us. Thus Proclus follows a very long tradition in arguing for the usefulness of the injunction to 'Know Thyself' (*gnôthi seauton*) in this way.

'Knowing our being' means placing ourselves in the three 'ranks of being' (4,5–18): 'undivided beings' (*tôn ameristôn ... ousiôn*), 'intermediate beings' (*tôn en mesôi tetagmenôn*), and 'beings divided in association with bodies' (*tôn meristôn peri tois sômasin*). Undivided beings are intellects (*noes*); intermediate beings are souls (particularly souls understood in separation from bodies); and divided beings are embodied souls.[82] For the Neoplatonist, 'we' – that is, ordinary human beings – are potentially *any* of these kinds of being. In the language of the 'scale of excellence' described above, if I act at the lower levels of natural or habituative excellence, then I am merely an embodied soul. If I begin to operate at the level of the philosophical forms of excellence, by displaying 'civic' forms of excellence such as justice or moderation, or by separating my soul from the body through the application of 'purificatory' excellence, then I am an independent soul. Again, if I have attained the peak of the philosophical forms of excellence by contemplating reality, then I am an intellect (*nous*). If I step even further beyond the philosophical forms of excellence to attain inspired or exemplary excellence, there is a sense in which I have become divine. The Neoplatonists' hagiographical literature suggests that they regard different philosophers, various characters in Plato's dialogues, and even Plato himself, as exemplifying different ranks of excellence in this hierarchy.[83] The completion or fulfilment (*teleiotês*) of each of these classes of being also occurs in different ways, either operating in eternity (for intellects), in the whole of time (for souls), or in a part of time (for immanent or embodied souls).[84]

Proclus' exhortation to self-knowledge relies on his view that each subject gains 'knowledge' (*gnôsis*) according to its own grade of being (*ousia*), rather than according to the being of its object (cf. e.g. *in Tim.* 1.11.15–19): we can 'know ourselves' as gods (*theoi*) only when we grasp our object – in this case, our own self – by unification with the object; as intellects (*noes*) only when we grasp our object in an intellectual manner; and so on. Proclus identifies us in our *current* position – that is, in our present status as 'unfulfilled' (*atelês*), or, in a wordplay that shall soon become apparent, 'uninitiated' (*atelestos*)[85] – as a 'student' embarking on the Platonic curriculum, who is, like Alcibiades in the dialogue, chiefly the 'rational soul' still subject to *pathêmata*. Thus he ascribes to us the ability to 'turn' upward or downward, towards intellect (*nous*) or towards partition. Alcibiades will subsequently be identified with the rational soul, which can be regarded as 'looking up' to intellect (symbolically, to 'Socrates'), or 'down' to the multitude who would rend him asunder into partition (symbolically, to the 'lovers'). As Plotinus articulated a similar point in *Enn.* 1.1 [53], 'we' are intermediate between intellect (*nous*) and multiplicity, with the potential to identify with either.

Like Alcibiades, 'we' – Proclus' students and readers – are souls with the demonstrated potential to 'turn upwards' and identify with intellect, but still subject to 'the misfortunes of the son of Clinias [sc. Alcibiades]': namely, the danger of falling into an entirely embodied state of multiplicity, rent apart into countless bodily appetites. Proclus proceeds to offer several arguments in favour of self-knowledge as the beginning of the philosophical curriculum, including divine authority. A crucial point here is the analogy drawn between the philosophical curriculum and the initiatory rites of the Mysteries, such that the beginning of the curriculum – self-knowledge – stands for 'initiation' and ensures 'purification'. This corresponds to the *Alcibiades* (6,3–7,8), where our being is carefully demonstrated and Socrates introduces us to the 'examined life' (*Apology* 38A) that can help us to care for our truer self.

Therefore, Proclus recurs to his original proposal that we seek self-knowledge in order to obtain the Good 'appropriate to us' (*to agathon to prosêkon hêmin*, 1,4). Crucially, he compares 'us' to Alcibiades *just before Socrates 'turns' him away from the multitude*. The 'reversion' executed by Socrates is just the transformation that philosophical education will bring about, and this again suggests that 'we' are addressed according to our place in the curriculum.

Proclus has offered a rich allegory. Socrates, in his overture to Alcibiades, represents intellect (*nous*) as it offers salvation to the rational soul; the lovers of Alcibiades represent the multitude underlying the world of becoming; and Alcibiades himself is the rational soul (*logikê psukhê*) at the moment of choosing between the higher life represented by Socrates, and the lower life to which the lovers have tried and failed to attract him. Each of these roles, Proclus suggests, has a corollary in the Mysteries: Socrates, the Good Spirit (*Agathos Daimôn*);[86] the lovers, the infernal or lower spirits (*daimones*); and Alcibiades, the initiate into the mysteries. The 'turning' of the soul is the 'self-knowledge' to which Apollo exhorts us (5–6), a purification (*katharsis*) that must precede the stage of initiation.

A symbolic exposition of a dialogue as a world or cosmos (*kosmos*) is common to the commentators after Iamblichus. Following Westerink, the fourth section of the *Anonymous Prolegomena to Platonic Philosophy* (probably a work of the sixth or seventh century, and at any rate to be dated at least a century after Proclus) offers a relatively comprehensible explanation of this idea as Proclus explained it:[87]

> It was in imitation of the creation of God [i.e. the cosmos] that Plato wrote dialogues, or it was because the cosmos itself is a kind of dialogue. For just as in the world there are superior or inferior existences, and the soul during her stay in the world sometimes conforms to the superior, sometimes to the inferior, so the dialogue also has its characters, the questioners and the

questioned, and our soul, sitting in judgement, now sides with the questioners, now with the questioned. Another reason, given by Plato himself (*Phaedr.* 264C) is that a literary work is comparable with a living being, and therefore the most complete literary work will resemble the most beautiful of living beings; the most beautiful living being is the cosmos, and the dialogue can be compared with the cosmos.

(*An. Prol.* 4, tr. Westerink 1962)

Proclus, I suggest, viewed the study of a dialogue within the school as a means of training the rational soul (*logikê psukhê*) by 'imitation' (*mimêsis*), to turn upward toward the intelligible.[88] What seems most distinctive of Proclus' treatment is his analogical identification of 'us' with Alcibiades, that is, with the rational soul: 'for we are subject to the same affections (*pathêmata*) as the son of Clinias' (7). Having established this analogy, Proclus endeavours to make the dialogue function as a model of the student's own transformation, produced by reading the dialogue, with the aid of an accomplished teacher: thus there is meant to be a sympathy between the student beginning the Platonic curriculum and Alcibiades in his first encounter with Socrates.

For Proclus, the dialogue functions as a kind of image or portrayal (*agalma*) of the cosmos, whose contemplation can directly affect the soul as it sympathises with characters in the text, chiefly through its appreciation for 'imitation' (*mimêsis*). The dialogue form, as the author of the *Prolegomena* continues, is particularly suited to 'capture our attention', as 'we are naturally fond of imitation, and a dialogue is an imitation of various characters'.[89] In this way, the soul may achieve the purification which, on Proclus' account in *in Alc.* 5–6, must precede illumination.[90]

This passage illustrates that it is the irrational part of the soul at which imitation (*mimêsis*) aims – that is, the part of the soul which is trained by 'habituation'. It is sensible, then, for Proclus to hold, as the author of the *Prolegomena* does, that this part of the soul is also affected – and in a beneficial way – by the *mimêsis* of the Platonic dialogue. Elsewhere in Proclus, we learn that human beings can also function in this way, as an image (*agalma*) of philosophy.[91]

The Platonic dialogue, as a 'cosmos', might be viewed as analogous to the unperturbed 'heavens' of the *Timaeus*, to which the eye turns to structure the motions of the soul.[92] (The 'heavens' were treated as the boundary of the world-order or *kosmos*). The *Alcibiades*, then, was placed at the outset of the curriculum as capable of drawing the 'eye of the soul' through these stages of reversion or 'turning', through a sympathy between the structure of the text and the 'cosmic' structure of the student's own soul, beginning at the level of the irrational soul and advancing to the rational soul (Alcibiades), intellect (Socrates), and finally to the divine or the Good.

Olympiodorus would use this principle of 'sympathy' to aid in his own pedagogical use of the *Alcibiades*. He strongly emphasises a fourfold structure within the being of Alcibiades, comprising the three grades of philosophical excellence (civic, purificatory, and contemplative) as well as the theurgic or paradigmatic excellence of 'inspiration' (*enthousiasmos*). He paraphrases Socrates as inviting Alcibiades to see himself in these four ways (paraphrasing *Alc.* 132D–133C: Olymp. *in Alc.* 7,11–8,14), and in doing so, invites his own students to follow Alcibiades' example.

5. Olympiodorus on the *First Alcibiades*

Olympiodorus' commentary contains several elements that Proclus' does not, particularly a *Life of Plato*, to be surveyed in more detail below. Like Proclus, his treatment of the dialogue begins with the traditional 'points to be studied': the target or subject-matter of the text (*skopos*), its usefulness (*khrêsimon*), its position in the reading-list (*taxis*), and its internal organisation or subdivision (*diairesis*). Olympiodorus deals at length with these four *topoi* of the standard introduction.[93] The *skopos* (target) of the dialogue comprises the second section of the first lecture (3,3–9.19); its *khrêsimon* (usefulness) begins the second lecture (9,20–10.17) and is followed by *taxis* (position) from 10,18–11.6; and *diairesis* (division) from 11,7–23. The examinations of the genre, at 13,11, and the title, at 3,5–8, are more limited.[94]

5.1. Olympiodorus on the target, usefulness, position and division of the *First Alcibiades*

Skopos

Olympiodorus begins (3,2–4,14) by expounding a target (*skopos*) based on the view of Proclus. Seven justifications are given for the theory that the *skopos* of the *Alcibiades* is self-knowledge: (1) the subtitle 'On the Nature of the Human Being'; (2) expressions such as the citation of the Delphic injunction to 'Know Thyself' at 124A; (3) the distinction of 'me' from 'what belongs to me' and 'what belongs to my belongings', and the ensuing identification of Alcibiades with his self, whom Socrates alone has loved, but his body with his belongings; (4) the interchangeability of the just and the advantageous, which only holds within soul (*psychê*); (5) Plato concludes the discussion once he has demonstrated that the human being is the soul; (6) Socrates leads Alcibiades to self-knowledge along the same path which he followed himself, namely that enjoined by the Delphic oracle; and (7) the expression 'self' (*auto*) and 'the self itself' (*auto to auto*). Proclus had interpreted 'self' to indicate the soul as Plato subdivided it, including reason, spirited-emotion and appetite, but 'self-itself' as indicating the rational soul alone.

Damascius (at Olymp. 4,15–5,16) offers a similar but distinct explanation. The *skopos*, he suggests, is not about self-knowledge unqualifiedly (*haplôs*), but about *civic* self-knowledge, i.e. the knowledge appropriate to those beings that associate with bodies. He establishes this, we are told, from the *Alcibiades'* account of the human being as a rational soul using the body as an instrument (129E–130C). Only the *civic* person uses the body as an instrument: he needs *thumos* and *epithumia* in order to act on behalf of his fatherland. The purificatory person is engaged in the process of freeing himself from the body, a process which culminates in the sympathy (*sympatheia*) that facilitates contemplation and the release of the soul: 'For the soul of the contemplative person, by being active [*energousa*] in accordance with that which is most divine within it, is in this way freed from its shell-like, pneumatic vehicle' (5,7–9). Hence we find here something like Plotinus' view in *Enn.* 3.4 that the soul is able to 'actualise' a way of life below or above that of the rational soul. Olympiodorus proceeds to adduce the authority of Homer for this view: when Odysseus 'strips off his rags' at *Od.* 22.1, he represents the quintessential soul attaining its freedom. 'In other words,' Olympiodorus continues, 'the contemplative person who has separated himself from such "rags" is truly "much-contriving".'

He sums up Damascius' view as follows: 'the goal of the dialogue concerns knowing oneself in a civic way, given that the body is indeed an impediment to the pure and contemplative person, and the pure person is distinguished by moderation of the passions (*metriopatheia*), and the contemplative one by freedom from them (*apatheia*)' (5,13–15).

Here, presented with an apparent divide between the doctrines of Proclus and Damascius, Olympiodorus' celebrated exegetical flexibility comes to the fore. 'Since we plead Proclus' cause', he remarks at 5,17, 'we must bring Damascius into agreement with him'. In fact, his harmonising endeavour results in a remarkable foray into creative territory (6,5–8,14). First, Olympiodorus repeats Proclus' view (152–54) that Socrates and the Platonic philosophy differ from the others, in that they heal souls not by opposites (*enantia*) but by *like* things (*homoia*). Faced with a lover, for instance, Socrates will say 'learn what is the love of beautiful things'; faced with a hedonist, he will say 'learn what is truly easy'. Accordingly, faced with a budding statesman (*politikos*), Socrates embarks on a discussion of *civic* self-knowledge. From this it is clear, Olympiodorus suggests, that Proclus agrees with Damascius' view that the *skopos* of the dialogue is civic self-knowledge.

Olympiodorus continues (7,11–8,5) with a paraphrase of *Alc.* 132D–133C (the analogy of the eye) which he proceeds to interpret in terms of the ladder of excellence (8,5–12). He concludes with a discussion of the famous injunction of the Delphic Oracle. He explains its origins as follows (8,15–21): in antiquity, suppliants were pressing for advice about external affairs, such as children, offices of state, and war, but failed to recognise that the sole solution to all their external problems was the knowledge of themselves. The Oracle, perceiving this, 'set in writing that they think about themselves and get to know themselves first, and the other things [about which they inquired] subsequently' (20–1).

From this inscription, Olympiodorus derives the crucial result that 'the human being is the rational soul' (9,1–2). For the injunction to 'Know Thyself' only suits the rational soul: the lower soul is incapable of 'turning back upon' itself (9,6), and the heavenly beings do not need to 'get to know' themselves, since they already do (9,8–11). This, therefore, is the message of Apollo to human beings (9,11–12); it corresponds to the mirrors which the Egyptians set up before the holy places in their temples (9,12–13), representing the same idea in the form of a riddle. Finally, in 9,16–19, Olympiodorus observes that Plotinus' treatise *What is the Living Being and What is the Human Person* (1.1) shares the *skopos* and the outcome of the *Alcibiades*.

Khrêsimon

Olympiodorus considers the 'usefulness' of the dialogue at the beginning of the second lecture. Its usefulness is threefold: it contributes to the soul's immortality, since self-knowledge is accomplished through reversion upon oneself, and everything which reverts upon itself is immortal (10,1–7);[95] second, to the knowledge (*gnôsis*) of all beings, since by knowing the soul we know the formulae (*logoi*) of all beings which it contains (10,7–11);[96] third, to knowing what is good for the soul and what is harmful to it (11–16; cf. Proclus, *in Alc. I*). Thus the utility of the dialogue is, as we have already seen in Proclus, directed towards the good of the soul, viz. self-perpetuation, and the development of its being, as well as representing an epistemological advance in self-understanding.

Taxis

The initial location of the *Alcibiades* is defended on Plato's own authority (*Phaedrus* 229E–230A): it is 'laughable' for someone to rush to know anything else while remaining ignorant of himself, so self-knowledge has to come first (10,19–20); one should pursue the philosophy of Socrates 'Socratically', and Socrates came to philosophy from the Delphic Oracle (11,1–3). And finally, in an especially interesting analogy, Olympiodorus indicates that 'one must consider that this dialogue is like the fore-gates of temples, and just as those lead on to the holy of holies (*aduton*), likewise the *Alcibiades* must resemble the fore-gates, and the culminating dialogue of the curriculum, the *Parmenides*, must resemble the holy of holies' (11,5–6).

Diairesis

The tripartite division of the dialogue into 'refutation' (*elenktikos*, 106C–119A), 'exhortation' (*protreptikos*, 119A–124A), and 'midwifery'[97] (*maieutikos*, or assisting in the birth of ideas, 124A–135D) derives from Proclus *in Alc.* 13–15. Proclus ascribes it to Iamblichus: 'First therefore comes one section that takes away ignorance from the reason ... next after this is placed a part of the dialogue, which proves that we must not be content with physical advantages and so fall short of practices that accord with fully fulfilled excellence; and third after these is the part that provides the recollection of our true being and the discovery of the correct treatment, and brings a fitting end to the whole theme of the discussions' (tr. O'Neill 1965). For Proclus and Olympiodorus, Socratic 'midwifery' operates by teasing out the soul's innate grasp of the Forms, that is, by stirring up the process of 'recollection' of the Forms, or in Neoplatonic terms, of the intelligible world.[98]

Olympiodorus offers a detailed treatment of each section from 11,7–16. He ends with a study of the exchange of positions with which the dialogue ends: Socrates becomes the beloved, and Alcibiades the lover (12,17–19); for this is the object of love, namely reciprocal love (*anterôs*, 12,20).[99]

5.2. Olympiodorus' interpretation: climbing the ladder

As we have seen above, Olympiodorus follows the Iamblichean tradition in representing the *Alcibiades* as the 'fore-gate' to the temple of which the *Parmenides* is the *aduton*, the 'holy of holies'. But for the Neoplatonic tradition, as I argued above, the specific function of this 'fore-gate' is to mediate from the natural (*phusikos*) level of excellence to the 'rungs' of philosophical excellence. Similarly, for Plotinus (*Enn.* 3.4.3; see above), we must turn from a natural (*phusikos*) and perceptual (*aisthêtikos*) way of life to a rational (*logikos*) way of life. Olympiodorus agrees with his predecessors that the *Alcibiades* facilitates such a transition at this introductory stage. So he adopts Damascius' definition of the target or subject-matter (*skopos*) of the dialogue as 'civic self-knowledge', introducing the *Alcibiades* as a bridge from the natural grades of excellence to civic excellence, the first rung on the philosophical ladder.

'Civic', for Olympiodorus, refers to that level of soul which associates with bodies: at 4,19–20, as we have seen, Damascius is said to have explained that 'only the civic person uses the body as an instrument', as opposed to the cathartic and contemplative persons, who do not need to use it. Olympiodorus comes back to this point repeatedly. The 'civic' agent must find his appropriate place as a part in the whole, to which he has the relationship of *politês* or 'citizen' to *polis* or 'state'. What, then, is this 'body', which the civic person employs as an instrument, but the purificatory and contemplative persons do not require? Olympiodorus, and Damascius before him, appear to have in mind spirited emotion (*thumos*) and appetite (*epithumia*). So, in the passage cited above (4,15–5,16), we read that 'the civic person uses the body as an instrument, since he is sometimes in need of a spirited emotion (*thumos*), as on behalf of his fatherland, but also of an appetite (*epithumia*) for doing his citizens good'.

These faculties of spirited emotion (*thumos*) and appetite (*epithumia*) are familiar from Plato, *Republic* 4, as the two lower aspects of the soul which, when it is in a just condition, is ruled by reason (*logos*). These are also the two 'mortal parts' of the soul in the *Timaeus*, whose bodily seats are described from 69D to 72D: these are concerned with pleasure and pain, nutrition, *aisthêsis*, and so forth. The true, 'immortal part' of the soul is securely lodged in the head, whose spherical shape mirrors the spherical shape of the cosmos. *Thumos* and *epithumia* have their seat in the vehicle (*okhêma*) upon which the head 'rides', namely the trunk and limbs. But when we talk about the needs of the civic person, we are not really concerned with the physical trunk and limbs, which are rather a vehicle (*okhêma*) than the 'body' (*sôma*) proper: our interest is instead in the parts of the soul, whose use distinguishes the civic man from the cathartic and contemplative.

I would like to draw attention to the way in which Olympiodorus describes each of these philosophic forms of excellence as a *way of life*,[100] following Damascius in speaking of a 'civic person', a 'purificatory person', a 'contemplative person', and an 'inspired person', who live their respective lives, defined by Olympiodorus (following Damascius) as the soul using the body as an instrument (civic), the soul reflecting on itself (purification),[101] the soul reflecting on its betters (contemplative), and the soul in a state of union with the divine (inspired). This, I think, should be considered in the context of the preceding tradition. Plotinus pointed out that it was possible, having once established the place of the soul, for it to ascend by 'turning' its metaphorical 'eye' to the level of intellect (*nous*), 'our transcendent mode of being' (*touton huperanô hêmôn*) which each knower possesses 'whole in the first level of soul' (*holon en psukhêi têi prôtêi*, 1.1.8). It may ascend even to the divine.

In the treatise on our allotted *daimôn* (3.4), Plotinus describes this process in greater detail: it is the 'choice' (*prohairesis*) of the soul – which contains all things in potentiality – to 'energise' or 'practise' a particular life (3.4.2–4): the vegetative life, the appetitive life, the spirited life, the reasoning life, the intellectual life, or the divine life. Depending on its choice, its afterlife will be of a plant, an animal, a man, a daimon, or a god. Therefore the goal is likeness to god (*homoiôsis tôi theôi*), that is, to achieve godliness in this life so as to remain a god in the next. But the first step is to raise ourselves, or 'escape' (*pheugein*, cf. *Theaet.* 176A8–B1), from the life of nature and perception to the life of the reasoning soul (*logikê psukhê*), recognising that *this is who the human being (anthrôpos) is* (3.4.2, 12). The life of the soul is more authentically 'us' than any perceptible thing, which is in a sense a reflection of the soul's activity (5.1.2). Later Athenian Neoplatonism, preserved in Proclus, systematised this development, presenting a sequence of self-knowledge, self-care, and ultimately unity with the divine – beginning with the realisation that the human being is the rational soul. Here begins the usefulness of the *Alcibiades*, which proves this point: the human being is rational soul alone.

Olympiodorus adopted these steps and presented them as the ladder by which Platonic philosophy, in its dialogue form, becomes a source of 'benefit' for human souls striving to pass from the 'natural' (*phusikos*) forms of excellence to the 'philosophic' excellences and finally to 'inspiration'. As I suggest below, he employs the *Life of Plato* as an allegory for this same ascent, to show its practical benefit in leading 'the good life', or obtaining *eudaimonia*. This 'benefit' he proceeds (19) to describe as immortality, knowledge of all beings, and what is good for the soul, namely *aretê* for the purpose of *eudaimonia* (10,11ff.).

Olympiodorus divides the main body of the *Alcibiades* into three sections, refutation (106C–119A, Olymp. 62,20–142,3), exhortation (119A–124A, Olymp. 142,3–170,3), and elicitation (124Aff., Olymp. 170,3ff.). He proceeds to map these three sections onto a familiar structure. In the first section, Socrates has healed Alcibiades' double ignorance about his soul; in the second, he has shown him how his soul pertains to his body and external possessions, and helped him to see that he is 'the rational soul using the body'; in the third, he has helped him look upwards to his truer self, the rational soul itself (170,3–171,19). These three categories correspond to the introversion, the 'downward' expression, and the 'upward' contemplation, respectively, of the *civic* soul. As Damascius put it (*in Phd.* 1.74), 'Soul has a threefold activity, the object being both the soul itself and what exists on either side, the lower and the higher; hence the three levels of life'. In each of these the soul can choose three different ways:

in civic life, that of ruling the lower, or of finding within itself the origins of its actions, or of *looking up* towards causes higher than soul.[102]

The final, 'upward' activity leads to the next stage of the philosophical curriculum, catharsis, followed by contemplation and finally inspiration. This is the way in which Olympiodorus concludes the commentary on the *Alcibiades*, and appropriately so, since the curriculum will proceed to the 'civic' *Gorgias* and the 'purificatory' *Phaedo*. In Lecture 28 (224,2ff. on 133C–135E), he explains how civic self-knowledge is about the human being as the soul using the body, namely, the subject of the *Alcibiades*. Cathartic self-knowledge is about the rational soul, not using the body, but reverting upon itself. Contemplative self-knowledge is about the rational soul reverting upon its betters. As we have seen, Olympiodorus understands this course of development to be the practical function of the Neoplatonic curriculum. He teaches the Platonic philosophy because this curriculum leads to *eudaimonia* and the good life, which he explains to be among its benefits. For him the very study of Platonism, which he offers in his lectures or *praxeis*, is sought by all human beings 'since they all wish to draw benefit from it, and are eager to come under the power of its streams and to render themselves full of Platonic inspirations' (1,6–9).

The advance of the soul through the higher levels of being is possible through 'Platonic philosophy' – because, as we have read in Proclus and in the *Prolegomena*, the dialogues present us with an ideal 'cosmos', a 'perfect living being', with which we are meant to sympathise. Through *theoria*, we are educated by the dialogue. By inviting us to imitate the characters, the dialogue directly affects even the irrational, 'habituated' part of the soul. The emphasis falls on us as individual readers to follow the example of the *Life of Plato* and 'ascend' in the curriculum, beginning by locating ourselves correctly within the 'cosmic' hierarchy represented by the dialogue.

5.3. Olympiodorus on the individual (*to atomon*)

I would also like to draw attention to Olympiodorus' special effort to locate the 'individual' (*to atomon*) in this hierarchy. In Lecture 26 (209, 22), Olympiodorus speaks about three categories of 'self' which are presented in the *Alcibiades*, an observation whose Proclan and Damascian implications he has already discussed (203,20–204). These are *auto* (self); *auto to auto* (self itself); and *auto hekaston* (each self). Olympiodorus reaches the conclusion that 'self' is the rational soul 'using the body and the passions as an instrument' (210,27), that is, 'the civic soul' (27–8), while 'self itself' is the rational soul, contemplative and purificatory, pure and untouched. 'Each self' is the *atomon* (210,4–16), generally translated the 'individual'. Olympiodorus reports Proclus at 204,3–11, repeating some of his own preliminary remarks on the *skopos* of the dialogue:

> For the text says that if we are to ascertain what 'self itself' is, we must also learn what 'each self itself' is, since it is not enough simply to ascertain the human being, but we must know also what the *atomon* is, because the task in hand is to help Alcibiades find out who *he* is – namely, his soul: and *actions are concerned with particular circumstances* (*praxeis peri ta kath' hekasta katagignontai*).

This final remark helps to understand Olympiodorus', and indeed Damascius' and Proclus', use of the phrase *ho kath' hekasta anthrôpon*, literally something like 'the one-by-one person', to describe *auto hekaston* and the 'individual'. Olympiodorus objects on several occasions, including immediately following this sentence (204,8–12), to a 'Peripatetic' definition of the individual (*atomon*) as an 'assembly (*athroisma*) of accidentals'.[103] How, then, does he propose that we define it? Olympiodorus reports and endorses Proclus (210,13–16):

> If we discover the common human being (*koinos anthrôpos*), we shall in fact, as it seems, discover the human being one-by-one (*ton kath' hekasta*), which we also need: in fact, this is that for which we care. The discussion is about Socrates and Alcibiades. The one [sc. the common] implies the other [sc. the one-by-one] (*ei de mê to a', oude to b'*).

This phrase *kath' hekasta*, as Proclus has told us above, refers to the 'particular circumstances' with which ethical actions or deeds (*praxeis*) are concerned. The relationship between the language of the particular (*hekaston*) and that of the 'individual' goes back to Aristotle; in *Metaphysics* B the *kath' hekaston* can be defined precisely as the 'one in number' (3.4, 1000a1–2). Thus Proclus observes, according to Olympiodorus, that the individual (*atomon*) or 'each self' (*auto hekaston*) is so named (*kalei*) 'from its activity concerning individual things' (*ek tou peri ta atoma energein*, 210,5). What is made clear in Olympidorus' report of Proclus is that these 'individual things' (*ta atoma*) are particular *deeds* (*praxeis*), that is, the particular deeds which, say, Alcibiades carries out (cf. 204,3–11). Therefore 'the individual' (*to atomon*) is so named as the agent of *praxeis*, involving actions which are 'concerned with particular circumstances' (*praxeis peri ta kath' hekasta katagignontai*). Hence this person is described 'one-by-one' (*ho kath' hekasta* [sc. *anthrôpos*], 210,14). This is the person whom Olympiodorus identifies with the embodied 'civic soul' (210,27–8), the one who is concerned with these particular acts one-by-one (*kath' hekasta*). His soul, as Proclus puts it, is divided in association with bodies, as it uses the body as an instrument to instantiate ethically meaningful actions (*erga, praxeis*). In this sense, when we speak of the 'individual', there is more to it then simply meaning 'me' as opposed to 'you' (or 'Socrates' as opposed to 'Alcibiades', as Olympiodorus and Proclus put it here). A person is considered *kath' hekasta* just insofar as she is concerned with particular acts (*praxeis*, 204,3–11). This is the quality of the civic soul, which – so long as it is 'looking down', as Damascius puts it, and 'ruling what lies below' – needs to use the body as an instrument for this reason, in order to generate acts 'one-by-one', in sequence.

Plotinus uses the distinction between universal (*katholou*) and particular (*kath' hekaston*) somewhat similarly in his treatment of the human person (*Enneads* 1.1), which also relies partly on the *Alcibiades*. To paraphrase Plotinus' discussion, the *Alcibiades*' independent and separable soul, which 'uses' the body (1.1.3) – the 'self itself' (*auto to auto*) in Olympiodorus' parlance – is the first rank of the soul (*psukhê hê prôtê*, which possesses wholeness and universality (1.1.8). It is regarded as 'each self' (*auto hekaston*) when it engages in particular actions and experiences particular impressions (*prattomena kai doxazomena*, 1.1.1,7). This now appears to have been Proclus' interpretation also. It is the rational soul (*logikê psukhê*), regarded as separate and 'as a whole', that exists 'in the whole of time'. But regarded in its particular acts, like the impressions of a seal-stone in wax, it is regarded as 'soul partitioned in association with bodies'. Above these two resides intellect (*nous*), completing the tripartite ontology that Proclus teases out from the *Timaeus*. Therefore 'we' must begin by reverting upon ourselves, recognising that we are essentially rational soul (*logikê psukhê*), and then, as Damascius has it, proceed to revert upon our betters.

In Olympiodorus' treatment, to discover 'what we ourselves are' does not only refer to determining and establishing the position of 'soul' in the hierarchy of being – although it means that, too. Olympiodorus preserves Proclus' formulation that we must focus on the identity of the individual (here,

'Alcibiades', representing, as I have suggested, the student), because at the level of the 'civic soul', we are concerned with the actions that are specific to him, *kath' hekasta*. To begin Platonic philosophy with the *Alcibiades* and 'civic self-knowledge' implies that Platonic philosophy must begin with the individual, at the level of his actions and particular choices, and only on that basis proceed to purifying the soul (*katharsis*, the soul reverting on itself), contemplation (*theôria*, the soul reverting on intellect), and divine inspiration (*enthousiasmos*, presumably answering to unification or *henôsis* in Plotinus and Proclus, as Olympiodorus refers to this 'inspiration' as 'union with the divine').

It seems especially clear in Olympiodorus' case that he linked the Platonic curriculum with individual transformation (see again §2.1 above). Strengthening this view further is Olympiodorus' introduction of his commentary through a *Life of Plato*, which, as I will argue, also suggests that Olympiodorus saw the course of Platonic education as an analogy for the advance of the student throughout the grades of excellence. If this interpretation is correct, then the *Life of Plato* here may be compared to the *Life of Proclus* composed by Marinus, which, on Henry Blumenthal's account, represents the master as living out the *scala virtutum*, beginning from the potential of natural excellence (*phusikê aretê*) to the completion of the hieratic.[104] The *Life* is translated in this volume (Olymp. *in Alc.* 2,14–3,2). Below, I argue briefly that it should be treated as an allegory for the individual student's progress through the grades of excellence.

5.4. Olympiodorus on the *Life of Plato*

Several aspects of the *Life* are certainly intended to reflect the course of the Neoplatonic curriculum,[105] whose language it often explicitly employs (as at 2,46–8): the tripartite soul, for instance, is presented together with its proper care, *logos* through letters, *thumos* through music, *epithumia* through gymnastics (2,45–8). Examples of 'civic' excellence are then clustered in Plato's journeys to Sicily; examples of 'purificatory' excellence in his journeys in the East; an example of 'contemplative' excellence in his foundation of the Academy; and an example of 'inspired' excellence in his final dream (where he is rendered ungraspable or *alêptos*, 2,158), representing the fourfold division that will rapidly become familiar to the reader of Olympiodorus' lectures.

If one is sympathetic to this view, it is possible to reconstruct the *Life* as a Neoplatonic exemplar of self-knowledge after the pattern of the *Alcibiades*. Thus the introductory account of Plato's divine origin implies Plato's doctrine that the soul pre-existed the body. Embodied learning, then, is a matter of recovering the soul's knowledge from its pre-embodied condition (cf. *Meno* 98A, *Phaedo* 72B–78B), that is, Plato's view that the soul existed before birth and can learn by being reminded of the knowledge it had then. The tripartite or embodied soul of Plato's *Republic* 4 is naturally presented next, together with its proper care. As we noticed above, the soul has three parts, namely reason (*logos*), spirited emotion (*thumos*), and appetite (*epithumia*), cared for by the study of letters, music, and gymnastics (45–8). Plato then engages the arts, another common theme in *Republic*. The arts represent the 'lower activity'[106] of the soul, beginning with painting[107] and concluding with poetry. It is Socrates who, at this juncture, 'turns' Plato's eye to philosophy (76–86), which is also, on the view of both Proclus and Olympiodorus, Socrates' function in the *Alcibiades*. Subsequently Plato studies with Cratylus (who, through his eponymous dialogue, represents the study of linguistic items, especially the question whether names refer to beings by nature or by convention) and Archytas (the Pythagorean, representing the mathematicals); this education brings him to the outskirts of soul.

Next, therefore, comes the division of the soul's achievement into the 'philosophic' grades of excellence (*aretai*): first the civic excellences, represented in Plato's efforts at constitutional change in Sicily, in his tenacity in enacting his ideals, his freedom of speech (*parrhêsia*), and his loyalty to his friend: second, the purificatory forms of excellence are represented in his study with the priests of Egypt and the magi of Persia: and finally, contemplative excellence is represented in the foundation of the Academy,[108] with which Plato passes into the realm of *nous*.[109]

Plato then passes beyond the reach of *nous*, into a transcendent realm where he is 'inaccessible' to the exegetes (*alêptos*, 158); his expressions are formulated not only naturally (*phusikôs*) and ethically (*êthikôs*), but also theologically (*theologikôs*). The significance of his earlier appearance as the swan in Socrates' dream (83–6), and as the son of Apollo (17–28), is clear in his nature, which is now divine: he has come to reside at the level accessible only by inspiration, or 'prophecy'. Thus he, like his companion soul Homer (162–4), is deserving of the epithet divine (*theios*), and, from beginning to end, he constitutes the perfect image of the Neoplatonic initiate.

This is, of course, one of many possible interpretations of the *Life*'s structure; but it is, I think, the one that Olympiodorus would offer. His *Life* gathers the existing elements in the tradition of Plato's life and combines them in a form which lends itself to structural exegesis. He employs the same method at 7,11–8,5, when he paraphrases the text of the *Alcibiades* into a structure which he proceeds to interpret in precisely these terms of fourfold hierarchy (8,5–14). Such an interpretation would also add a chapter to the history of the ladder of human excellence and its application to narrative biography and late antique hagiography.

I would argue, then, that Olympiodorus' presentation of the *Life of Plato* represents the inclusion of the full cycle of excellences in the Platonic curriculum, the 'non-rational' cultivation of appetite and spirited emotion, followed by the rational cultivation of civic, purificatory and contemplative excellence, and finally the supra-rational accomplishment of divine or theurgic, 'inspired' excellence. This cycle is presented narratively for the student's benefit, as a pattern to imitate. (By presenting a myth for imitation, Olympiodorus cultivates the 'irrational' forms of excellence, which can be cultivated through imitation, as well as the 'rational' *aretai*.) Much like the *Alcibiades* itself, this *Life* can be read, in Olympiodorus' sense, as a Platonic Myth.

It also represents the training that Olympidorus himself offers, based on the curriculum of the Athenian school; and its ultimate expression remains the action or *praxis* of the individual. This focus on the individual student, I suggest, underlies the curricular focus of the *Alcibiades*, which is designed to take up the reader at a particular 'level' of activity (*energeia*), and, through imitation and analogy, to raise him up to reason and prepare him for the remainder of the curriculum. At the same time, however, the *Alcibiades* contains the *whole* curriculum: like Plato's life, the dialogue gestures toward purificatory and contemplative and inspired excellence. And this, again, is the feature of the *Alcibiades* which was said to have been drawn out by Iamblichus: we are now in a position to understand his statement that it contains philosophy 'as if in a seed' in the context of the Platonic curriculum as a whole. By making the individual the focus of philosophy in this way, I think Olympiodorus presents us with a later Neoplatonism which is intended to

serve, not a dusty museum-piece of metaphysical abstractions, in E.R. Dodds'
famous turn of phrase, but a manual of practice and discipline, not unlike the
Handbook of Epictetus that served to begin the prior 'habituation' of the
student.

In Olympiodorus' treatment, then, we have the completion of the function
of the *Alcibiades* in the curriculum: drawing the student from *phusikê aretê*, it
introduces him to our inward civic 'constitution' (*politikê aretê*), including the
recognition that the self is the soul alone; the *Alcibiades* teaches us that this is
the 'higher' soul, and that the self includes both the *katholou* and the *kath'
hekasta anthrôpos*, which Proclus will call the 'unpartitioned' soul and the 'soul
partitioned in association with bodies'. The dialogue eventually advances as
high as 'likeness to God' (*Theat.* 176B) and also includes the application of this
lofty knowledge in deeds or *praxeis*. Thus it anticipates the entire curriculum
in one whole.

6. The text of Olympiodorus' lectures: this volume

This volume translates Olympiodorus' first nine lectures *On the Alcibiades*
(1,3–90,24). Following a brief preamble on the value of Platonic philosophy
(1,3–13) and the *Life of Plato* (1,13–3,2),[110] this includes Olympiodorus'
treatment of the target, usefulness, position, and division of the text (3,2–13,8);
his study of 103A–106B, which he regards as the 'proem' (13,10–62,17,
including commentary on the different kinds of lovers and an excursus on
Socrates' *daimôn* and the nature of *daimones* more broadly); and the beginning,
according to Olympiodorus' division, of the 'elenctic' or 'refutative' part of
the dialogue from 106C–119A (62,20–142,3). The subsequent sections are
exhortation (119A–124A, Olymp. 142,3–170,3) and elicitation (124Aff.,
Olymp. 170,3ff.)

The lectures are entitled 'from the voice' of Olympiodorus (1,2): they were
perhaps delivered over about ten weeks[111] around the middle of the sixth
century AD.[112] The phrase 'from the voice' (*apo phônês*) describes notes taken
by a pupil during a lecture or tutorial.[113] For the sixth-century AD philosophy
student, working up a record of the master's remarks was regarded as a valuable
pedagogical practice, and perhaps also a kind of 'spiritual exercise'.[114] Similarly,

a philosopher working alone might make substantial progress by following and adapting a predecessor's written commentary.[115]

Editing or translating such notes can be a challenge: as E.R. Dodds noted, 'the task of reconstructing a course of lectures from students' notebooks is full of difficulties' (1957, 357; cf. Westerink 1982, VIII–IX). In spite of Westerink's caution that '[t]he editor cannot be held responsible for all the blunders and inaccuracies of the text' (1982, IX), I tend to agree with Dodds that obvious errors of fact should not be attributed to the lecturer (1957, 357), particularly when these can be easily explained by auditory or palaeographical error. I have generally erred on the side of correcting errors of fact and obvious slips of the tongue or ear: for examples, see below, 2,20, 45,2, and 61,8, with notes.

The archetype of all the surviving copies of the text is Marcianus graecus 196 (*c.* 900 AD). It is in very good condition, and so the transcripts that derive from it are mostly useful for filling the lacuna between folios 119–20 (2,94 *Epeidê* to 20,9 *hupo*). The manuscripts and textual and linguistic issues associated with the text are concisely discussed by Westerink (1982, VII–XIV). Westerink's edition is outstanding, as Dodds (1957) judged, and is a thorough development from the only earlier edition, by Creuzer, which was based on one of the transcripts.

7. Conclusions

This overview has been broad, but hopefully helps to establish the geography for Olympiodorus' commentary as an introduction to his system of thought, and to Alexandrian Neoplatonism more broadly. We have sketched Olympiodorus' social and intellectual environment (§1), located the *Alcibiades* in the framework of the 'scale of virtues' that guided his teaching (§2), and briefly reviewed the reception history of the dialogue through late antiquity (§§3–5). I hope to have offered an interesting explanation for Iamblichus' selection of this dialogue as the head of his influential Platonic curriculum: it *had* to begin the curriculum due to its place in the scale of excellences (*aretai*), mediating from natural (*phusikê*) to civic (*politikê*) grades of achievement. I have also argued that Olympiodorus develops an interesting focus on the individual, understood as the agent of particular moral actions (*praxeis*) when she is exercising civic excellence; this is suggestive, I think, that the sage continues to act morally 'in the world' after achieving the peak of human excellence.[116] Finally, I have argued that, just as the scale of excellences (*aretai*) was expressed in late antique biographies such as Marinus' *Life of Proclus*,[117] it is represented in Olympiodorus' *Life of Plato*, which is prefixed to the *Alcibiades* commentary precisely because the student will learn from both Alcibiades and Plato as exemplary models. Hence the Platonic *Alcibiades* appears (at least to the Neoplatonists who comment upon it) to be a kind of early ancestor of their school of late antique hagiography.

The fortunes of the *Alcibiades* over nearly a millennium represent the changing fortunes of a certain school of Platonism, according to which the human being who has discerned her true nature as soul (*psukhê*) begins a programme of philosophical self-cultivation, but instead of withdrawing from society, instead pursues the betterment of her community. The *Alcibiades* thus helps to bridge a gentle tension between the civic altruism of Plato's Socrates in, say, the *Apology*, on the one hand, and the call to independence from physical and social demands that seems to be issued in the *Phaedo*. (The Neoplatonists were especially sensitive to such tensions, for they were 'unitarians' about the dialogues, maintaining that every Platonic text expounded the same system, though perhaps at different levels for different audiences; they were therefore particularly awake to these concerns.)

By 'stacking' these two models as civic and purificatory grades of excellence, respectively, and allowing for the successful philosopher to 'return' to benefit his community (as Olympiodorus evidently understood himself to be doing), the Neoplatonists could regard the *Alcibiades* as the starting-point for the journey recommended by Socrates and Glaucon for the philosopher-kings in *Republic* 7: those philosophers who have ascended to the light of day, who have mastered the ladder of human excellence, will return to the 'cave' to teach and help others.[118] Olympiodorus, perhaps, was not as quiet in his 'little fortress' (*teikhion*) as it first appeared to us.

As an historical side note, the ancient vogue of the *Alcibiades* seems to track the currency of the approach to Plato that would, in the course of time, become Neoplatonism. It enters the stage of history alongside the early glimmerings of the movement that we call 'Middle Platonism', and comes into its own as a curricular foundation-text near the dawn of Neoplatonism proper. With the resurgence of a Neoplatonic worldview in the Renaissance, the *Alcibiades* also resurged in the Academy of Marsilio Ficino, functioning as the 'gateway' to the Neoplatonic Plato. Its multilayered metaphysics of the mysteries and initiation (*teleiôsis*), its search for excellence (*aretê*) and the quest for godliness, carried much less appeal for the careful philologians of the nineteenth century, and on Schleiermacher's terms the *Alcibiades* could be called nothing but 'very poor'. But in the later twentieth century, alongside a renaissance of scholarly interest in Neoplatonism in general, the *Alcibiades* was also back on stage. It offers an interesting case study in the interdependency of a root text and the commentary tradition and philosophy that develop in dialogue with it.

Appendix: Testimonia to the *First Alcibiades*, ordered by century

Adapted from Carlini 1964

Century	Citation	Reference Type*	Referring Author	Referring Work
IV BC	132D11–133B11	fort. resp.	Aristoteles (ps.)	Magn. Moral. II 15 (p.1213, a13–24)
I	119C10–E9	fort. resp.	Cicero	De officiis I 87
	130E2–9	fort. resp.	Cicero	Tuscul. I 52, De rep. VI 26
I AD	104B5–6	resp.	Persius	IV, 3
	113B8–C7	resp.	Persius	IV, 8–16
I–II	106D5–6	resp.	Epictetus	Diss. II 12,23
	129E3–130D8	fort. resp.	Epictetus	Diss. II 12,20–1
	131D8	cf.	Epictetus	Diss. III 1, 42
	106E7	resp.	Plutarchus	Alc. 192E
	121D1–2	cf.	Plutarchus	Phoc. 755C
	122A8–B2	cf.	Plutarchus	Lyc. 49F
	122A8–B2	resp.	Plutarchus	Alc. 192A
	123A1–5	cf.	Plutarchus	De prof. in virt. 79A
	132E7–133A3	fort. resp.	Plutarchus	De facie in orbe lunae 942D
	132E7–133B11	fort. resp.	Plutarchus	De audiendo 40D

(Continued)

Appendix (Continued)

Century	Citation	Reference Type*	Referring Author	Referring Work
II	115A9–116D5	resp.	Albinus	Isag. 158,35–6 Hermann
	121E4–122A3	cit.	Apuleius	Apol. 30, 7–13 Helm
	113C3	cf.	Aristides	Or. 46 497 (II, p. 387,13–14 Dindorf)
	118B6–C2	cf.	Aristides	Or. 46 471 (II p. 368, 8–100 D.)
	118C3–5	resp.	Aristides	Or. 46 207 (II p. 167,14–15 D.)
	120B2–4	cit.	Diogenianus	I 73 (Corpus paroem. graec. I, p. 193 Leutsch-Schneidewin)
	106D5–6	cf.	Galenus	Inst. Log. p. 38,3–5 Kalbfleisch
	103A5–7	resp.	Maximus Tyrius	VIII 6 (p. 92,9 Hobein)
	132A5–7	cit.	Maximus Tyrius	XXXV 6 (p. 409,1 H.)
	128C13	cit.	Pollux	II 155 (I p. 131 Bethe)
	129C7	cit.	Pollux	X 141 (II p. 232 B.)
II–III	106D5–6	cit.	Alexander Aphrodisiensis	In Met. 267, 12–13 Hayduck
	103A2–3	resp.	Athenaeus	187E
	118E3–7	cf.	Athenaeus	506D
	120A10–B1	cf.	Athenaeus	506D
	132A5–7	cf.	Athenaeus	506D
	109E1–7	cit.	Clemens Alexandrinus	Strom. V 17,2 Stählin (unde Theodoretus, infra)
	135C4–6	cf.	Clemens Alexandrinus	Strom. II 22,5
	123B4–5	cf.	Hermogenes	Peri methodou deinotêtos p. 445, 16–17 Rabe
III	130A1	resp.	Plotinus	I 1,3,3; VI 7,5,24 Bréhier
	132A5–7	cit.	Plotinus	IV 4,43,20–1 B.
III–IV	106A8–9	?	Iamblichus	ap. Olymp. in Alc. 59,22–60,12

	131A2–B8	cf.	Iamblichus	Protr. p. 28,19–29,10 Pistelli
	134E4–5	cf.	Iamblichus	ap. Stob. III 11,35
	135E1–3	fort. resp.	Iamblichus	De vita pythagor. p. 15,12–13 Deubner
	104E2	fort. resp.	Methodius	p. 254,7 Bonwetsch
	130A5–B12	resp.	Methodius	p. 311,8–10 B.
	103A1	cit.	Tiberius	Spengel, Rhet. Gr. III 76,7–8
IV	133C1–8	cit.	Eusebius	Praep. Ev. 551b (unde Theodoretus, l.c., V 39)
	132D6–133C7	resp.	Gregorius Nyssenus	De mortuis 509bd
	129A2–4	resp.	Julianus	Or. VI 188cd
	133C1–7	resp.	Julianus	Or. II 68d–69a
	112C4–5	fort. resp.	Libanius	Apol. Socr. 137 (V, p. 91,13 Foerster)
	130A1	resp.	Nemesius	De nat. homin. p. 37,7–10 Matthaei
	130C1–4	cf.	Nemesius	De nat. homin. p. 37,7–10 M.
	123A1–5	cf.	Themistius	Or. XIII 174c (p. 214,6–10 Downey)
	132A3–4	fort. resp.	Themistius	Or. 26 314a3–4 (p. 380,15–16 D.)
	107E6	cit.	Timaeus gramm.	Lex. Plat. s.v. (VI, p. 387 Hermann)
	120B2–3	cit.	Timaeus gramm.	Lex. s.v. andrapodôdê
IV–V	117E7–118A5	fort. resp.	Synesius	Dio X 52d (p. 262,5–6 Terzaghi)
	109E1–7	cit.	Theodoretus	Graec. Affect. Cur. I 84 (p. 24,22–25,5 Raeder)
V	105A9–C6	resp.	Hermias	In Phaedr. p. 244, 10–13 Couvreur
	109E9–110A1	cf.	Hermias	In Phaedr. p. 42,26–8 C.
	131C11–D5	resp.	Hermias	In Phaedr p. 200, 17–19 C.
	132C7–133B11	resp.	Hermias	In Phaedr p. 196, 25–9 C.
	119A3–7	resp.	Proclus	In Parm. p. 624, 32–4 Cousin

(*Continued*)

Appendix (Continued)

Century	Citation	Reference Type*	Referring Author	Referring Work
	120B2–4	cit.	Proclus	In Tim. I, p. 102,12–13 Diehl
	127E6–7	cf.	Proclus	In Tim. III p. 252, 9–10 D.
	129B1–2	cit.	Proclus	In Remp. I p. 172, 3 Kroll
	129C5	cf.	Proclus	In Remp. I p. 171, 23–5 K.
	133B7–C7	resp.	Proclus	In Plat. Theol. I 3 (p. 7, 40–6 Portus)
	133C6–7	cit.	Proclus	In Tim. III p. 103,4–5 Diehl
	134E4–5	cf.	Proclus	In Tim. III p. 274, 26–7 D.
	135C6	cit.	Proclus	De provid. 23,18 Boese
	109E1–7	cit.	Stobaeus	III 1,191
	110D1–E3	cit.	Stobaeus	III 1,192
	115E7–116D5	cit.	Stobaeus	III 1,193
	120D13–122A8	cit.	Stobaeus	V 29,26
	122A5–6	cf.	Stobaeus	IV 7,26; Florilegium Monacense 241 etc. Carlini p. 173 ad loc.
	126B9–127D3	cit.	Stobaeus	IV 1,151
	127E9–131D5	cit.	Stobaeus	III 21,23
	132B5–134B6	cit.	Stobaeus	III 21,24
	134B7–135C13	cit.	Stobaeus	IV 1,152
	123B4–8	cit.	Syrianus	In Hermog. II p. 30,20–4 Rabe
V–VI	110E5–10	cf.	Damascius ap. Ol.	ap. Olymp. in Alc. 91,23–92,1
	113C5	cit.	Damascius ap. Ol.	ap. Olymp. In Alc. 106,2
	119C2	cit.	Hesychius	s.v. Alcibiades
VI	103A1	cit.	Asclepius	In Met. 18,31 Hayduck
	106D5–6	cit.	Asclepius	In Met. 256,21–3 H.
	118D7–119A7	resp.	Asclepius	In Met. 10,18–19 H.

	103A6	cit.	Choricius Gazaeus	210,7 Foerster-Richsteig
	109D3	cf.	Choricius Gazaeus	p. 30, 5 F.–R.
	114B11–C1	cit.	Elias	In Porph. Isag. p. 33,29–31 Busse
	115E7–9	cit.	Elias	In Categ. p. 122, 14–15 B.
	126D10–11	cit.	Elias	In Porph. Isag. p. 33,20–1 B.
	129E11–130C2	resp.	Elias	In Porph. Isag. p. 22,33–5 B.
	111D11–112A2	resp.	Olympiodorus	in Gorg. p. 35,15 Norvin
	116C1–D3	resp.	Olympiodorus	in Gorg. p. 104,8–10 N.
	130D4–6	resp.	Olympiodorus	in Phaed. p. 48, 12–13 N.
	132A3–4	cf.	Olympiodorus	in Gorg. p. 192, 30–193,2 N.
	115E7–9	cit.	Philoponus	Aetern. mundi p. 445,12–15 Rabe
	104A8–B2	cit.	Priscianus	Inst. XVIII 122 (II p. 264 Hertz)
	104E1–2	cit.	Priscianus	Inst. XVIII 122 (II p. 265 H.)
	104E6–105A1	cit.	Priscianus	Inst. XVIII 123 (II p. 266 H.)
	105A4–5	cit.	Priscianus	Inst. XVIII 124 (II p. 265 H.)
	105E5–106A1	cit.	Priscianus	Inst. XVIII 124 (II p. 265 H.)
	106A1	cit.	Priscianus	Inst. XVIII 123 (II p. 265 H.)
	115C10–11	cit.	Priscianus	Inst. XVIII 125 (II p. 266 H.)
	121D5–8	cit.	Priscianus	Inst. XVIII 254 (II p. 336 H.)
IX	119C4	cit.	Photius	Lex. s.v. Alcibiades

* Abbreviations: resp. = corresponds; fort. resp. = perhaps corresponds; cf. = refers; cit. = cites.

Notes

1 Brown 1992, 117.

2 Translations from Olympiodorus' *Gorgias* commentary here and following are taken from Jackson, Lycos and Tarrant 1998, sometimes lightly adapted for compatibility with other translations in the essay. Translations from the *Phaedo* commentary are taken from Westerink 1976.

3 On Olympiodorus, see for example Opsomer 2010; Saffrey 2005; Tarrant 1997; and Wildberg 2008. For his social and political environment, see Watts 2006, ch. 5; Westerink 1990; Jackson et al. 1998, 1–33. As 'the distinguished philosopher' (*ho megas philosophos*), Olympiodorus' teaching routine and philosophy were influential on the following generation of Christian teachers of Plato and Aristotle at Alexandria.

4 These particular lectures are often dated relatively early by various features, including reliance on Ammonius and perceived philosophical simplicity. In the remainder of this volume Olympiodorus will be cited as follows: *Proleg. in Cat.* = *Prolegomena to Logic and Aristotle's Categories* (ed. Busse 1902); *in Alc.* = *On Plato's Alcibiades* (ed. Westerink 1956), *in Gorg.* = *On Plato's Gorgias* (ed. Westerink 1970, tr. Jackson et al. 1998), *in Phaed.* = *On Plato's Phaedo* (ed. and tr. Westerink 1976), *in Meteor.* = *On Aristotle's Meteorology* (ed. Stuve 1900). The numbering system is page,line (divided by a comma) except where a chapter-heading based system is now more standard, as in the *Phaedo* and *Gorgias* commentaries.

5 Here and following, Olympiodorus' commentary on the *Gorgias* is cited by chapter heading in Westerink 1970, as adopted by Jackson et al. 1998.

6 See Watts 2008, chs 8–9; Watts 2010, ch. 1.

7 As Brown (1992, 117) puts it, 'the fear generated by the murder of Hypatia still hung over the city . . . '.

8 The *Republic* was not taught in the Platonic philosophy curriculum that derived from Iamblichus, but some of Olympiodorus' students may have known this and other Platonic texts from their study of rhetoric. On the Alexandrians' use of the Iamblichean curriculum, see for example Jackson et al. 1998, 14–15, Westerink 2010, 1962, and Mansfeld 1994, 88.

9 Olympiodorus' commitment to the value of Platonic philosophy for the good life is on vivid display in the opening lecture of his course *On Plato's Alcibiades* (discussed below). He mentions 'theurgy' approvingly as a virtue in his lecture on the *Phaedo* (8.2), and while he is careful to explain that 'the philosophers' worship not stone images but what they represent (*in Gorg.* 47.5), his remark suggests that the practice is still current and, as far as Olympiodorus is concerned, correct as a means of grasping intelligible being and the divine.

10 On the contemporary situation, told from Damascius' vantage point, see Athanassiadi 1999.

11 See for example Kaster 1988, 201–2.

12 Ammonius (*c.* 435/45–517/26), who was followed in the chair by a mathematician called Eutocius and then by the young Olympiodorus himself, had previously instituted an 'agreement' of some kind with the Christian authorities in Alexandria (so Damascius 118B: Athanassiadi 1999) on account of which he was able to continue teaching at the public expense. Whatever Ammonius' arrangement might have been, it seems reasonable to suppose that Olympiodorus followed in his footsteps, perhaps restricting the subjects or manner of his teaching or religious practice, and so was able to secure the professorship from Christian or governmental hostilities. It has been hotly debated whether the 'agreement' attributed to Ammonius by Damascius came down to a particular doctrinal compromise, or a commitment not to teach theurgy, or even some nominal confession of Christian creed. Sorabji 2005a argues that the agreement stipulated against the advocacy of pagan ritual that caused problems in 486; this would imply only minor restrictions on subject matter. (See also Sorabji 1990, 12.)

13 There is an epigram attributed to Olympiodorus in the *Greek Anthology*: 'Had the writing of Plato not checked my impulse, / I would have loosened by now the grievous, baneful bond of life' (*Anth. Gr. Appendix* 177). If genuine, however, this is likely to reflect Olympiodorus' characteristic exegesis of the *Phaedo* rather than an autobiographical remark.

14 See Tarrant 1997, 182–3. For the concept of *paideia* in Hellenised Egypt and late antiquity more broadly, see Cribiore 2001, Kaster 1988.

15 *Daimones*: Olymp. *in Alc.* Lecture 3, 15,3ff. Eternity: *in Gorg.* 11.2, 65.26, and *in Meteor.* 118.10–119.8. Theurgy: *in Phaed.* 8.2.1–20, on which see also below, §2.1.

16 I use 'Christianity' here to speak in general terms of the diverse Christian sects and doctrines that populated Alexandria in Olympiodorus' day, which might have been perceived by him collectively as the customary culture (*sunêtheia*) of the majority (*hoi polloi*). Mossman Roueché has kindly sensitised me to the dangers of treating these as a monolith. The particular beliefs of a Christian student would have been unlikely to interfere with their studies, but could be safely compartmentalised while they studied to become a gentleman and, often, future civil servant (*kalos k'agathos, mousikos anêr*); on that long-standing tradition in late antiquity, see Watts 2006, ch. 1. It is unlikely that Olympiodorus faced serious or dangerous hostility in Alexandria, which prized higher education, as her heavy investment in lecture-theatres testifies (Derda et al. 2007), but like any good lecturer, he appears acutely aware of the need to cater to his audience in terms that they will understand and find relevant to their lives and culture.

17 Two dialogues titled *Alcibiades* survive in the Thrasyllan corpus of Plato, one 'Greater' or 'First', and the other 'Lesser' or 'Second'. Today, the *Second Alcibiades* is widely acknowledged to be by an author other than Plato; the authorship of the *First Alcibiades* is still contested (see §3.1 below). Throughout this introduction and the translation, I will often refer simply to *Alcibiades* or *Alc.* to mean the *First Alcibiades*.

18 On Proclus and his thought, see Chlup 2012, Siorvanes 1996.

19 Westerink 1976, 23. Harold Tarrant has also stressed Olympiodorus' primary commitment as a teacher of Hellenism, a 'classicist' or 'champion of some ancient heritage that needed to be kept alive', while drawing out his views on the common ground of Platonism and Christianity. Indeed, Olympiodorus regarded himself as a teacher first and foremost, as an expounder of Hellenic *paideia* (Tarrant 1997, 188–92), the 'token of shared assumptions' that made a Mediterranean gentleman (Kaster 1988, 15) and had drawn students to pursue a higher education in Alexandria for centuries.

20 In the translation below, I have generally preferred to transliterate, rather than translate, the Greek word *daimôn*, which can refer to any divine power or apportioner (of destiny). In the later ancient technical sense mostly relevant to Olympiodorus, *daimôn* usually references a 'spiritual . . . being inferior to the gods' (LSJ A II 2).

21 On this treatment of *daimones*, see Renaud 2011.

22 Cf. Olymp. *in Cat.* 117,30 and *Meteor.* 264.3.

23 Tarrant 1997.

24 On this point, see also *Republic* 2, 377A, and Jackson et al. 1998, 290 n. 876.

25 See Griffin 2014c. This is what Jan Assmann has called 'syncretistic translation' (Assmann 2008, 146–7), building on Glen Bowersock's assessment of Hellenism (1990, 5).

26 Olympiodorus perhaps doubted that *real* disagreement is possible between genuinely accomplished philosophers. After all, they have achieved 'contemplative excellence' (*theôretikê aretê*; see below, §2.1) and therefore share a common vision of reality as it really is. Of course, some who call themselves philosophers (such as the Democriteans at Olymp. *in Alc.* 92,6) may not be deserving of the name, in its strictest sense.

27 These two lectures represent the beginning of the Aristotelian and Platonic curricula respectively.

28 This formulation, literally 'beautiful and good', is the standard description of an aristocratic hero in Homer, and also had currency in classical Athens as the description of a gentleman.

29 See Watts 2006, 6. On the cycle of liberal education leading up to philosophical studies, see Hadot 1984.

30 For examples of Olympiodorus' deployment of the hierarchy of virtues in his exegesis of the *Phaedo*, see Gertz 2011, 66–70.

31 Westerink 1976, 116–18 (n. ad Olymp. *in Phaed.* 8.2), offers an excellent summary of the textual sources for the scale of virtues. The complete hierarchy may have been developed by Iamblichus, although the list tabulated earlier appears mostly in sources later than Marinus, such as Damascius (*in Phaed.* 1.138–44 Westerink), Simplicius (*On Epictetus' Handbook*, 2.30–3.2 Duebner), and Olympiodorus *On the Alcibiades* (4,15–8,14 Westerink). Plotinus distinguished the cardinal 'civic excellences' (*politikai aretai*) of *Republic* 4 from higher *aretai* which he termed 'purifying', a distinction for which the Neoplatonists cited *Phaedo* 82A–E (where good reincarnations result from the practice of 'civic' excellences such as moderation and justice, but only philosophy delivers genuine 'purification'). Porphyry, drawing on Plotinus, already gives us the basic stages of 'civic', 'purificatory', 'contemplative', and 'exemplary' *aretai*. And Plotinus, in *Enn.* 1.3 and elsewhere, already studies a kind of natural excellence which is most basic to our being, and is shared even by plants.

32 Damascius *in Phaed.* 1.138, Olymp. *in Phaed.* 8.2,2–3. The name and the concept derive from Aristotle *Nic. Eth.* 6.13, 1144b3–9.

33 Damascius *in Phaed.* 1.139, Olymp. *in Phaed.* 8.2,3. Again, the name and the concept are partly inspired by Aristotle *Nic. Eth.* 2.1, 1103a17.

34 For a wider picture of later ancient education or *paideia*, see for example Watts 2006, ch. 1, Cribiore 2001, Kaster 1997; for its function specifically in these philosophical schools, see Hadot 1984.

35 Damascius *in Phaed.* 1.140, Olymp. *in Phaed.* 8.2,9–12.

36 Damascius *in Phaed.* 1.141, Olymp. *in Phaed.* 8.2,9–12.

37 As in Plotinus' ontology: see for example *Enneads* 5.1. For the later Neoplatonist elaboration of this system, see Proclus, *Elements of Theology* (Dodds 1963).

38 Damascius (*in Phaed.* 1.172) explains: 'To some philosophy is primary, as to Porphyry and Plotinus and a great many other philosophers; to others hieratic practice, as to Iamblichus, Syrianus, Proclus, and the hieratic school generally. Plato, however, recognising that strong arguments can be advanced from both sides, has united the two into one single truth . . . '. Damascius himself remarks that philosophers turn to the hieratic art to ground their own axioms, as the other sciences turn to philosophy! (*in Phaed.* 2.109). Iamblichus also recognises the distinction between two 'currents', one represented by himself and the other by Porphyry (*De Myst.* 2.11, 96,7–10). See also Chlup 2012, 16–32.

39 Chlup 2012, 168–84 offers an excellent summary of Neoplatonic theurgy, with
   references.

40 Hermias *in Phaedr.* 99,14–16; Proclus *De Sacr.* 150,24–151,5; Marinus *Life of
   Proclus* 18–19. Iamblichus had especially emphasised Egyptian symbolism and
   ritual practice, and Marinus reports that Proclus spent time explaining the
   meaning of other cultures' rites to their priests.

41 For instance, Proclus released Attica from a drought and healed a friend's daughter
   (Marinus *Life of Proclus* 28–29). Outward theurgy can also benefit the
   practitioner's own practical situation (Hermias *in Phaedr.* 96,4–8), but unlike the
   'magician' (whom the Neoplatonists regarded as a manipulator of sympathies
   within nature: cf. Plot. *Enn.* 4.4.32), the theurgist does not aim to 'compel' nature to
   his will, but to clear obstacles to the gods' beneficent action in the world.

42 Adopting Radek Chlup's helpful elaboration of the later Neoplatonists' distinction
   between 'external' and 'internal' theurgy (Chlup 2012, 168–84).

43 See Proclus, *Chald. Phil.* 1.206,6–11; *in Tim.* 1.211,27–8; Iamblichus *De Myst.* 3.6.
   Dillon 2002, 291 suggests that the procedure of inward theurgy involves 'a series
   of spiritual exercises based on the contemplation of images of light'.

44 Damascius *in Phaed.* 1.143, Olymp. *in Phaed.* 8.2,12–20. I take this to be – at least
   for Olympiodorus and Damascius – a different sort of practice from Porphyry's
   'exemplary' or 'archetypal' excellence in *Sent.* 32, since this practice belongs to the
   'theurgist' (Olymp. *in Phaed.* 8.2,20), although the goal of achieving and
   remaining in the intelligible realm is the same.

45 On the Oracles, see Majercik 1989 and the still valuable, monumental study by
   Hans Lewy, now revised and updated in Lewy 2011. On their role in Neoplatonism
   in particular, see Saffrey 1981.

46 Damascius *in Phaed.* 1.144.

47 But now in a 'unitary' rather than 'existential' manner, as Damascius rather
   gnomically remarks (1.144,2–3).

48 Treating the final 'theurgic' stage of excellence as one, rather than breaking out two
   separate stages, was likely the earlier view; see Westerink 1976, 117, n. ad loc.
   Olympiodorus might also have simply avoided talking about a separate hieratic
   stage of excellence in the course on the *Phaedo*.

49 For contemplative *theôria* and social *praxis* in Neoplatonism, see recently the
   essays by Linguiti (on Plotinus and Porphyry) and van Riel (on Damascius) in
   Bénatouïl and Bonazzi (2012); on the application of these ideals, see also Dillon
   1996.

50 The soul contains the building-blocks, for example, for the formulaic definition of
   a human being: 'rational animal'. By grasping this formula or rational principle
   (*logos*) within, the soul simultaneously grasps the structuring formula or rational

principle (*logos*) that guides the generation of human beings in the world. For the Neoplatonist, there are, in principle, as many of these structuring formulae available to the soul as there are eternal Forms in the intelligible world.

51 See Griffin 2014c.

52 See Hoffmann 1987, Griffin 2014a.

53 Proclus' commentary is extant to 116AB; Damascius' is lost (but it seems very likely, based on Olympiodorus' references, that he wrote one); Olympiodorus' own commentary is complete. See §3.4 below for a more detailed discussion of Proclus' and Olympiodorus' surviving commentaries.

54 I will argue below that this term has a special meaning in regard to the curriculum of the Platonic dialogues.

55 Including 'many considerations of logic, the elucidation of many points of ethics and such matters as contribute to our general investigation concerning happiness, and the outline of many doctrines leading us to the study of natural phenomena, or even to the truth regarding divine matters themselves, in order that as it were in outline in this dialogue the one, common, and complete plan of all philosophy may be comprised, being revealed through our actual first turning towards ourselves. It seems to me that this is why the divine Iamblichus gives it the first position among the ten dialogues, their whole subsequent development having been, as it were, anticipated in this seed' (tr. O'Neill 1965).

   Here and following, translations from Proclus *in Alcibiadem* are lightly adapted from O'Neill 1965, with some modifications. The best modern translation available is that by Segonds (Tome 1: 1985; Tome 2: 1986).

56 On this treatise and Plotinus' sources, see Aubry 2004, 15–61.

57 See Gill 2007, 194.

58 'Our argument shows that the power and capacity of learning exists in the soul already; and that just as the eye was unable to turn from darkness to light without the whole body, so too the instrument of knowledge can only by the movement of the whole soul be turned from the world of becoming into that of being, and learn by degrees to endure the sight of being, and of the brightest and best of being, or in other words, of the Good' (tr. Jowett.). For the imagery of 'looking up', compare also *Timaeus* 47B–C: the soul must 'look up' to the heavens in the *Timaeus* to recognise the motion of intellect (*nous*), and formulate its own motion accordingly.

59 This quality has counted against both *Alcibiades* and *Theages* in modern-day judgements of authenticity: see Joyal 2000, ch. 4.

60 In that curriculum, the philosophical virtues appear to embrace the study of natural philosophy and theology under the heading of the 'contemplative' virtues.

61 Blumenthal 1993a. On the idea of the 'practical' activity of the sage in late antiquity, see also Dillon 1996.

62 As Dillon points out, such a 'journey' was also already presented allegorically by Origen in his exegesis of the wanderings of the Children of Israel in the Desert (Num. 33), in the 27th *Homily on Numbers*: cf. Dillon 1996, 104.

63 Edited by Segonds 1985–1986, 2 vols. My English translations are normally lightly adapted from O'Neill 1965.

64 We have already discussed Iamblichus' reference to the *Alcibiades* as containing Plato's knowledge 'as if in a seed' (fr. 1 Dillon 1973). Proclus' opinion is cited above. Olympiodorus called the *Alcibiades* 'the entrance-gate to the works of Plato', whose holy of holies (*aduton*) was the *Parmenides (in Alc.* 11, 1). A millennium later, Marsilio Ficino followed suit in describing it as follows: 'Candidissimus Platonis nostri liber, qui Alcibiades inscribitur, Alcibiade ipso venustior et omni carior auro' (quoted in Friedländer 1957, 231).

65 Dobson's translation of Schleiermacher's introduction to the *Alcibiades* is reprinted at Schleiermacher 1836, 328–36.

66 Schleiermacher 1836, 329.

67 For the reception of the figure of Alcibiades in the broader Platonic tradition, see Johnson and Tarrant 2011; for Olympiodorus, see in particular Renaud 2011. While we cannot discuss Alcibiades himself in any historical detail here, readers interested in exploring the developing of the figure may find Gribble 1999 valuable for an introduction to the character of Alcibiades and his literary influence.

68 Friedländer 1957, ch. 17, 231–43.

69 See for example Joyal 2003: (1) Would Plato really have written a work that manifestly aimed to serve as an instruction to his own writings? (2) Does the *Alcibiades* fail to serve as an implicit protreptic for the reader, as Plato's aporetic dialogues usually do? (cf. Slings 1999, 163–4). (3) The *Alcibiades* refers to Socrates' divine sign as 'the god' (*ho theos*), which none of the certainly-genuine works do. Is this an indication of inauthenticity?

70 An excellent overview of its reception history can be found in the introduction to A. Segonds' excellent Budé edition of Proclus' commentary on the *Alcibiades* (Segonds 1985), x–civ. I also offer a brief sketch of its reception below.

71 Diogenes Laertius (3.56–62). Notably, the *Alcibiades* joins other targets of modern criticism in the Fourth Tetralogy: the *Second Alcibiades*, the *Hipparchus*, and the *Rival Lovers*. Another point of interest is the joint focus of this tetralogy on 'the education of the young': on this point see H. Tarrant, *Plato's First Interpreters* (Ithaca: Cornell University Press, 2000), p. 118.

72 A. Carlini, *Platone: Alcibiade, Alcibiade secondo, Ipparco, Rivali* (Turin: Boringhieri, 1964), pp. 401–3.

73 In the appendix to the introduction, I have adapted Carlini's index, omitting the commentaries of Proclus and Olympiodorus (but including other references from Proclus and Olympiodorus), and adding the citations from Carlini's apparatus criticus, with his introduction of each (*resp.*, *fort. resp.*, and *cit.* where the citation is explicit). I have added the date for each witness from the *Thesaurus Linguae Graecae*.

74 For the notion of *philia* within an individual, cf. *Phaedrus* 279C and *Republic* 9, 589A; for justice as a common structure in individuals and groups, see *Republic* 1, 351C–352A.

75 For example, *Alc.* 105A and Xen. *Mem.* 1.2.16, and more importantly the theme of self-care at Xen. *Mem.* 1.2.53–5 and *Alc.* 128B–133C.

76 In Segonds 1985, see for Iamblichus, xxi–xxxiv; Syrianus, xxxv–xxxix; Proclus, xxxix–lii; Damascius, liii–lxix; Olympiodorus, lxix–civ.

77 It is also worth noting that Olympiodorus' commentary is preserved from a student's notes, whereas Proclus' commentary is an independent treatise by his own hand; this difference may also account for some of the difference in simplicity.

78 On Proclus' philosophy, see Chlup 2012 and Siorvanes 1996. For his commentary on the *Alcibiades*, see Segonds 1985, xxxix–lii.

79 On the Aristotelian curriculum preceding the Platonic, see Hadot 1991; Hadot 1992; and Mansfeld 1994, 92. On the ancient titles of the *Metaphysics*, see Ross 1924, xxxii, and on the possibility of a 'Roman edition' by Andronicus of Rhodes, who may or may not have influenced the structure of the compilation that became our *Metaphysics*, compare Barnes 1997 and Primavesi 2007, with an excellent recent overview in Hatzimichali 2013. The modern nomenclature, *Meta ta phusika*, probably dates to Andronicus (first century BC). The earliest title, *On First Philosophy*, is probably reflected in Olympiodorus' title *Theology*.

80 On this see also the introduction to Segonds 1985, cited above.

81 In Neoplatonist metaphysics and ethics, multiplicity represents a challenge to the soul, which is essentially striving for unity. See §2.1 above and Proclus, *El. Theol.* pr. 1.

82 The outline of this taxonomy is fundamentally Neoplatonic, drawing primarily on the *Timaeus* (especially 35A), a text which Proclus has already introduced in the commentary. Several propositions of the *Elements of Theology* explain his analysis of these three ranks of being. 'Indivisible existence' refers to intellect (*nous, El. Theol.* pr. 171), and this participates the Unities (*henades*) that are beyond being (pr. 129); 'intermediate existence' refers to Soul (pr. 190); and 'being divided in association with bodies' is inseparable from its substrate, and extended somatically, so as to belong to what it informs: that is, this is the immanent soul, or the

combined 'living being'. This threefold ontology of (indivisible) intellect, (intermediate) separate soul, and (divided) inseparable soul, touches, at its upper bound, divine unity (*to hen*, cf. *El. Theol.* pr. 129), and, at its lower bound, bodies (*sômata*).

83 See Griffin 2014b: Socrates also often represents an intellect (*nous*), as he does later in Proclus' commentary. Alcibiades, here in Plato's *Alcibiades*, is treated as a person on the lowest rung of philosophical virtue, who is (as Proclus describes him) an example of the Rational Soul. Also, Plato himself is frequently assigned the epithet *theios* (divine), and Olympiodorus' *Life of Plato* (as I suggest below) is suggestive that he has attained the divine height of virtue. Aristotle, perhaps, is treated as obtaining the level of intellect, as he earns the epithet *daimônios* (intermediate between divine and human).

84 Thus intellect (*nous*), as Proclus explains here, obtains completion in Eternity (*aiôn*), whereas Soul finds its completion in Time – the separable soul in all of time, but the immanent soul in portions of time (*El. Theol.* prr. 55, 175). Thus here, the 'partitioned' or 'divided' soul is fulfilled 'in a portion of time', while the whole soul, viewed *katholou*, is fulfilled in the *whole* of time, and is 'composed in indissoluble bonds' (Proclus' citation from *Timaeus* 43A, referring to some extent to the 'circularity' of time; see Sorabji, *Time, Creation and the Continuum* (1983), 184–90). Time may be, for Proclus, known in parts or as a whole. Intellect, however, is fulfilled in Eternity, and needs no such composition (see Sorabji 1983, 255 and 263 on Proclus' view that God's knowledge of things temporal is timeless). It is in this way that Good differs for the *taxeis* of being: 'for those who have been allotted undivided (*ameristos*) being, their good is eternal (*aiônios*), but for those who have been allotted divided being, their good is naturally in time (*kata khronon*) and lies in motion (*kinesis*), while to those that lie intermediate, according to the measure of their existence (*hupostasis*), so is their completion considered, requiring time, but of the first order, and able to measure out non-bodily periods' (4,13–18).

85 Cf. *Phaedo* 69C.

86 On Socrates' *daimôn* and daimonic associations in particular, see Renaud in Johnson and Tarrant 2011. Cf. Plotinus, *Enn.* 3.4.3, 21–4 on the daimon's role in rescuing the soul, and the soul's ability to actualize the daimonic life. In the same treatise Plotinus suggests that the true philosopher, who is morally good (*spoudaios*), is spiritual or daimonic (3.4.6), and elsewhere he explains how this is: the morally good person is able to improve those outside himself without sacrificing his vision of the intelligible world within him, and his contemplation is a kind of vision all at once (3.8.6, 35–40). Socrates, symbolising both intellect and the 'good spirit' (*agathos daimôn*) for Proclus, may serve such a role.

87 Westerink, in his edition, has suggested that this section of the *Prolegomena* might draw on Proclus' lost *Prolegomena* – to which Proclus may be alluding at *in Alc.* 10,3–14, when he refers us to his fuller remarks on the dialogue as a cosmos 'in other works' (*en allois*). Westerink argues that this is a case where the full treatment of the *Anonymous Prolegomena* is a useful witness to Proclus' own, now lost *Prolegomena*. Westerink points out that the second part of the *Prolegomena* (chs 2–11) is closely connected with Proclus, in one case by a direct reference (ch. 10), in others by references in other writings of Proclus to a similar work of his own hand (chs 5, 9, and 10).

88 L.G. Westerink, *Anonymous Prolegomena to Platonic Philosophy* (Amsterdam, 1962), esp. xli.

89 We might add that Alcibiades himself is cited for this 'capturing of our attention': 'In a conversation, people are kept awake by asking and being asked; Alcibiades, indeed, was so stirred by Socrates' talks, that he said of himself: "Socrates, when I listen to you, my heart pounds as if I were in a trance, and tears spring to my eyes" ' (*Symp.* 215E).

90 One might compare Aristotle's account of the viewer of tragedy, although the Proclan conception of purification or *katharsis* seems very different. In fact, Olympiodorus reports in his *Life* that Plato went to study with the tragedians, 'the teachers of Greece', and that 'he went to these to draw from the tragic art the gnomic and solemn and heroic quality of its subjects', 2,50. Proclus, in his *Commentary on the Republic*, explains this episode in Plato's life as follows: 'Socrates, meeting Plato for the first time (who was then giving serious attention to tragedy) and having demonstrated to him that tragedy offers no good to men, turned him away from imitations of this sort [*tês toiautês mimêseôs*] and, in some way, turned him to the composition of those Socratic writings in which he proved tragedy to be neither educative nor beneficial but to be at a third remove from truth, with no share of knowledge or of correct opinion about the things which it imitates and aiming not at our intelligence but at the irrational part of our soul' (*in Remp.* 1.205,4–13, tr. Riginos 1976, 222).

On Proclus' treatment of tragedy and poetry in general, his Fifth and Sixth *Essays on the Republic* are particularly valuable, studied by Sheppard 1980 and more recently, with particular reference to Homer, by Kuisma 1996. The same view of poetry as a 'cosmic' requiring exegesis prevails, and the notion of a deeper underlying 'mystery' in the words of Homer and Hesiod traces its roots to *Republic* IV. On the issue in general in Neoplatonism, see Lamberton 1986.

91 Proclus describes his teacher, Syrianus, as follows: 'he came to human beings as the exact type of philosophy (*philosophias typon*) for the benefit of souls down here, being equal in worth to the *agalmata*' (*in Parm.* 618.9–11).

92 On this difficult concept, see Betegh 2003.

93 See Mansfeld 1994, 10–11. On the points to be discussed in approaching a
   Platonic dialogue in particular, see Hadot 1990, 32–4, 46–7; Westerink et al. 1990,
   lix–lxxvi, and Hoffmann 2012, 613–14.

94 The fifth item in the standard *schema isagogicum* discussed by Mansfeld 1994,
   authenticity, is omitted by Olympiodorus – as we noted above, it is probable that
   the standard position of this dialogue in the Iamblichean curriculum, and its
   suitable treatment of its theme, exempted it from doubt.

95 Compare Proclus, *Elements of Theology* prr. 44–6 and 186–7.

96 The Neoplatonists could draw partially from their interpretation of Aristotle *DA*
   3.6–8 for this view.

97 On Socratic 'midwifery' in general see M. Burnyeat, 'Socratic Midwifery and
   Platonic Inspiration', *BICS* 24 (1977) 7–17.

98 For the later Neoplatonists' pedagogical analysis of Platonic recollection, see for
   example Simplicius *in Cat.* 12,26–13,4, with Hoffmann 1987 and Griffin 2014a.

99 Compare *Symp.* 222B, where Alcibiades himself warns that Socrates has allegedly
   tricked Charmides, Euthydemus, and other youths 'by pretending to be their
   lover (*erastês*), but he ends up instead as the one that they love (*paidika*)'
   (*exapatôn hos erastês paidika mallon autos kathistatai ant' erastou*). Reciprocity is
   an important theme in Plato's discussions of *erôs*. Compare *Phaedr.* 255C–E: 'As a
   gust of wind, or an echo, bounces off smooth hard surfaces and is carried back to
   whence it came, so too the stream of beauty goes back [from the lover] to the
   beautiful boy. It passes through his eyes, which are the natural route to the soul.
   When it arrives, . . . it fills the soul of the beloved in its turn with love. He is in
   love, but he does not know with what; . . . he has not realised that he has seen
   himself in his lover, as if in a mirror; . . . he contains an image of love, a
   counterlove' (tr. Denyer ad *Alc.* 135E). One may compare the doctrine that 'the
   interlocutor is the speaker'.

100 For this terminology, see Hadot 1995.

101 It may not seem immediately obvious why the soul's self-reflection belongs to the
   tier of purificatory virtue. A plausible explanation is that purification liberates a
   being from lower principles (Proclus *El. Theol.* pr. 158), and the soul is able to
   reflect on itself only as it liberates itself from the body.

102 In the triadic structure familiar throughout later Neoplatonism, these ways
   correspond to the soul's proceeding from its own level of being, remaining at its
   own level of being, and reverting to its own level of being.

103 'The Peripatos erred concerning the *atomon*, considering it to come about by a
   combination of accidentals. Consequently, they define it as follows: "whose

aggregation could never occur in any other case"; the Peripatetics made the superior from the inferior, viz. the accidental.' According to Porphyry (*Isagogê* 7,22) an individual is 'constituted (*sunestêke*) of features whose assemblage (*athroisma*) will never be found the same in anything else'. (tr. O'Neill) See Barnes 2003, 342–5 and Sorabji 2006, 138–42 for analysis of this definition and its contentious history.

104 Blumenthal 1993a.

105 On which see, with Mansfield (1994), Siorvanes 1996, 114–15.

106 Cf. Damascius *in Phaed.* 1.74 on the three activities of each hypostasis.

107 Which, according to Olympiodorus' account, concerns the 'mixing' (*mixis*) of parts of colour, corresponding to the division associated with bodies.

108 Dedicated to the Muses, not coincidentally the handmaidens of Apollo.

109 The solitude of the misanthrope Timon is, on this interpretation, not coincidental: his misanthropy indicates his lack of care for the political associations which constitute the lower activity of soul, but his name, *Timôn*, nevertheless implies the 'honour' that is accorded to the nobler beings (147).

110 The *Life* has been treated as a separate work since its first publication in 1692, and was omitted in Creuzer's edition of the text. For the reader's convenience, I have marked 3,2 as the beginning of 'Lecture 1 *On the Alcibiades*' proper, but this is somewhat arbitrary, since the manuscript begins labelling the lectures with Lecture 2 (*praxis sun theôi B*, 9,20).

111 If we take *prôên* in Lecture 4, 34,8 as meaning 'the day before yesterday' (LSJ A II), pointing back to Lecture 3, 14,20–6.

112 Only Olympiodorus' *Meteorology* commentary can be dated with confidence, to sometime not long after 565 AD, thanks to Olympiodorus' reference to a recent comet (*in Meteor.* 52,31). The *Alcibiades* commentary may have been about a decade earlier. The *Gorgias* commentary is often thought to be quite a bit earlier, as it seems less mature (Jackson et al. 1998, 3–4).

113 See Richard 1950; Hoffmann 2012, 615–16.

114 See Marinus *Life of Proclus* ch. 12, 295–300; ch. 13, 318–31, translated in Sorabji 2005.3, 2(a)10. Proclus may have discussed the points to be examined with a teacher in a treatise entitled 'Sunanagnôsis', or 'Explication of a Text under the Supervision of a Master' (Hadot et al. 1990, 26, 34; for this translation, Hoffmann 2012, 608). For the concept of a 'spiritual exercise' in antiquity, see Hadot 1995, 2002.

115 See Simplicius *in Cat.* 3,2–9; Hoffmann 2012, 615; Hadot 1978, 147–65; 1996, 41–60.

116 See further above, §2.

117 Damascius' *Life of Isidore* may be somewhat different from others like the *Life of Plato* or the *Life of Proclus*, if Damascius does not portray Isidore as obtaining all the tiers of virtue that are theoretically available.

118 Perhaps with some relevance to the continuing debate regarding the ethical status of the late antique sage: cf. Sorabji 2005.1, 15(a), Linguiti 2012, Van Riel 2012, Schniewind 2003, 2005, and Chiaradonna 2009.

Textual Emendations

The edition of Westerink (1982) is excellent and clear. I have rarely deviated from Westerink's printed text, primarily to accept conjectures offered either by Westerink himself (in his apparatus or addenda), or by Dodds (1957).

2,20:   For *en ia'* read *en [hen]deka* (Dodds)
2,62:   For *hoss' eidon tekeessin* read *hoss' idon en tekeessin* (correcting from Olymp. *in Phaed.* 1.5,16)
23,16–17:   Read *legetai <prosektikon, to de epi tais orektais dunamesi legetai> suneidos* (a supplement suggested by Westerink, comparing Damascius *in Phaed.* 1.271)
27,7:   For *enantioutai* read *enantiousthai* with M
31,1–2:   For *protreptên* read *propetê*, as suggested by Westerink
45,16:   For *di' autôn* read *dia tên*, as suggested by Westerink
55,16:   For *hous* read *oun*, as suggested by Westerink
73,9:   For *ouk esti gar <henos moriou>*, read *ouk estê gar*, as suggested by Dodds

Olympiodorus

Life of Plato

and

*On Plato
First Alcibiades 1–9*

Translation

Commentary on the *Alcibiades* of Plato [transcribed] from the voice[1] of the distinguished philosopher Olympiodorus

[On beginning Platonic philosophy]

Aristotle begins his own *Theology*[2] with the statement that 'all human beings naturally reach out for knowledge; and a sign of this is their love of the senses'. But in beginning Plato's philosophy, I would go a step further and say that all human beings reach out for Plato's philosophy, because all people wish to draw benefit from it; they are eager to be enchanted by its fountain, and to quench their thirst with Plato's inspirations.[3]   1,5

[Platonic inspirations]

There are four of these in [Plato], in four of his dialogues. One, in the *Timaeus*,[4]   2,1
he delivers with inspiration after he has become divinely possessed, and portrays the Demiurge addressing the heavenly [bodies], whom he calls the 'young gods', about the administration of affairs here [on Earth]. (That is also why Iamblichus entitled his commentary on this dialogue *On the Speech of Zeus*.)[5]

The second inspiration occurs in the *Republic*,[6] where he became possessed   5
by the Muses and portrayed them recounting in detail the dissolution of the constitution that he had constructed, when he says: 'everything that has come to be must necessarily pass away'.

The third inspiration occurs in the *Phaedrus*,[7] where Socrates was possessed by the nymphs as he philosophised under the plane tree about love (*erôs*).   10

The fourth occurs in the *Theaetetus*,[8] where he became philosophically inspired in his portrayal of the leader of the philosophical chorus (*koruphaios*), that is, the contemplative philosopher.[9]

It is, then, for the sake of these inspirations that everyone comes to the philosophy of Plato.[10]

[Life of Plato][11]

But come, let us also describe the parentage and life (*genos*)[12] of the philosopher,
15 not for the sake of 'much-learning',[13] but rather to help and prepare those who
approach him: for this is no 'Nobody',[14] but rather the 'one who reverts human
beings'.[15] For the story goes that Plato was born the son of Ariston, son of
Aristocles, from whom he traced his family to Solon the lawgiver (which is
also why, in emulation of his ancestor, he wrote the *Laws* and the *Composition
of the Republic*, in 12 and 10[16] books respectively): and he was born from his
20 mother Perictione, who was descended from Neleus, son of Codrus. Now they
say that a vision (*phasma*) of Apollo coupled with his mother Perictione, and
appeared to Ariston in the night, instructing him not to have intercourse with
Perictione until she gave birth, and he acted accordingly.[17] And when Plato was
25 born, his parents took the newborn and placed him on Mount Hymettus,
wishing to make sacrifices on his behalf to the gods there, Pan, the Nymphs,
and Shepherd Apollo. And as he lay there, the bees approached and filled
his mouth with honey from their honeycombs,[18] so that the saying came true
of him,

> from whose tongue flows speech sweeter than honey.[19]

30 And he also calls himself in every way 'the fellow-servant of the swans',[20] since
he came forth from Apollo; for the swan is Apollo's bird.

[The education of Plato]

When Plato reached the appropriate age, in order to pursue the usual course in
reading and writing (*koina grammata*) he initially studied under Dionysius the
grammarian, whom he actually mentions in the *Lovers*,[21] in order that his
teacher Dionysius would not lack a share in the enduring memory attached to
35 Plato. Then, after him, he availed himself of a teacher of gymnastics, Ariston of
Argos,[22] by whom he was reportedly given the name 'Plato' (he was previously
called Aristocles after his grandfather).[23] He was given this name because of
two parts of his body that were particularly 'broad' (*platus*), his chest and his
brow, as the images of him set up everywhere tell us, since this is how they
appear. But others say that he was not renamed for that reason, but rather on
40 account of the 'breadth' (*to platu*), the flow, and the open expanse of his

unconstrained style, just as they say that Theophrastus was renamed on account of the divine (*theios*) quality of his expression (*phrasis*), having been called Tyrtamon before.[24] And Plato had as his music teacher Draco, the pupil of Damon, whom he mentions in the *Republic*.[25]

Athenian youths were taught these three subjects – I mean reading and writing, music, and wrestling – not just for the subjects' own sake,[26] but in the case of reading and writing to structure the reason (*logos*) within them; in the case of music, to master their spirited emotion (*thumos*); and in the case of wrestling and gymnastics, to rekindle their appetite (*epithumia*) when it waned.[27] ([Plato's] *Alcibiades* was evidently taught these three subjects as well, which is why Socrates says to him, 'but you refused to learn the pipe', and so on.)[28]

And he also studied under painters, from whom he had help in the mixing of colours, and he refers to these in the *Timaeus*.[29] After this he was taught by the tragic poets, who were called 'the teachers of Greece'; he went to these for the gnomic and solemn qualities to be found in (*apo*) tragedy and for the heroic nature of its subjects.[30] And he participated in the dithyrambs that were performed in honour of Dionysus (who is called the 'overseer of becoming').[31] For the dithyramb was dedicated to Dionysus, from whom it also took its name: Dionysus was the 'Dithyramb' because he came forth from two (*duo*) portals (*thurai*), from Semele and from the thigh of Zeus. As a matter of fact, the ancients were accustomed to call effects by the names of their causes, just as they also call wine 'Dionysus'. That is why Proclus[32] says on this subject,

All that they prophesied to the parents, I beheld in the children.[33]

That Plato had also practised the dithyramb [at this time] is clear from the *Phaedrus*,[34] a dialogue that abounds in dithyrambic style,[35] when we consider that this was reportedly the first dialogue that Plato wrote.[36]

He especially enjoyed both the comic poet Aristophanes and Sophron, from whom he had some help in the representation of the characters of his dialogues. He reportedly enjoyed them so much that when he died, [the works of] Aristophanes and Sophron were even found on his couch. And he personally composed the following epigram for Aristophanes:

The Graces, when they sought to take up a sacred space (*temenos*) that would never fall, found the soul of Aristophanes.[37]

And he put [Aristophanes] in a comic situation in the *Symposium*, reflecting the fact that he had help from him in comedy: for when he made him sing a
75   hymn to Love (*Erôs*), he portrayed him falling into hiccoughs in the middle, so that he was unable to complete the hymn.[38]

And he composed tragic and dithyrambic poems, as well as some others. He burned them all after he had experienced the lifestyle of Socrates, with words like these:

Hephaestus, come forth as thou art: Plato now has need of you.[39]

80   And a certain Anatolius, a grammarian, once won considerable success here [in Alexandria] by quoting this line to Hephaestus, who had been appointed governor of the city, giving it the following form:

Hephaestus, come forth as thou art: Pharos now has need of you.[40]

They say that when Socrates was about to receive [Plato], he dreamed that a wingless swan was seated on his knees, and straightaway it grew wings and
85   flew up into the air, and let out a sweet-voiced cry, so as to enchant everyone who heard it: and this showed the future glory of the man.[41]

After the death of Socrates, [Plato] resorted next to Cratylus the Heraclitean as his teacher, for whom he also composed a dialogue of the same name, entitling it *Cratylus, or On the Correctness of Names*.[42] After [his time with] this
90   man, he went to Italy. Upon finding there a school that had been established by the Pythagoreans,[43] he had Archytas the Pythagorean as his next teacher: and his dialogue the *Philebus* is reportedly also named after a certain Pythagorean, and he also refers to Archytas in that dialogue.[44]

[Plato in Sicily][45]

And since the philosopher should be a 'sight-lover'[46] of the works of nature, he
95   also went to Sicily, in order to behold the craters of the fire in Mount Aetna – it was not for the sake of the 'Sicilian table', O noble Aristides, as you claim.[47] And in Syracuse he visited Dionysius the Great, who was the tyrant of that city, and he attempted to transform his tyranny into an aristocracy;[48] in fact, that is the reason why he went to him. And when Dionysius asked him, 'Whom among
100   human beings do you regard as happy (*eudaimôn*)?' (since he thought that the philosopher would refer to him out of flattery), Plato answered 'Socrates'.[49] And

he asked him again: 'What do you consider to be the work of the statesman (*politikos*)?'; and he answered, 'To make his citizens better'.[50] And he added a third question: 'What then? Do you suppose it is trivial to dispense justice correctly?' (For Dionysius had a reputation for dispensing justice correctly.) 105 But Plato answered, not shrinking back in the least: 'A small thing, yes, and the least part [of the statesman's work]: for those who hand down the right verdicts are like menders, who repair torn clothes'.[51] And he added a fourth question: 'Do you not consider the tyrant courageous?' 'He is the most cowardly of all', Plato replied; 'for he fears losing his life even to his barber's shears'. And so 110 Dionysius, enraged by these answers, proclaimed to Plato that he must escape Syracuse before sunset. And that was the ignominious fashion in which Plato was ejected from Syracuse.

The cause of his second journey to Sicily was that, after the death of Dionysius 115 the Great, his son Dionysius succeeded to the tyranny, and his uncle on his mother's side was Dion, who had become Plato's associate (*homilêtês*) on his first journey. So Dion wrote to him, 'if you join us now, there is hope of transforming the tyranny into an aristocracy'. Then, after Plato had undertaken his second journey for this reason, he was accused to Dionysius by his bodyguards of 120 plotting to transfer rule to Dion and depose Dionysius, and then arrested by [Dionysius] and handed over to Pollis of Aegina, who was on a trading voyage to Sicily, for sale [as a slave].[52] And he, after bringing [Plato] to Aegina,[53] found Anniceris the Libyan, who was about to sail to Elis in order to compete in the four-horse [chariot race]. So when [Anniceris] chanced upon Pollis there, he 125 purchased Plato from him, winning greater glory in this act than any victory in a chariot race [could bring]. Aristides also remarks about this [episode] that no one would have heard of Anniceris, had he not ransomed Plato.[54]

The reason for his third trip to Sicily was that Dion had been arrested by Dionysius, deprived of his property, and cast into prison. He therefore wrote to 130 Plato that Dionysius had promised to release him, if Plato came back to him. He readily undertook this third journey as well to help his friend. And that covers the philosopher's time abroad in Sicily.

[Plato in Egypt and Phoenicia]

One should be aware that he also journeyed to Egypt, to the priests there,[55] and learned the priestly skill[56] from them. And this is why in the *Gorgias*[57] 135 he says, 'No, by the Dog, god of the Egyptians': for the power that the sacred images (*agalmata*) [of the gods] have among the Greeks, animals have among the Egyptians, by representing each of the gods to whom they are dedicated.

140   Since he wished to encounter the Magi as well, but was unable to reach them because of the war being joined in Persia at that juncture, he arrived in Phoenicia, and upon encountering the local Magi, acquired the skill of the Magi.[58] And this is why in the *Timaeus*[59] he is plainly experienced in the skill of sacrifice, discussing the [prognostic] signs of the liver and [other] entrails and other matters like this. But these events should have been recounted before explaining his [second and third] voyages to Sicily.[60]

[The foundation of the Academy]

145   When he reached Athens he established a school in the Garden of Academus, marking off a certain portion of this gymnasium as a sanctuary for the Muses.[61] And the misanthrope Timon would keep company only with Plato there.[62] And Plato attracted very many to learning, both men and women, preparing [the latter] to attend his lectures looking like men (*andreiôi skhêmati*),[63] and
150   demonstrating that his love of wisdom was superior to any love of work.[64] For he dissociated himself from Socratic irony, from frequenting the Agora and the workshops and from pursuing the young to engage them in conversation: and he also dissociated himself from the solemn dignity of the Pythagoreans – keeping the doors closed, and 'Himself said so'[65] – by conducting himself more sociably (*politikôteron*) towards everyone.

[The exegesis of Plato]

155   Now when he had made many into his lovers (*erastai*) and had benefited large numbers of them, he dreamed as he was on the point of death that, having turned into a swan, he was moving from tree to tree, and in this way was causing extreme toil for the hunters. Simmias the Socratic interpreted this dream as follows: that Plato would be difficult to grasp for those succeeding him who wished to explain him (*exêgeomai*): for the commentators (*exêgêtai*)
160   who attempt to pursue the concepts (*ennoiai*) of the ancients are like bird-catchers, and Plato is difficult to grasp since it is possible to interpret his words

on the level of natural philosophy (*phusikôs*), ethics (*êthikôs*), or theology (*theologikôs*) – in short, in many different senses[66] – as is also the case with the [words] of Homer. For these two souls are said to have embraced every mode,[67] which is why it is possible to take the words of both of them in all manner of ways.

When he died, the Athenians buried him lavishly, and inscribed upon his tomb: 165

Two did Apollo bring forth, Asclepius and Plato,
The one to keep our soul healthy, the other our body.[68]

And that covers the parentage and life (*genos*) of the philosopher; next we   3,1
must proceed to the subject before us.

[Lecture 1 on the *First Alcibiades*][69]

[The goal of the Alcibiades *according to Proclus: seven supporting arguments]*

Now then, the target (*skopos*)[70] of the present dialogue, according to Proclus,[71] is self-knowledge: and this is confirmed by a plurality of arguments.

First by the title: for the dialogue is entitled the 'Greater Alcibiades, or On   5
the Nature of a Human Being'. (It is 'greater' since there is another 'lesser' *Alcibiades* by Plato,[72] just as there is a 'greater' and a 'lesser' *Hippias*).

Next [he establishes that the target is something like this] on the basis of certain expressions in the dialogue; for example, it is stated in it 'But, my good friend, being persuaded by me and by the inscription at Delphi, "Know   10
Thyself".'[73]

And in addition in the dialogue before us the following three designations are distinguished:[74] 'me', 'what belongs to me', and 'what belongs to my belongings'. And [he argues] from the statement that all who were in love with the body of Alcibiades did not love Alcibiades [himself], but rather one of his possessions, and it was Socrates alone who loved Alcibiades himself.   15

Furthermore [he argues] from the assertion that the just and the advantageous are in this work interchangeable, from which it is clear that this discussion is about the soul: for to [the soul] alone is the just advantageous,

since it is not advantageous to the composite [of soul and body]: for example,
4,1   the death of Menoeceus[75] was just, since he died on behalf of his fatherland,
but it was not advantageous to the body that perished.

And [he also argues] from the fact that [Plato] concludes the discussion
once he has demonstrated, at the end of the dialogue, that the human being is
the soul, on the ground that all of the prior assumptions are made for the
purpose of establishing this [conclusion].

5   And also because Socrates strives not only to lead his beloved (*paidika*)
upwards, but to do so along the very path by which he has himself been led
upwards: for it is reported that he came to philosophy from the Pythian
inscription, 'Know Thyself'.

And, further, from the use in the work of the following expression – 'self',
'the self itself'. Now Proclus takes this [expression] one way, and Damascius
10   another. For Proclus says[76] that 'self' is the tripartite soul (*hê trimereia tês
psukhês*), or simply the soul, and that 'the self itself' is the rational soul: but
Damascius approaches this differently and says that 'self' is the rational soul,
while 'the self itself' the highest and most intellectual part of the soul.

This is the goal [of the dialogue] according to Proclus.

[The target of the Alcibiades *according to Damascius]*

15   But Damascius[77] conveys its goal more exactly and more truly when he says
that it is not about knowing oneself unqualifiedly, but about knowing oneself
as a civic person (*politikôs*).[78] And he establishes this from the definition of the
human being in this dialogue as a rational soul (*psukhê logikê*) that uses the
body as an instrument. Only the civic person uses the body as an instrument,
20   since he is sometimes in need of spirited emotion (*thumos*), for example [in
fighting] on behalf of his country, but also of an appetite (*epithumia*) for doing
his citizens good.[79] But neither the purificatory person (*kathartikos*) nor the
contemplative person (*theôrêtikos*) need the body. For a purificatory person is
5,1   the soul freeing itself from the body, though the 'chains' nevertheless remain
and are not released as [they were] from the Ambracian youth;[80] instead, they
are released through sympathy.[81] For it is possible for beings even here [sc. in
the perceptible world] to exist above [sc. in the intelligible world] in a
contemplative manner, because of a certain kind of sympathy, and also for
5   beings above to exist here, when the soul sheds its wings, descends here and

becomes aflutter about [this world], because of its love of the body. And the contemplative person is a soul that has been released from the body, while again here [in this world] we become intellectually aware (*noein*) of a release on account of the independence [of the soul from the body]. For the soul of the contemplative person, by being active (*energousa*) in accordance with that which is most divine within it, is in this way freed from its shell-like, pneumatic vehicle.[82] And on this subject the Poet says

    10

    Adroit Odysseus then stripped off his rags . . .[83]

In other words, the contemplative person who has separated himself from such 'rags' is truly 'adroit' (*polumêtis*).[84]

So, then, the target of the dialogue concerns knowing oneself as a civic person, if indeed the body is an impediment to the purificatory and contemplative person, and the pure person (*kathartikos*) is distinguished by moderation of the passions (*metriopatheia*), and the contemplative one   15 (*theôrêtikos*) by freedom from them (*apatheia*). That is Damascius' position.

[The target of the Alcibiades *according to the commentators*:[85] *a reconciliation of the views of Proclus and Damascius*]

Now if it is necessary for us, who plead Proclus' cause, to bring Damascius into agreement with him, then [Damascius] does say that the target [of the dialogue] is civic self-knowledge *primarily* (*proêgoumenôs*), [but not exclusively].[86] And we should explain this in a plausible way. For when   6,1 Socrates was watching Alcibiades 'dashing into civic life (*ta politika*)'[87] he realised that he would not readily tolerate questioning about knowledge of his soul (i.e. himself), unless [Socrates] also discussed his present appetite. This is what the Platonic philosophy is like, and in this it possesses a great   5 superiority over the other [schools]: for Socrates' admonishments are like painless purifications, or medicines drenched in honey. For [Socrates] does not heal (*epanorthoun*) souls by [applying] the opposites [of their current conditions], as Hippocrates[88] prescribes for bodies when he says 'opposites are cures for opposites'; nor in the way that Aristotle[89] exhorts us to   10 check spirited emotion (*thumos*) with appetite (*epithumia*), and appetite with spirited emotion, inasmuch as these are opposites; nor as the Pythagoreans do, through the 'tasting' of the passions, i.e. 'with the tip of the finger', as they put it:[90] for one could never heal the person who is aflame with the passions, they say, without some small concession to them. (And this is also why in the Poet [sc. Homer], Athena is depicted as urging Pandarus to break his oath,[91] on

7,1 the ground that he is painfully eager to do so – for if we reasoned otherwise, it would be very strange to suppose that the god was issuing a summons to wrong-doing – and this is why the Poet also depicts [Pandarus] being punished through his tongue, [as the spear enters] into that [organ] with which he broke his oath.)[92]

And so Socrates does not heal souls in this way, like those we have just
5 mentioned, but rather by [applying medicines] that are *similar* [to the soul's current condition]:[93] if someone is a lover, by saying 'learn what the love of beautiful things is'; if one is a lover of wealth, we say 'learn what self-sufficiency is'; if one is a lover of pleasure, 'learn what the easy life truly is, which the Poet even attributes to the gods by speaking of "the gods who live at ease".'[94] Therefore Socrates, by also being such [a teacher] to Alcibiades, converses with
10 him about civic self-knowledge, and incorporates [a conversation] about purificatory and contemplative [self-knowledge]. For he says in the present work, 'Just as, if the Demiurge had told the eye, "Look at yourself", it would have been unable to do so on account of its not being self-moving, but would have looked [instead] at another eye, and not at any random part of it, but at the one entrusted (*empepisteumenon*) with optical activity (which is also called
8,1 the "pupil" (*korê*), because of the appearance of little images in it), so too should you, Alcibiades, since you have blinded the self-moving in you by giving yourself over to non-rational activities, look away to me – that is, to the soul of Socrates – and not to any random part of this, but to the highest part, and you
5 shall see in me intellect and god.'[95]

Now by saying 'look away to me', he has indicated that the target of the dialogue is self-knowledge in a civic sense; and by saying 'not to any random part,' that it is also [self-knowledge] in a purificatory sense, for self-purification is the province of the highest part of the soul; and by saying 'you shall see in me intellect', [he has indicated] that it is also [self-knowledge] in a contemplative sense, for engaging with the realities in accordance with his intellect befits the
10 contemplative; and through saying 'and god', [he has indicated] that it is also [self-knowledge] in an inspired sense, for we are inspired according to the divine in us, which is simple, just as is the divine itself. After all, it is through

being independent and simple that children and country-dwellers experience inspiration to a greater degree:[96] inspiration cannot be captured by imagination (*aphantasiastos*), which is why it is undone by imagination, because that is its opposite.[97]

And since we have mentioned the Delphic inscription, 'Know Thyself', it should be realised that it was not inscribed before the inner shrine to no purpose, but since it beheld everyone as they arrived – whether they came to inquire about their children, like Laius, or about offices of state, like Cylon, or about wars, like Croesus, while, in line with that [famous] Megarian saying,[98] leaving oneself out of the reckoning – it was therefore set in writing that they think about themselves and get to know themselves first, and the other things [about which they inquired] subsequently.

And through the injunction, [the Delphic inscription] revealed what was enjoined: that the human being is the rational soul. For [the inscription] says 'Know Thyself', and this was addressed to the soul, which has a capacity for knowledge (*gnôstikos*). Consider that the body does not gain knowledge, nor does the combination [of soul and body] in respect of the body. Nor does the vegetative [soul] come to know.

But someone might object that even if this [sc. the vegetative soul] does not [gain knowledge], still the non-rational soul [as a whole, i.e. spirited emotion and appetite] does. But the inscription is not discussing this [level of soul], for it adds on 'Thyself', whereas the non-rational soul cannot get to know itself, since it cannot revert upon[99] itself, but only the rational soul does that. Yet [it is further objected] the heavenly [beings] also have knowledge, and indeed know themselves, since they turn back [upon themselves]. But the phrase 'Know Thyself' does not apply to them either, for in saying 'Know', [the inscription] speaks of being transformed from ignorance to knowledge, namely a [process of] fulfilment (*teleiotês*) for the soul, whereas those [heavenly beings] always know [and so their knowledge is already complete]. So it is speaking only with reference to the rational soul.

Equivalent, then, to this inscription at Apollo's [shrine] are the mirrors in Egyptian temples, since they are set up before the holy places and possess the same power as the Pythian inscription (for they set them up for self-knowledge, since [the Egyptians] always indicate realities through riddles, just as the Greeks do through written words).

And again, what the first treatise (*kephalaion*) in the *Enneads* is for Plotinus – [the one called] *What is the Living Being and What is the Human Being* [*Enn.* 1.1 (53)], in which [Plotinus] demonstrates that the combination [of body and soul] is a living being (*zôion*) and the soul a human being (*anthrôpos*) – that is what the *Alcibiades* is for Plato, and it has the same kind of target.

That is the content of the lecture (*praxis*).

20

Lecture 2

With the god's favour[100]

103A   SOC. Son of Clinias, I think that you are wondering . . .[101]

After [our discussion of] the target, which is threefold – including the views adopted by Proclus, by Damascius, and by the commentators (i.e. the view shared by the commentators)[102] – come, let us also get into detail about the usefulness (*to khrêsimon*) of the present dialogue, which is also threefold.[103]

[The usefulness (khrêsimon) of the dialogue]

10,1   For us, the present dialogue contributes in the first place to [grasping] the soul's immortality (*athanasia*) and everlasting nature (*aïdion*); and this follows naturally. For if [Plato] is discussing the process of getting to know oneself in this [dialogue], and it is by reverting upon ourselves that we get to know

5   ourselves,[104] and the philosophers have demonstrated in countless treatises that everything which reverts upon itself is eternal and immortal, then here [in this dialogue] we shall get to know that the soul is immortal.

Second, it also contributes to our knowledge (*gnôsis*) of all beings (*panta ta onta*): for if we know the soul, we shall also know the formulas (*logoi*)[105] that it holds within itself; and it holds the formulas of all beings and their patterns

10   (*tupoi*), since it serves as their image (*indalma*); and therefore the knowledge of the soul contributes for us to the [knowledge] of all beings.[106]

Third, [it contributes] to knowing what is good for the soul and what is harmful to it.[107] For consider that if the human being (*anthrôpos*) happened to be a body, it would find fulfilment (*teleiotês*)[108] in size and beauty; and if it happened to be spirited emotion (*thumos*), in the love of honour; and if it happened to be appetite (*epithumia*), in the love of pleasure: by the same token, since it is [in fact] reason (*logos*), i.e. the rational soul (*logikê psukhê*), excellence of character (*aretê*)[109] is solely sufficient for its well-being (*eudaimonia*), while   15 defectiveness of character (*kakia*) [suffices] for its ill-being (*kakodaimonia*). For, as Plato says, the soul shall go forth into the next world possessing nothing except its excellence and defect of character.[110]

So much for the usefulness [of the dialogue].

[The position (taxis) of the dialogue]

As for its position (*taxis*) [in the curriculum], it should be said that [this dialogue] must come first in order of all the Platonic [works]. For as [Plato] says in the *Phaedrus*,[111] it is laughable for someone who is in a rush to know everything else to remain ignorant of himself. Secondly, [this dialogue must   11,1 come first] since it is necessary to learn the [views] of Socrates in a Socratic way, and Socrates reportedly came to philosophy from the [utterance] 'Know Thyself'. Also, one should consider that this dialogue is similar to the fore-gates [of temples], and just as those [fore-gates] lead on to the Holy of Holies (*aduton*), so one should liken the *Alcibiades* to the fore-gates, and the   5 *Parmenides* to the Holy of Holies.[112]

[The division (diairesis) of the dialogue]

As for the division (*diairesis*) [of the text] into sections (*kephalaia*), it should be recognised that this dialogue is divided into three: [a section of] refutation (*elenktikon*), [another] of exhortation (*protreptikon*), and [a third] of midwifery (*maieutikon*).[113]

In the [section] of refutation [106C–119A], [Socrates] demonstrates that [Alcibiades] is doubly uneducated: both because he is ignorant of civic affairs (*ta politika*), and because he thinks that he does understand them. For he is ignorant because he has neither learned from a teacher nor inquired into   10 (*zêtêsas*) [knowledge] by himself. [That follows] because knowledge arises in two ways, either by the learning which comes through teachers (*didaskaloi*), or by inquiry on our own part: and it is better to know by inquiring oneself than by learning from someone else, considering that the self-moving is also

superior to that which is moved by another (as Aristotle says in the *Rhetorical*
15   *Arts*),[114] and the self-originated (*autophuês*) to that which is taught by another.
Thus he demonstrates that Alcibiades, as we have explained, does not
understand civic affairs (*ta politika*) in even one of these ways. For he did not
study [this] under teachers: he learned only reading and writing, music, and
wrestling, and moreover there was clearly never a time when, considering
himself to be ignorant, he approached a teacher (for even when he was a child
and very young, when playing dice he used to say to the others, swearing an
20   oath, that 'I'm being cheated!' (*adikoumai*), as though he knew exactly what
was just (*dikaios*): nor, clearly, did he inquire [into it for himself]. As a result, he
did not know the goal (*telos*) of the civic person from these [sources] – namely,
the just, the advantageous (*sumpheron*), and even the beautiful. So much for
the [section] of refutation.

12,1   The [section] of exhortation [119A–124A] is the one in which Socrates
exhorts him to conquer his antagonists by wisdom (*sophia*), for it was an
ancestral tradition among the Athenians to conquer by wisdom. (The enemies
of the Athenians were the Lacedaimonians and the Persians, as the
Peloponnesian and Persian [wars] demonstrate).

5   The [section] of midwifery [124A–135D] is the one in which Socrates,
through a line of questioning appropriate to [Alcibiades'] nature, makes
Alcibiades prove that the human being is the soul, so that he himself is his own
teacher: here, then, is the [Platonic] doctrine (*dogma*) that the answerer is the
speaker.[115] For this is the sort of person that Socrates is, acting as midwife to
souls for the birth of ideas (*logoi*): which is also why they say that he is the son
10   of Phainarete, who was a midwife (*maia*) – like Hermes [the son of Maia].[116]
For just as the doctor merely removes discharges from eyes, and [so removes]
impediments to the functioning of vision, and just as midwives bring babies
into the light but do not *put* them into the persons who give birth, similarly
Socrates acts as a midwife for souls (*psukhai*), and does not *put* theories into
the young, as though into lifeless (*apsukhos*) vessels.[117] As a matter of fact, he
15   himself says in the *Theaetetus* that 'the god has made me act as midwife, and
prevents me from producing'.[118]

Then at the end of the dialogue he finishes by exchanging their roles (*to
skhêma tês tukhês*), and makes himself, who was previously the lover, the
beloved and Alcibiades, who was previously the beloved, the lover. For this is

the goal of the art of love, namely, the reciprocation of love.[119] And Socrates has
a lover's disposition (*erôtikos*), as he also says in the *Phaedrus* to Love (*Erôs*):   20
'that art of love which you gave me, Master, please do not take away from me,   13,1
nor disable through some anger or other cause'.[120] Alexander too, after seeing a
certain army in a miserable state, reportedly said, 'May the man who put so
many in this condition come to a bad end (*apoloito kakista*)'.[121] At the end, too,
[Socrates] concludes the dialogue by comparing his love to the storks: since   5
the storks too, having first been nourished by their parents, finally nourish
them in their old age, and in this way they change [their respective positions].

That is the content of the lecture.

Lecture 3

With the god's favour

**Soc. Son of Clinias, I think that you are wondering why I, who was the first   10
person to become your lover, am the only one who doesn't abandon [you]   103A
now that the others have left off, [and also why I never even spoke to you in
so many years, when the others mobbed you with conversation. The cause
of this isn't human; I was prevented by some daimon, whose power you too
will later learn. But now, since it doesn't oppose me any longer, I have come   103B
to you. And I have good hopes that it will not oppose me again in the
future].**

Because the dialogue is about love (*erôtikos*), [Plato] uses the proem to explain
three differences between the divinely inspired (*entheos*) lover and the crude
(*phortikos*) lover.[122]

[The differences between the crude and divine lovers]
The first difference is that the crude lover wonders at his beloved (*ta paidika*),
whereas the divinely inspired lover is the object of [his beloved's] wonder. And
[Socrates] illustrates this in the words, 'Son of Clinias, I think that you are   15
wondering . . .' – that is, 'at me'.

The second difference is that the crude lover coordinates his passion with
the bloom of youth[123] and soon abandons his beloved, whereas the divinely

inspired lover accompanies his beloved from swaddling-clothes to grave,
20   provided that the physiognomic signs[124] of the begotten declare him worthy of
love. And [Socrates] makes this clear when he says, 'I, who was the first man to
become your lover, am the only one who doesn't abandon you now that the
others have left off', indicating that he follows his beloved before they do,
alongside them, and after them.

And the third difference is that the divinely inspired lover is present (*sunesti*)
with his beloved in a godlike way (*theoeidôs*), that is, without physical presence:
14,1   for just as the radiance of the divine (*to theion*) is present in every place, yet its
essence (*ousia*) is in no place (since it is not confined in place), the divinely
inspired lover is present in a way that imitates this same mode [of presence].
But the crude lover is present with his beloved [only] when he wants to engage
5   in acts (*energein*) at the level of bodily sensation, at the lowest level [of
sensation] at that, namely, touch. He has made this clear in his statement, 'Since
the others mobbed you, but I didn't say a word over so many years' [103A],
showing that he is absent insofar as he is silent, but present insofar as he follows
and loves [Alcibiades].

These are the differences [presented] here, but [Plato] also presents a fourth
10   difference of the same kind (*toiautên*) in the *Phaedrus*:[125] namely, that the
presence of the crude lover injures the beloved, in body and soul and outward
[possessions]: in body, because [the lover] wants to make him effeminate and
unmanly; in soul, since he wishes him to be unintelligent (*anoêton*), with a
view to making him suggestible about doing what [the lover] wants; in outward
[possessions], since he also [wants him] to be poor, so that he is dependent on
15   [the lover] and willing [to provide] him with pleasures. In fact, he even wants
him to be fatherless, motherless, and unloved, so that he has no one to keep
him from his company. But the divinely inspired lover is not like this. He is
present, not for these kinds of reasons, but [to bring about] the good for his
beloved, by reverting [his attention] to fine and beautiful things (*ta kala*).

20   Since, then, we have learned the differences between the inspired lover and
the crude lover, we should examine why they are called by one and the same
name ["lover"] in spite of the stark differentiation and opposition between
them, and not [by different names] as the [other] opposites are – for example,
'moderation' (*sôphrosunê*) and 'indulgence' (*akolasia*).[126] Well, we reply that
Love, thanks to the superabundance of his power, has been able to shape[127]

even [these] opposites for his own purposes. For 'all love is madness straining',[128]   25
insofar as both [kinds of lover] want to 'give birth in beauty'[129] – the inspired
[lover] to learning in the soul, and the crude [lover] to living beings in the
body.

[The daimonic[130] cause of Socrates' presence and the order of daimons]

But [Socrates] says that the cause of his godlike presence, and of his not
speaking to [Alcibiades] until now, 'is not human', but is 'some daimonic   15,1
opposition' [103A5]; and this makes sense. For if the effect (namely, the godlike
presence) is more than human, surely the cause of the presence is divine to a
much greater degree.[131]

Because the 'daimonic' was mentioned in this passage, the commentators   5
have been obliged to pay close attention to the theory (*logos*) of daimons.[132] It
should be understood that there are three divisions (*diaphorai*) of daimons,[133]
because some are daimons by analogy (*kat' analogian*), others by essence (*kat'
ousian*), and others by relation (*kata skhesin*).[134]

Now those that are *essentially* daimonic are really the standards (*gnômones*)
for those that are analogically and relatively so, because those that are *superior*
to essential daimons are daimonic in an analogical sense, while those that are   10
inferior to them are [daimonic] by relation [to them].[135]

[Those that are] analogical are so called because, inasmuch as these are
primary,[136] they possess the formulas (*logoi*)[137] of the essential daimons: in
other words, they are daimons in a causal way (*kat' aitian*), because what [has
a property] *causally* is necessarily prior to what [has that property] *existently*.[138]
The orator Isocrates also demonstrates that these [sc. gods] are called daimons,
when he says, 'honour the daimonic, always, and especially when the city   15
does';[139] and Homer [says] '[Athena returned] into the midst of the other
daimons' [*Il.* 1.222];[140] and Orpheus portrays Zeus as saying to his own father,

Make straight our race, glorious daimon.[141]

For in these cases, the name 'daimon' is bestowed on the divine.

The souls of those who have lived well are called 'daimons' by relation – for   16,1
instance, the souls of the golden race, which depend upon (*skhetikôs ekhousai*)
daimons, and which are themselves addressed as 'daimons'. Thus Hesiod, too,
says about them:[142]

They are called holy daimons dwelling upon the earth (*epikhthonioi*),
5   noble, warders-off of evil, guardians of mortal humans.

As we said, then, the name 'daimon' is threefold.

We should also investigate how they [sc. the commentators] arrived at the concept (*ennoia*)[143] of claiming that daimons exist. We assert, then, the following:[144]

[1] Our soul, which streams with life and bubbles over with it, is unable to exist without engendering life (*zôopoiein*).

(a) For there are times when [soul] is inactive with respect to its cognitive [faculties] (*kata tas gnôstikas*), for example when it is
10   overcome by lethargy, but this is never the case with respect to the life-engendering [part of the soul].[145]

[2] The ovoid (*ôioeidês*) or luminous (*augoeides*) vehicle was invented (*epenoêthê*) for [the soul at a time] when the shell-form (*ostreïnos*) body was not always attached to it.[146] This vehicle has two names:

(a) [It is called] 'ovoid' on account of its shape (*skhêma*), for it is not altogether spherical like the heavenly [bodies], but less spherical [than them], and for this reason they say that it sometimes suffers
17,1   'distortion' (*diastrophên*), but certainly isn't destroyed; because it is of the same essence (*ousia*) as the heavenly bodies, that is, of the fifth body, and therefore also everlasting (*aïdios*);

(b) it is called 'luminous' from its essence (*ousia*), because it is transparent and aetherial.

[3] Just as they assigned this luminous vehicle to the soul,[147] in order that,
5   being fastened all through it (*dia pantos*), it might always engender life, in the same way, in the case of the heavenly bodies, which cannot cease from activity (*energein*), they fastened this essentially daimonic race to
˙   them. (For our souls are not always fastened to them on account of our shedding our feathers and descending into becoming).

[4] This [daimonic race], then, being intermediary, is the interpreter for [people] here [on earth] of [messages] from the gods.[148]

10   But since [this race] interprets every attribute of the heavenly beings, because there are six things [to be distinguished] in the heavenly beings, it – I mean the

race of *essential* daimons – has also been divided into six. In the heavenly beings, then, are [found]:

Divinity (*theotês*),
Mind (*nous*),
Rational Soul (*psukhê logikê*),
Non-Rational Soul (*psukhê alogos*),
Form (*eidos*), and
Matter (*hulê*),[149]
[and] therefore the different types of daimons are equal in number.[150]

Those [daimons] who link us to the Divinity of the heavenly [beings] 18,1 are called 'divine' (*theioi*), who preside over (*ephestêkasin*) [divine] inspirations.

Those who link us to the Mind [of the heavenly beings] are called 'intellective' (*noêroi*): they preside over common concepts (*koinai ennoiai*), by means of which, beyond demonstration, we know certain [truths] among the common concepts even without demonstration (*anapodeiktôs*).[151]

Those that [link us] to the Rational Soul are called 'psychic'. Concerning 5 them, the poet [Homer] says,

And a daimon will advise you on the rest,[152]

and

First a daimon breathed it in my mind, [to weave] a great web.[153]

Those that link us to the Non-Rational [Soul] of the heavenly beings [are 10 called] 'non-rational' (*alogoi*).

Those [that link us] to the Form of the heavenly [beings] are called 'formal' or 'form-like'. That our forms *are* linked to the forms of the heavenly, is clear from their growing and shrinking along with the heavenly [beings], for the humours wax and wane with the moon (*selênê*), and so do hairs, for which 15 reason we see that those who live a priestly life do not cut their hair while the moon is waxing. And epilepsy (*to selêniakos pathos*) also makes this clear, and heliotropic plants, and moon-stones too, by waxing and waning with the 19,1 moon; and similarly oysters, and just about everything. For this reason, this saying was well addressed to the moon:

You build everything up when you are waxing,
and crush everything when you are waning.[154]

Next, the [daimons] who fasten this matter here to the matter of the heavenly [beings] are called 'material'. Since they stand guard over [this matter]
5 by doing this, they do not allow it to be utterly destroyed, although it is in a state of flux (*rheustos*). For Orpheus, too, speaks

of matter heavenly, starry, and boundless deep,[155]

on the basis that matter is threefold and that one kind, which functions as the substrate for the seven spheres, is 'heavenly'; another, which functions as that for the stars, 'starry'; and [a third], which he has called 'boundless deep'
10 (*abussos*) because it is lowest (*eskhatos*) and in flux, earthly (*khthonios*).

But since we have stated that the first form in the heavenly [beings] is the divine (*to theion*),[156] we must understand that among the gods, some are beyond the cosmos (*huperkosmioi*) (to which our souls are fastened, but no body of any kind), and others within the cosmos (*enkosmioi*) (to which only bodies are fastened). And of the [gods] within the cosmos, some are heavenly
15 (*ouranioi*), others aetherial or fiery, others airy, others watery, others earthly, and others under Tartarus (*hupotartarioi*), as the poet also says,

And they call those under Tartarus . . .[157]

20,1 And of the earthly ones, some rule the regions of the globe (*klimatarkhai*), while others maintain the cities (*polioukhoi*), and others belong to the house (*katoikidioi*).

[Our allotted daimon]

But we should ask which of the aforementioned six types of essential daimons they say is allotted to each person.[158]

Well then, they say that those who live according to their own essence (*kat'*
5 *ousian*) – that is, as they were born to live (*pephukasi*) – have the divine daimon allotted to them,[159] and for this reason we can see that these people are held in high esteem in whatever walk of life they pursue (*epitêdeuein*). Now [to live] 'according to essence' is to choose the life that befits the chain from which one is suspended:[160] for example, [to live] the military life, if [one is suspended]

from the [chain] of Ares; or the life of words and ideas (*logikos*), if from that of Hermes; or the healing or prophetic life, if from that of Apollo; or quite simply, as was said earlier, to live just as one was born to live. 10

But if someone sets before himself a life that is not according to his essence, but some other life that differs from this, and focuses in his undertakings on someone else's work – they say that the intellective (*noêros*) [daimon] is allotted to this person, and for this reason, because he is doing someone else's work, he fails to hit the mark in some [instances].[161]

But so much about the allotted daimon of each person.

[The allotted daimon of Socrates]

Concerning the allotted daimon of Socrates, [the commentators] say that three 21,1 points are important to pick out (*exairetos*).[162]

First, that it always used to turn him aside [from a course of action], and that whenever it did not turn him aside, this was a sign of encouragement.[163] That is, since Socrates was beneficent and always eager to help everyone, like a spirited horse eager for the race, he needed the bit rather than the whip.

Second, that his allotted daimon was divine,[164] and he makes this clear: for 5 he says in the present dialogue that 'My guardian is better and wiser than yours' [124C], and when the young man asks, 'Who is that?' he replies, 'A god, Alcibiades, a god.'[165]

Third, that he seemed to hear the voice [of the god], not because [the god] was actually talking, but [because] a kind of emanation (*ellampsis*) of [the god] 10 was present in the region of his acoustic organs, and he took this to be a voice.[166] In the same way we observe even now in common usage (*sunêtheia*)[167] that those who live the priestly life, when they suddenly catch the scent of a sweet fragrance, will say (since in their case too an emanation is present in the region of the olfactory organs) that it is 'the presence of an angel'.

[Our allotted daimon in contemporary religious practice]

But since we have discussed our allotted daimons, it is necessary to recognise 15 that these matters are also recognised in common usage (*koinê sunêtheia*), albeit not by the same names. For instead of the 'daimon' they speak of the 'angel' of each of us; thus you can hear them refer to 'your angel' when they address those who lead the life most pleasing to god.[168] In fact, Plato would

22,1   have made use of a word like 'angel', except that he left this [entire] expanse (*platos*)[169] [of the daimonic realm], from the heavenly [beings] to the sublunar, undivided and didn't divide it up as the Chaldaeans[170] do. For they divided [the expanse] into three, angels, daimons, and heroes; and they said that the [region] close to the greater [beings] contained angels, the one close to us heroes, and

5   the one in the middle daimons, the intermediaries [thus] being in the middle.[171]

Moreover, [Plato] calls Love (*Erôs*) a 'god' at one point in the *Symposium*, but elsewhere 'a great daimon'.[172] And the reason why he says 'god' is clear; but he addresses him as 'daimon' because he is an intermediary, as Love is intermediate between essence (*ousia*) and activity (*energeia*), between the beloved and the lover; and [he addresses him] as 'great', since he acts beyond sensation

10   (*aisthêsis*), intellectively (*noerôs*). And for this reason Orpheus, too, says,

> shepherding our thinking, eyeless and fleet, Love,[173]

for Love is eyeless, in that he sees and hears by mind (*nôi*), if you consider the saying that

> mind sees and mind hears.[174]

That, then, is what the commentators say concerning daimons and their allotments; but we, for our part, will attempt to run through all this in a manner

15   that leads to reconciliation (*sumbibastikôs*) with the [views] that are current.[175] (After all, Socrates was condemned to the hemlock for introducing new daimonic [beings] (*daimonia*) to the youth, and believing in gods that the state

23,1   (*polis*) did not consider gods.)[176]

So it should be noted that the 'allotted daimon' is really the 'conscience' (*to suneidos*);[177] this is the 'crowning peak'[178] of the soul, that which is faultless (*anhamartêtos*)[179] in us, an unswerving judge and witness before Minos and Rhadamanthys to what [has happened] here [on earth].[180] This even becomes

5   the cause of our salvation, because it always remains faultless, and is not condemned alongside the soul for the latter's faults, but even 'recoils' because of them[181] and 'reverts' [the soul] back to the right.[182] And just as a child weeps in the wake of a dream because of some phantasm (*phantasia*) [that he saw there], even so does the conscience lead the soul back upward in the wake of its errors

10   (*plêmmelêmata*), as when [Menelaus] says [in Euripides, *Orestes* 395-6],

What ails you? What sickness is wasting you?

and [Orestes] replies,

My conscience (*sunesis*), as I know I have done terrible things.

And from the opposite perspective, the lyric poet [Pindar] says,

[For the person who is conscious of no injustice], hope is a nurse and a good nourisher in old age.[183]

Thus you would not go wrong (*hamartois*) by naming the allotted daimon 15 'conscience'. (But it should be recognised that the [species] of 'consciousness' (*suneidos*) concerned with our cognitive faculties (*gnôstikai dunameis*) is called <'attention', but the [species] concerned with our faculties of desire (*orektikai dunameis*) is called>[184] 'conscience' (*suneidos*), equivocally with the genus).[185]

[That is the content of the survey.][186]

[103A] Son of Clinias. This can be interpreted in three ways.[187] (1) Either the patronymic (*hê ek patros klêsis*) is used as an archaism, as the Poet [describes when he writes]:

calling each man by his father's name and his lineage, doing honour to all,[188] 20

or else, (2) since the young man cares for his reputation (*philotimos*) and takes pride on account of his father (who demonstrated his excellence at the battle 24,1 of Coronea[189] and died there), he wanted to be named from him (*enteuthen*) because of the praise associated with that; or else, (3) it is because a patronymic is lively (*diegêgermenos*) and appropriate to lovers – because they are the way they are and have a lot of manliness (after all, love (*erôs*) is either so named 5 from strength (*rhôsis*) and being strong itself, or from heroism (*to hêrôikon*)).[190]

Accordingly, by addressing [Alcibiades] by his patronymic, [Socrates] all but exclaimed

do not shame the generation of your fathers,[191]

turning him from this [world] toward knowledge of himself, [of] what sort of person he is and from what [causes he has sprung], and urging him towards 10 what is noble (*kalos*).

I think that you ... This [language] seems unworthy of Socrates'
knowledge, since it makes Socrates appear ambivalent and limited to
guesswork about his proposed subject from the very start. So what can we
say about this? That it indicates ignorance? Not at all, but instead [that
it indicates] the highest [level of] knowledge, to approach [different]
personalities (*prosôpois*) using a method that is appropriate [to each].[192] In this

15   case, since every young man (*neos*) cares about controversy and reputation –
not least when it comes to standing up to strong claims – Socrates approaches
Alcibiades cautiously, much as bird-catchers approach birds in a roundabout
way (*meth' hupostolês*) in order to avoid scaring off their quarry. Similarly,
when Socrates characteristically begins the conversation in an open-ended
way (*dia tou distaktikou*), he is aiming for the young man to be persuaded by

20   himself, and not to [approach the conversation] with a contentious attitude
(*enantioumenos*).

Are wondering ... The phrase is suitable to the target (*skopos*) [of the
dialogue], as wonder is 'the beginning of philosophy'.[193] For once we wonder
'*that* it is', we move on to '*why* it is (*dioti*)': and this is [what it is to do] philosophy,

25,1 to express the causes (*aitiai*) of things – assuming that philosophy is the
knowledge of beings (*onta*) insofar as they exist.[194] And [this is so] in another
way too – for Iris ['Rainbow'] is philosophy since she speaks about beings, and
the poets tell the tale that she is the daughter of Wonder.[195] And Iris herself

5   causes wonder when she appears in the air; [namely] wonder at how a
mathematical shape, the circle, emerges in such material [as air]. And a certain
shape is also called 'wonder' (*thauma*) among the geometers who work on
linear [shapes].[196]

Why I, who was the first person to become your lover ... He uses the
words 'one' (*heis*) and 'first' (*prôtos*) and 'only' (*monos*) of himself, but
'multitude' (*polloi*) and 'last' (*teleutaioi*) and 'mob' (*okhlos*) of the others.

10   And we should understand that the 'people' (*dêmos*) rank before the 'mob',
and the 'chorus' (*khoros*) before the 'people'. For the 'people' are better
organised (*eutaktoteros*) than the 'mob' (which is also why Paeanieus, to
slander the people [of Athens], says, 'if the people are a mob, it's the
most unstable thing of all', etc., using the word 'mob' for the people).[197] But

15   the chorus is better organised than the people, since it has much unity (*henôsis*)

and attends only to one chorus-teacher. So too Socrates, as a single individual, is on the side of good order, but he refers to the others as 'mobbing' [Alcibiades] (*di' okhlou*).

Moreover, it was appropriate for him to comment that [Alcibiades] 'wondered' that his first lover had not yet abandoned him, even after a long time. For the majority of people (*hoi polloi*) do not judge [the qualities of an individual] by referring to his [actual] condition (*hexis*), but by referring to the time [that he has spent in achieving it]. For instance, they actually suppose that 20 those who have spent the most time in school are wise, rather than those who have spent less time, even if the latter are really wiser. Thus [Socrates] means that 'you find yourself in a state of wonder when you reckon up the time that has passed since I first fell in love with you, and it's clear that [you do this] like one of the majority'.[198]

But I never even spoke to you in so many years: It is an Attic figure [of speech] (*skhêma*) to say 'in so many years' (*tosoutôn etôn*).[199] This means that 'I said 26,1 nothing for such a long time'.

And the cause of this isn't human: Of what? Clearly, of loving without [physical] presence. For it is not the cause of love unqualifiedly (*haplôs*), but of *godlike* love, because [Socrates] comments that the cause of the lover's failure 5 to speak to [the beloved] (i.e. godlike love) is something daimonic and not human. And he is right to say so; for the cause of a godlike effect also has to be divine.

Whose power you too will later learn: [That is, the power] of the daimonic [being]. This statement is meant to help the listener: because [Socrates] knows that [Alcibiades] is after power, he causes [Alcibiades] to expect that he will discuss matters dear to his own heart (*oikeios autôi*), 10 namely, what he wants.

In the phrase 'too . . . later', the word 'too' (*kai*) is [grammatically] superfluous. That is, it isn't part of the syntax (*sumplektikos*) here, but it functions as an expletive;[200] for [Alcibiades] did not 'both' (*kai*) learn about his power before this, so that he could 'also' (*kai*) learn about it later. The poet [sc. Homer] also uses it in this way, in the [line],

Eurytus, to whom Apollo himself gave too a bow [*Il.* 2.827], 15

For the 'too' is there not because [Apollo] had *also* handed over some other thing [earlier]; it's just an expletive.

Also, [Socrates]' use of the word 'later' is explained by his remark, a little later on [105E–106A], that 'When you were younger, for sure, and you were not yet full of such high hopes, I think the god prevented me from conversing with
20   you, so that I would not converse in vain – but now he has put me on the job, because now you may be ready to hear me'.

But now, since it doesn't oppose me: We should investigate why the daimonic power does not also oppose his approach to Alcibiades now, considering that [Alcibiades] is going to commit mistakes after this. For he deserted and then
25   advised the Lacedaemonians to fortify Deceleia in his homeland,[201] and before this he personally urged Pericles to wage the war through the writing of the decree against Megarians,[202] in order to avoid rendering an account of the
27,1 funds spent for the [sacred statue of] Athena by Pheidias – for this was his responsibility.[203] And another point: he caused the Mysteries to be mimed in the house of Polytion.[204]

[1] We offer the following reply [first]:[205] just as the sun does not shine selectively,[206] but shines even upon those who do not see it – even if, on account of their own unfitness, they fail to enjoy its rays – so too the daimonic power
5   did not prevent Socrates from conversing with Alcibiades, even if he was unfit.[207] (But against this [interpretation], I think, is the fact that the daimonic power continued its opposition until the present moment:[208] for why did it not allow him to converse at the very start?)

[2] Xenophon's solution [*Mem.* 1.2.24–5] is rhetorical, and here it is: that Alcibiades would have been worse than he [actually became], if he did not spend time with Socrates.[209]
10   [3] But the third solution is actually truer, that even if the [discussions] of Socrates were not going to benefit him in this life, then nevertheless in *another* life (*en heterôi biôi*) he would recollect these and be benefited,[210] recognising as true what was said before, and almost saying aloud,

I did not let him persuade me, and that would have been far better[211] –

15   The same applies when, even in one and the same life, we observe certain people thinking along these lines once their passions have subsided, and only giving in to them while they are in a rage.

So I have come to you: In fact, [Socrates] was present the whole time; so how can he say that 'now I have come to you, since the daimonic power did not oppose it'? Well, we reply that 'I have come' evidently refers to his perceptible [presence] and not, as before, his solely godlike [presence], which also lacked any [perceptible] presence.[212]   20

And I have good hopes that in the future: This also belongs to love (*erôtikos*), to regard benefiting the young man as a case of 'good hope' (*euelpistia*) on his behalf.[213] And the [word] 'good' is used here on account of Socrates, while 'hope' [is here] on account of Alcibiades. For hope is unstable, as Herodotus   28,1
also remarks, and is the 'waking man's dream'.[214]

It will not oppose: This is a fair statement; for if [Socrates] experienced no opposition before [Alcibiades] heard the words from his conscientious (*sôphrôn*) lips, it is clear that he will experience no opposition after Alcibiades has heard him out.[215]

Lecture 4

With the god's favour   5

Soc. Now I have been making a study of you all this time, and have just   103B
about come to understand (*katanenoêka*) [how you handle your lovers.
Even though quite a few big-minded men sprouted up, there was not one
of them who was not overwhelmed by you, through your spirit (*phronêma*),
and has now fled and gone. And I would like to run through the train of   104A
reasoning (*logos*) in virtue of which you are high-spirited. Now you say that
you need no man for anything: because the resources available to you
(*huparkhonta*) are vast, to the point of needing nothing, beginning
(*arxamena*) from the body, and ending (*teleutônta*) at the soul. For you
think in the first place that you are the most beautiful and great – and on
this front, it is certainly plain to everyone that you tell no lie – and next, you
belong to the most vigorous[216] lineage in your own state, which is itself the
greatest of the Hellenic states, and from there, through your father, there   104B
are available to you a multitude of the finest people as friends and family,

who would do you service if any need arose; and those such on your mother's side are no worse, nor fewer. And you count on a greater power than all of these I have mentioned together, I mean, Pericles, son of Xanthippos, whom your father left as Guardian for you and your brother – Pericles, who not only holds power in *this* city to do whatever he wishes, 104C but in all Hellas, and in many and great races of alien peoples. And I will add also the advantage of your wealth: but you seem to me to act proud about this least of all. On all these fronts, then, you make yourself big, and you have overpowered your lovers, and they, being inferior, have been overpowered; and this has not escaped you: for that reason, I know very well that you wonder what in the world I have in mind (*dianooumenos*) when I do not let go my love, and with what hope in mind I'm remaining when the others have fled].

Socrates is making two points here, one of which is human, the other divine. Naturally it is human to be in love, since this is common to all human beings: but it is divine to love without being [physically] present (*aparousiastôs erân*). He presents the cause of the second [kind of love] first, when he says that it is 10 a god or a daimon.[217] (In doing this he adopted the ancient [rhetorical device] of 'making the end of the last into the beginning of the next' [sc. chiasmus].[218] So Homer also says:[219]

> [She bore three children], Isander and Hippolochus and Laodameia:
> with Laodameia lay Zeus of the counsels . . .)

15 But now he will return to the first [kind] and express the cause of this – I mean, of [human] love. For he loves [Alcibiades in this first, human sense] because he looks down on the others, and he looks down on them for four reasons: [1] because of the beauty of [his] body, [2] because of his good birth, [3] because of his many friends, and [4] because he is proud of having Pericles as guardian. For [1] that he was beautiful in body is clear from the saying that he was 'beloved in common of all Hellas'; from the [saying] that the Herms were 20 sculpted at Athens according to his image and likeness; and from the comment of the Cynic Antisthenes about him, 'if Achilles was not like this, he was not in his bloom'[220] – about whom the Poet [sc. Homer] says, when he wants to praise Nireus for his beauty:[221]

Nireus, the most beautiful man who came beneath Ilion,
Beyond the rest of the Danaans next after perfect Achilles.　25

And [2] he was proud on account of his lineage, since on his father's side　29,1
he was descended from Ajax, and on his mother's side from Alcmaeon,
which was regarded as the greatest and foremost lineage in Athens and
all Hellas. And [3] he was proud on account of his friends, because – since
he was 'beloved in common of all Hellas' (as the saying goes) – he acquired
plenty of friends as a consequence. And [4] it was certainly with justice
that he revered Pericles as well, considering that he was his guardian, and　5
that he held the greatest power in his country – about whom the historian
(*sungrapheus*) [sc. Thucydides][222] says: '[Athens] came to be a democracy
in name, but in fact a rule by the first man'. And the comic [Eupolis] says
about him that

He beat the orators by sixteen paces in speaking.[223]　10

It is thanks to these [sources of pride], then, that [Socrates] says that Alcibiades
looked down on the others.

But if we consider that praising the youth gives him a cause for pride
(*huperopsia*) (since this makes him even more headstrong), and praising
someone to his face is the mark of a flatterer (for certain people flatter
others by praising them to their face), and praising a beloved, again, makes him
proud – [if we consider all of this], why does Socrates praise Alcibiades on　15
these grounds, despite the fact that he is a young man, and face-to-face, and his
beloved?

Well, we reply [first] that what appear to be words of praise now, as they are
uttered by Socrates, are in reality remonstrations and refutations (*elenkhoi*). It
was necessary for [Socrates], after all, before he offered refutations that were
unmixed [with praise] and plain, to offer some that were mixed, in order to
avoid arousing and frightening off his quarry; instead, he had to approach his　20
quarry noiselessly, as competent bird-catchers do. Moreover, that kind of　30,1
[harsh behaviour] would diverge from the Socratic character (*êthos*); for, as we
have often remarked,[224] Socratic encouragements are like purifications
drenched in honey and are unlike the [purifications] of others, for instance,
doctors' incisions and burnings.

Again, when [Socrates] tallies up natural kinds of excellence (*phusikai*
5   *aretai*) in the course of his praises [of Alcibiades], these too are objects of both
praise and criticism:[225] [1] [they are objects of] criticism, on the one hand,
because they arise from nature and not from discipline (*askêsis*) (which is why
they are frequently available even to slaves, so that Plato called these kinds of
excellence 'slavish');[226] but [2] [they are also] praiseworthy insofar as even
[merely natural excellences] are named 'excellences' (*aretai*), since all excellence
10   is praiseworthy. It is clear from this, too, that [Socrates'] refutations are offered
mixed with praise.

For again, [Socrates] remarks at the beginning of his praises, 'as *you* say' [sc.
'that you need no man for anything', 104A], and by this he means, 'as you say
and not I', just as the Tragedian [Euripides writes]:[227]

You hear this from yourself, and not from me.

31,1   And next, that 'you also say that you need nothing from anybody': for through
these [words], he hints at Alcibiades' rashness,[228] since this [sc. complete self-
sufficiency] lies beyond the weak reach of human beings, and especially of
Alcibiades, who is fond of his reputation and always keeping an eye on
everyone [for praise].[229] For only a god needs nothing.
5   And third, that he says: 'you think your resources are great and you are
proud of these', by which he means, 'your reverence isn't of yourself, but what
lies *outside* of you, since you have left yourself "out of the reckoning (*logos*)", as
the Megarian [oracle] goes'.[230]

And fourth, that 'your pride starts with bodily goods and ends with the
[goods] of the soul, which was a mistake. For you suppose', he means to say,
'that you are incomparably beautiful, but it was unfitting to revere yourself for
10   your beauty, which will pass with the season (*opôrâi*)'. For Plato also writes in
the *Epigram of Laïs*:[231]

[She dedicated] her mirror to the Paphian [sc. Aphrodite] – for she was
unwilling to behold herself as she was, but she was unable to behold herself
as she used to be.

Here, he shows that one should not be proud on beauty's account alone.
15   Again, [Socrates] comments that 'You are also proud on account of your
good birth', as if to say, 'If we adopt your standards for self-reverence, it's

possible that your ancestor was a slave twenty-five generations back.'[232] Another refutation comes when he remarks that 'You think your friends are your servants': for if, as the Pythagoreans have it, 'friendships are equalities',[233] and according to Aristotle 'a friend is another self',[234] why should [friends] be our 'servants' any more than we ourselves are? And 'you are mistaken to be proud of Pericles as a guardian', since this man had been shown in the *Gorgias*[235] not to be a [true] statesman (*politikos*). For he made his citizens neither noble nor good, but on the contrary, he made them worse: for he made them arrogant when they were angry, by providing them with dockyards, harbours, and allies; consider, too, that the comic poet praises Aristides alone [among statesmen], since nobody good came after him.[236]

32,1

5

　　But since every false belief takes its start from a true one (for the false, as a 'falling away' from the true, draws substance from it (*parhuphistatai autôi*) and depends upon it, lacking the power to exist in its own right: for the true, through its abundance of power, influences even its contrary the false, and there is no such thing as a total darkening (*amaurôsis*) of the common concepts)[237] – [for all these reasons] we need to articulate Alcibiades' grounds for thinking that what *appeared* good was [in fact] the greatest good, and then becoming proud about it.[238]

10

　　We say, then, that when he was boasting about beauty, he had *intelligible* beauty in his mind, and he held onto an image (*phantasia*) of it, but since he lacked the power to obtain it truly, he started 'fighting over shadows',[239] over the perceived and apparent – as the poetic verse has it,[240]

15

> And all about this image (*eidôlon*) brilliant Achaians and Trojans hewed at each other, and at the ox-hide shields strong circled guarding men's chests . . .

Again, he revered himself for his good birth, since also in the All (*to pan*), what emanates from 'better-born' causes is treated as more deserving of honour, and superior. Thus Plato, too, comments that what derives from an unmoved cause is eternal and imperishable.[241]

20

　　Likewise, [Alcibiades revered himself] on account of his friends, because the origin (*arkhê*) of all things, which is one and single (*mia kai hen*), is also a unity: and friendship is like this, since, as a process of unification (*henôsis*), it is directed toward the One (*to hen*).[242] And [he revered himself] for his

33,1

guardian (*epitropos*) Pericles, since he had in mind the concept (*ennoia*) of his
allotted [daimon] – for that is our true 'guardian' (*epitropeuei*).

And finally (*teleutaion*), Socrates says that 'you are wealthy, too, Alcibiades,
5   but because you despise money and care about your reputation, you don't
think it's worthwhile to be proud over your wealth'. Indeed, it is clear that
[Alcibiades] despises [money], for the story goes that once, when the Athenians
were summoned to the Assembly concerning their revenue, he voluntarily
handed over ten talents from home.[243]

Now caring for one's reputation (*to philotimon*) is superior to caring for
money and caring for pleasure, because spirited emotion (*thumos*), from which
10   the love of honour derives, has a purpose which is separable [sc. from the body].
For it provides a motivation (*orexis*) that resists grief, and a drive (*ephesis*) to
defend [ourselves] against anyone who previously wronged [us]. But the
purpose of appetite (*epithumia*) – which is the source of our care for money and
pleasure – is not separable, but it has been smothered by the body, either by
filling up whatever it's missing, like food and drink and other such things
imported from outside, or else by letting out whatever is overflowing, like semen
15   in sexual [activities]. There are also other ways in which spirited emotion is
more honourable than appetite: for when reason (*logos*) and appetite (*epithumia*)
engage in battle, spirited emotion becomes the ally of reason, and, like a noble
and well-born soldier, it takes up arms against appetite on reason's behalf.[244]

[That is the content of the survey.]

[103B] So I have just about come to understand: The text of the passage
20   supports (*sumphônos*) our comments. For Socrates is present, and through
these words he expresses the cause of the first – I mean, of [the first kind] of
love: and so 'just about' was said on Alcibiades' account, but 'understand' is said
on Socrates' own account. For if we do not interpret it along these lines, then
the force of his words 'just about' and 'understand' will be reversed: for this
[former language] does not fit [Socrates'] knowledge (*epistêmonikos*), but the
34,1   [phrase] 'just about' does suit Alcibiades, since he is young. (Alternatively, it
might make for more effective persuasion, considering [Alcibiades'] character
(*êthikôs*), like the phrase 'I think' above.)

How you handle your lovers: Here it is clearly [necessary] to understand
(*noein*) the second cause [sc. human love], since Socrates says that

he loves Alcibiades on account of the latter's scornful treatment of his other lovers.   5

Even though quite a few great-minded men sprouted up: We need to investigate why he calls the crude lovers 'great-minded' (*megalophronas*).[245] Well, we reply that the [reason] is just what we said the other day (*prôen*)[246] about Love (*Erôs*), namely, that he influences even his contrary through an abundance of power, with the result that both [the divine and crude kinds] are called 'lovers' by a common name; likewise, here too we say that great-   10 mindedness (*megalophrosunê*) has also provided a share of itself to its opposite, with the result that even the crude lovers are called 'great-minded'.

It is also worth noting that [Socrates] has used appropriate language to address the young man in each case. Since he knows that [Alcibiades] is practically bursting to enter public life (*ta koina*) and rushing after a military command (*stratêgikos*), he describes him using words that reflect [the very qualities] by which the young man hopes to achieve the positions that he seeks.   15 For here he says 'great-minded', then 'overwhelmed by your spirit', and again 'have fled', and each and every one of these [phrases] suits the statesman (*politikos*).

[104A] I'd like to explain the reason (*logos*) why you felt yourself so superior:[247] Socrates uses these words to acclimatise the young man to a life lived with purpose (*kat' aitian*). Consider that Alcibiades might have scorned his other   20 lovers, not due to pride and great-mindedness, but rather due to an empty conceit (*khaunotês*) of the soul.[248] But instead [Socrates] addresses him as someone who scorns them for a *reason*, not out of ignorance, but rather due to a kind of knowledge that can't be articulated (*aporrhêtê epistêmê*), thus drawing him toward life lived with a cause, as we have already remarked. For when [Socrates] says, 'the reason why you felt yourself so superior . . ', it was not *entirely*   25 because of some 'reason' or other that [Alcibiades] looked down on them.

You say [that you need] no one: These appear to be words of praise, but   35,1 refutations (*elenkhoi*) are intermingled with them. For at the beginning he says, 'as *you* say . . . '.

That you need no one for anything: A second refutation: for it does not belong to human power (*dunamis*) to need no one for anything, and especially [not to

the capacity] of Alcibiades, who wants to be a statesman and a leader of people
5   (*dêmagôgos*), and hence needs *many* [things].

For your resources: A third refutation.

Beginning from the body: A fourth refutation, if at least he demonstrates through this that [Alcibiades] honours bodily goods before goods of the soul.

For you *think* that you: He means, 'for you do not *know* with precision
10   (*akribôs*), but you only surmise'.[249]

In the first place are the most beautiful and great: This is the first of the four indictments described in [our preceding] survey (*theôria*), on the strength of which Alcibiades proudly looked down on his lovers – namely, that he is beautiful.

And it is plain to everyone to see, that you do not lie: Here he secretly refutes
15   Alcibiades, and does not praise him (which is what he appears to do). For just as the good in the god cannot be articulated in words, likewise the good in us participates in something beyond articulation. And if now he says, concerning [the good that is] present to Alcibiades, that it is 'clear to everyone to see', it is plain that this is a base thing and not truly 'good', so that even in these [words] there is a refutation.

20   **And next, you belong to the most vigorous lineage:** This is the second [indictment] on the strength of which Alcibiades proudly looks down on his
36,1   other lovers. And we have pointed out[250] that there is a refutation here as well: after all, what if his ancestor twenty-five generations back was a slave?

5   **[104B] [Friends and family] who, if anything *were* needed, would come to your aid:** Here again is another refutation: for we will come to the aid of our friends no less than they will come to ours, at least if 'friendships are equalities', according to the Pythagoreans, and 'a friend is another self', according to Aristotle.

And you count on a power greater than all I have mentioned: Note that here
10   too, following everything that has been said, he has offered a speech that is appropriate (*oikeios*) to the young man, since he says 'you count on a power . . .':

that befits a military commander's work, and the young man is rushing to become one of these. And we have often pointed out[251] that Socrates tries to guide his conversations in the necessary direction by using [topics] that are similar (*tôn homoiôn*) [sc. to the interlocutor's existing interests]. So he is all but shouting aloud, 'Learn what is *true* power: knowledge (*epistêmê*)!' (For as he says in the *Theaetetus*,[252] 'there is nothing more powerful than knowledge 15 existing in soul'; for this alone, and the good life, can't be seized by tyrants nor taken away.)

And I will also add the advantage of your wealth: Socrates offers this second reason for his love of Alcibiades, after the first, which was divided into four. This [second reason] is that Alcibiades is also 'great' in regard to his wealth, and 20 actually greater than many wealthy people are. And he takes this up right away in the next [sentence], commenting, 'and you seem to be proud of this least of all'. For he means that 'you aren't proud at all of your wealth, since that you 37,1 don't revere yourself over this, because you don't care about money (*philokhrêmatos*)'.

You have conquered your lovers: In these [words] too, Socrates again entices the young man with the appropriateness of his language, in order to elevate 5 him. For he says 'you have conquered' and again, 'being no match for you, they were conquered': and Alcibiades welcomes all of these [remarks].

And these [facts] have not escaped you either: With these words, Socrates turns Alcibiades back toward himself and toward self-knowledge, acting to the advantage of the dialogue's target (*skopos*).[253] And in general, just as self- 10 knowledge has a recurrent nature (*apokatastatikos*), likewise this discussion is recurrent, thanks to the present sentence and the following one: for at the beginning, [Socrates] said that 'I think that you wonder'; and now he says this, that 'it has not escaped you'.[254]

Then Socrates' arguments converge in the sentence, '**From this, I know very clearly that you are in a state of wonder**'.[255] And it is certainly fair to wonder 15 at how, at the beginning (prior to the demonstrative arguments) he made the phrase 'you wonder' less certain by adding 'I think', but now (after the demonstrative arguments) he said 'I know well', unambiguously: for he used the [language] that was most useful in each case.

Lecture 5

With the god's favour

20 Alc. As a matter of fact, Socrates, perhaps you don't realise that you just
104D beat me to the punch. [I had already decided to come and ask you that very question: what in the world do you want? What do you hope to achieve when you crowd in on me, always making sure you're present wherever I am? Yes, I really do wonder what you're up to, and it would be a great pleasure to find out.

Soc. Then you'll listen to me with full attention . . . and I have in you a
104E listener who will stay to hear me out? Look out: it would be no wonder if I found it as difficult to stop as it was to start.

Alc. By all means . . . Speak, good man, and I will listen.

Soc. Speak I must, then. It is difficult to play the lover with a man who doesn't give in to lovers; all the same, I must dare to speak my mind. Alcibiades, if I saw that you were content with the advantages that I just
105A mentioned . . . I would have set aside my love long ago; at least, that's what I persuade myself. But now I'm going to show you your own, rather different plans. From that, you'll realise that I've had you constantly in mind.

You see, as you seem to me, if one of the gods asked you, 'Alcibiades, would you rather live with what you now possess, or would you rather die on the spot if you weren't permitted to acquire anything greater?' – it seems to me that you would rather die. But now I'll tell you exactly what your real
105B hope in life is. You think that as soon as you present yourself before the Athenian people, as indeed you expect to in a very few days, by presenting yourself you'll show them that you deserve a greater reputation than Pericles himself, or anyone else who ever was. Having shown that, you'll be the most influential man in the city, and if you're the greatest here, you'll be the greatest among the other Hellenes, and not only among the Hellenes . . .

And if that selfsame god were then to tell you that . . . you weren't
105C permitted to cross over into Asia . . . I think you'd rather not live with only that to look forward to; you want your reputation and your influence to saturate all mankind, to so speak. I don't think you regard anybody as ever

having been much to speak of, except perhaps Cyrus and Xerxes. I'm not guessing that this is your ambition – I know it well.]

Since we have finished learning from Socrates' words of reason (*logoi*), come, let us   38,1
examine Alcibiades' utterances (*phônai*) too.[256] Now, it is appropriate that we have
attributed 'words of reason' to Socrates, but 'utterances' to Alcibiades. For 'words of
reason' are appropriate to human beings, but 'utterances' to irrational (*alogos*)
[animals].[257] Since, then, Socrates has more in common with reason (*logoeidesteros*),
whereas Alcibiades is less rational, let us treat their respective speeches accordingly.   5

We have [so far] learned two things from Socrates' words: first, that Socrates
loves Alcibiades, and second, that he loves him in a godlike manner (*theoeidôs*),
that is, by attending him silently. And [we have learned] that – using an archaic
style[258] – [Socrates] articulated the cause of the second [divine kind of love]
first, namely, that it is a daimonic or divine opposition. Then, in conclusion
(*teleutaion*), he introduced two causes of the first [human kind of love]: one,   10
that [Alcibiades] looks down on his other lovers (which, as [Socrates] says, he
does for four reasons: beauty, good birth, friends, and [having] Pericles as his
guardian); and second, that he has not been captured by the affection of caring
for money (*philokhrêmaton pathos*). For caring for money, although superior to
caring for pleasure (for that – I mean caring for pleasure – is the lowest (*eskhatos*)
affection of all), is nevertheless inferior to caring for one's reputation.[259] For the   15
lover of reputation does exactly the same things that the good person (*spoudaios*)
does, but the lover of reputation does them for reputation's sake (*dia timên*),
whereas the good person does them for the good – just as the empirical doctor
does exactly what the scientific (*logikos*) doctor does,[260] even though one acts
with reason (*logos*), the other without reason or cause (*aitia*).

Since, then, in these [lines] we have learned about Socrates' arguments, as
we have already remarked, let us now get into detail about the remainder, i.e.   20
Alcibiades' utterances. And these utterances express wonder at four [features]
of Socrates: [1] the good timing (*eukairia*) of his words; [2] his essence (*ousia*);
[3] his power (*dunamis*); [4] his activity (*energeia*).[261]

[Four causes of Alcibiades' wonder at Socrates]

[1] Now [Alcibiades wonders at] the good timing of [Socrates'] words when he
says this: 'You just beat me to the punch' – as if to say, 'if you hadn't just beaten

25   me to it, I would have asked you first why in the world you've been following
      me around for so long'. And consider: were there no need for the daimonic and
39,1 divine to lead the human (but [they do, for] this is what it amounts to for [the
      daimon] to encourage Socrates to approach Alcibiades and converse with him,
      by not *dis*couraging him); and if the actual were not prior to the potential
      (which it is in principle,[262] <even if not in time>;[263] and Socrates operates at
      the level of actuality, but Alcibiades at the level of potentiality) – if all that
5   had not been so, then (he says)[264] he would not have just beaten Alcibiades to
      the punch. So [Alcibiades] expresses wonder at [Socrates'] good timing on
      these grounds.[265]

         Now, good timing (*eukairia*) has the potential to achieve the very greatest
      results. Consider that 'opportunities (*kairoi*) are the souls of therapy',[266] and as
      Aristotle puts it, 'opportunity is time as it seizes the moment of need (*to deon*)',
      and 'time as it seizes the right [moment] (*to eu*)';[267] and just as nature defines
10   the appropriate place (*topos oikeios*) for each body, so too she assigns a *time* to
      each action (*praxis*), which is called its 'opportune' moment (*kairos*).[268] (On
      another note, an [entity] that needs fulfilment (*teleiôsomenon*)[269] must maintain
      a suitable attitude toward the agent that fulfils it, just as if it were present, even
      if it is not present; and conversely, the agent of fulfilment should maintain such
      an attitude to that which is to be fulfilled, just as if it is present, even if it is not
15   present.[270] But this is a matter of attitude, not of timing, or rather, good timing).

         [2] Second, [Alcibiades] expresses wonder at [Socrates'] essence when he
      says, 'what do you want?' [104D]: for what we want is good.[271] Through this
      phrase, then, he has expressed wonder at the similarity of [Socrates'] essence to
      the Good (*agathoeides*).[272] For we all want good things: and if we also do things
      that are bad (*kaka*), it is not because we *want* them, but because they *seem*
      [desirable] to us, as [Socrates] remarks in the *Gorgias*:[273] in that dialogue, with
      the god's favour (*sun theôi*),[274] we will also discover (*gnôsometha*) the distinction
20   of what we want from what *seems* [to be wanted].[275] Subsequently in our
      passage too, he calls [Socrates] 'good'.

40,1   [3] Third, he expresses wonder at [Socrates'] power (*dunamis*) when he says,
      'always making sure you're present, wherever I am'. Now this belongs to a power
      that is sleepless and unwearied, which is also why Athene is called 'Unwearying'
      (*Atrutônê*).[276] Hence it is an indication of the greatest degree of power to be
      present everywhere, always.

[4] Fourth, he expresses wonder at his activity (*energeia*), when he says 'you crowd in on me' (*enokhleis*): and this – I mean 'crowding' him like this –   5
amounts to unhindered and unceasing activity. For the [phrase] 'you crowd' (*enokhleis*), used just now, is not identical with the [phrase] 'in a mob' (*di' okhlou*), used earlier [103A]: consider that there, he described the crude lovers, those who wanted to act on him by means of touch (*haptikôs*), as being 'in a mob'; but here, he uses the words 'you crowd', meaning 'you obstruct me (*aporein*)', which derives from the metaphor of people walking in a crowd and   10
being at a loss about how to move forward, just as if they are prisoners.[277] For 'obstruction (*aporia*) is a prison of the soul',[278] which is why its remedy (*iasis*), like the remedy of imprisonment, is called 'release' (*epilusis*). And Aristotle also comments in *On Interpretation* [17a35–7], 'And this much is said in reply to the sophists as they crowd in (*enokhlêseis*)', in other words, to 'obstructions'; and he also labelled obstruction a 'crowding' (*okhlêsis*), using the metaphor of   15
a crowd. So 'you crowd' [does mean] 'you obstruct me' (*aporia*). This, then, is what Alcibiades has to say.

[Socrates' reply]

Next, Socrates imitates the leader of the philosophical chorus (*koruphaios*) – he who requires the fewest words, because he develops his first principles (*arkhai*) from the non-hypothetical.[279] (For [his principles derive] from our common concepts (*koinai ennoiai*), which have been agreed as a consensus,[280]   20
whereas the other skills (*tekhnai*), drawing their principles from hypotheses, demand many arguments: for instance, the medical [skill] takes its principles (*arkhetai*) from the hypothesis that human bodies are [composed] from the four elements; but it is the job of the first philosopher [i.e. metaphysician] to *prove* that hypothesis, namely, first that [the elements] are four and secondly that our bodies are [composed] from them).[281] Hence Socrates, imitating the   41,1
leader of the philosophical chorus (*koruphaios*), as we have said, and taking his principles from the non-hypothetical, demands little from Alcibiades, and what [he does request] is nothing too costly: first, to hear what he has to say, and then to answer his questions.[282] Next, with the young man nodding his   5
agreement to do this, Socrates adds that 'if you do this, it is in my ability to bring you that power which your other lovers did not have the power to [provide]'.[283]

Next, we should look into the third reason why he is in love with [Alcibiades], namely, because the lover kindles Love and is lifted up to this [condition], in
10   order that he can keep the young man paying even closer attention to his words. Hence he explains that the elements and marks of the divinely inspired lover are the following two: namely, it is necessary for the divinely inspired lover to possess both judgement (*krisis*) and compassion (*sumpatheia*). For if he lacks either of these, he will not be like this [sc. a divine lover]: for if he has judgement but not compassion, he will be a knowledgeable but not a truly good (*spoudaios*) lover; and conversely, if he has compassion but not judgement,
15   he is only a crude lover. Thus it is necessary that both be present.

And where does [Socrates] state this? In the passage where he says, 'It would be no wonder if I found it as difficult to stop as it was to start' [104E]. For the [phrase] 'difficult to start' indicates judgement (since he knew that Alcibiades was unprepared [before now]), whereas the [phrase] 'difficult to stop' indicates
20   compassion, and [Socrates'] longing for more of his beloved. Aside from this (*allôs*), the difficulty in starting was due to Alcibiades himself, since (as we have remarked) he was unprepared: but Socrates' difficulty in stopping is due to himself. For Socrates, who is always longing to help youths and to do them good,[284] will not stop until he brings his beloved to fulfilment.[285] So he says that 'it was difficult (*khalepon*) even now to approach you': and he is right to use the
42,1   word 'difficult' instead of 'easy' or 'impossible'. For it was not easy, since it was not feasible for [Alcibiades] to divert Socrates in the same way as he scorns his other lovers; nor, for the same reason, was it impossible. That is, once he began
5   to scorn the other [lovers], Socrates' approach was no longer impossible; for it had been impossible for him to hear Socrates out without looking down on the others.

Having said this, and having kindled love to this point, [Socrates] reveals the third reason [for his love] when he adds that, 'because I scorn your resources, I love *you*, and I have not abandoned you for all this time – because
10   I know you really don't desire these appearances'.

Now it is not the case that all human beings desire the same experiences (*pathê*) – for example, one cares for reputation, another cares for money and riches, another cares for pleasure.[286] And the pleasure-lover longs for divine ease, about which it has been said, 'the gods who live at ease'[287] – that is the kind of *idea* that this person has in mind, but since he is unable to attain it, he fights over shadows (*skiamakhein*), the reflections and expressions of this [higher idea].[288] And the money-lover longs for fulfilment and self-sufficiency,[289]   15 because self-sufficiency and fulfilment are divine – and so he desires this; but since he is unable to attain [the real thing], he grasps after it by loving money. And again, the reputation-lover longs for the god who is sufficient and freely giving, even if he is unable to attain this. (But being fulfilled (*teleion*) and being sufficient (*hikanon*) are not identical; for fulfilment is just needing nothing from another, whereas sufficiency is a matter not only of having no needs, but   43,1 also being able to *give* freely to others. And the reputation-lover wants to *appear* to be such a person). And since Alcibiades thinks little of his own resources, this is the approach that Socrates deploys. For he introduces the god   5 [into the conversation] when he asks him 'whether you prefer, Alcibiades, to let the life of great works fall by the wayside and to be content with what you have, or to die?', and then, offering an answer himself on Alcibiades' behalf, [replies that he would] 'prefer to die'.

After this, he divides up Alcibiades' entire life, and says that 'you hope to approach the people in a few days and to advise the Athenians'. Now this was   10 at the stage just preceding adolescence (*ephêbias*); in ten days, as Proclus relates, [Alcibiades] was to be enrolled among the Ephebes (*ephêboi*),[290] and it was the custom that no one could give advice to the Athenians before being enrolled among them. 'And so,' [Socrates] continues, 'you are about to offer advice, and you suppose that on this basis you will get a reputation, and then be honoured in the city, and not only here, but also in Attica and Hellas, then   15 among the Hellenes and throughout all Europe – and not here alone, but even in Asia and through the whole earth: and you will count no other person as worthy of notice and wonder beyond yourself, save Cyrus and Xerxes.' So says Socrates.

[The god questions Alcibiades: 105A–C]

But come, let us look into the god's questions, and the philosopher's answers   20 to the god on behalf of Alcibiades, [and consider] what lessons (*dogmata*) we should take away from the god's questions and the philosopher's answers. And first of all, let us articulate the reason why [Socrates] made a god question Alcibiades, and then made himself answer on [Alcibiades'] behalf.

25   Well, then, he made a god pose the questions for three reasons:[291] [1] first, in order that the young man might not deny his own words, since we have all learned to trust that the divine is aware of even our chance movements, if indeed it is true that

44,1   All things are full of god, and he hears all things, right through rocks and through the earth and within a man himself, who has concealed his thought (*noêma*) in his breast.[292]

[2] The second explanation would be that Socrates staged this scene because of his fondness for tragedy. Certainly [Socrates] is keen on this kind of thing: hence, just as the [tragedians] often produce a 'god from the machine'

5   (*mêkhanê*) to resolve disasters[293] (as in the *Alcestis* of Euripides, the playwright put Apollo in the house of Admetus),[294] so Socrates similarly introduced a god in this case. [3] According to a third explanation, it is because Socrates, who is a lover, wants to bring himself into union with his beloved, both as a consequence of his compassion [for him], and because the divine is a unity (*henas*) beyond being; meanwhile, he wants to

10   fulfil his beloved according to his judgement (*krisis*), and the divine also acts for fulfilment (*teleiôtikos*).[295] And he made himself answer for Alcibiades, since the interval (*meson*) between god and Alcibiades was wide, and it would have been empty (*kenon*), had Socrates not placed himself in this [mediating] position.[296]

But let us look at the remainder [of the lemma], what lessons (*dogmata*)

15   emerge from the god's questions. (For the questions and answers themselves have already been stated). From the questions, then, it emerges that lives (*bioi*)

45,1   [come about] by choice (*kath' hairesin*) and not by the compulsion of necessity: for he says, 'What do you want?' So too in the *Timaeus* responsibility (*aitia*) lies with the one who chooses, but 'the god is blameless (*anaitios*)' [*Republic* 10, 617E; cf. *Timaeus* 42D];[297] and again in *Republic*, 'you will choose a daimon; a

5   daimon will not be allotted to you'. For it is up to us (*en hêmin*)[298] to choose a life of a certain kind; but it is *not* up to us whether we who made the choice will act out (*prattein*) the consequences of that life, but this is compelled by necessity – just as it is up to us (*eph' hêmin*) to throw a stone, but the stone's landing, once it is released, is not up to us.[299] So we must express it in the poetic verse,

. . . Yet I am not responsible (*aitios*),
But Zeus is, and Destiny, and Fury the holy wanderer . . .[300]   10

And the following lessons [emerge] from the [god's] answers: [1] that it is more profitable not to exist than to exist badly;[301] for he says, 'You, I think, would choose to die rather than live like this.' [2] Second, that the body is an impediment to obtaining excellence (*aretê*), from the same [sentence] – for if he prefers to die, it is clear that he chooses this because the body is an impediment to what he desires (*epithumei*). [3] And the third lesson is that you   15
should not give advice (*sumbouleuein*) to your advisees with a view to your own reputation (*timê*), but instead, with a view to benefiting[302] those who listen to you. Alcibiades, on the other hand, wants to approach the people with [his own] reputation in view (*dia timên*). [4] Fourth, that you should judge the reputation-lover by the quality of the people who honour him, and not by those who happen to find him worthy of wonder – just as Alcibiades wants to be an object of wonder to Hellenes and barbarians and all human beings.[303] [5]   20
Fifth, that the examples (*paradeigmata*) which he introduced were dissimilar (*anomoia*) [from one another], namely, Cyrus[304] and Xerxes:[305] for Cyrus was called 'father' on account of his gentle character and tolerance toward his subjects, whereas Xerxes [was called] 'despot' on account of his extreme irascibility and use of overpowering force (for this man was aroused [to anger] not only against human beings, but even against nature herself and the   46,1
elements: as Aristides says, 'he strode on the sea by yoking the Hellespont, and he sailed the land by cutting Athos, and he hid the sun when he gave the order to fire');[306] and Darius[307] was a mean between these, who was called 'the dealer'   5
on account of his love of money. For he ordained the tribute for the Persians, as Herodotus says, and he was the one who secured his own throne by a horse's whinny,[308] since it was the Persian custom for children to succeed to kingships.
    That is the content of the survey (*theôria*).

[104C] As a matter of fact, Socrates, perhaps you don't realise that you just   10
beat me to the punch . . . See how the text agrees with what was said in the survey (*theôria*).[309] In these words, you see, Alcibiades expresses wonder at Socrates' good timing – which has the greatest power (*dunatai*) in all things, as has been demonstrated. For Socrates would not have just beat him to the punch, were it not for the reasons we have explained.

15   **[104D] What in the world do you want?** Here he expresses wonder at the
essence of [Socrates], which is good: for what we want is good. And we have
commented[310] that what is [truly] wanted is not the same as what *appears* to be
[wanted], as had been explained in the *Gorgias* [467C–468D].

What do you hope to achieve when you crowd in on me? He made [Socrates']
activity (*energeia*) clear in the phrase, 'you crowd'. But the phrase 'you crowd'
(*enokhleis*) used just now, and the phrase 'in a mob' (*di' okhlou*) used earlier do
20   not come to the same thing, as we have learned.[311] And next he expresses
wonder at [Socrates'] power (*dunamis*).

Always making so sure you're present, wherever I am.[312] See how he has also
conveyed [Socrates'] power here. For it belongs to a power that is sleepless and
unwearied to be present and accompanying everywhere.

25   **And it would be a great pleasure to find out.** It has also been explained in the
47,1   survey[313] that even the pleasure-lover does not long for this *apparent* pleasure,
but rather for *true* [pleasure]; not, however, being able to obtain it, he fights
over a shadow, namely, its appearance. And the phrase 'a great pleasure' has
provided us with the opportunity to make this observation (*epistasis*): for the
passage is appropriate to the pleasure-lover.

5   **Then you'll listen to me ...** Here Socrates imitates the leader of the
philosophical chorus and asks for little, in keeping with the philosophy that
does not rely on hypotheses.[314] And he says here that 'it is in my ability to bring
you that power which your other lovers did not have the power to [provide]', in
order that [Alcibiades] will listen to his words now, and answer him a little
later on.[315]

10   **And I have in you a listener who will stay to hear me out?** This was intended
as a question, and it ought to be read this way [sc. interrogatively].[316] The reply
to him makes this clear: for [Alcibiades] adds 'by all means' after [Socrates] has
asked the question.

**[104E] Look out: it would be no wonder if I found it as difficult to stop as it
was to start.** Here we should articulate the third reason [for Socrates' love],[317]
15   but he has not done so, in order that he might kindle his love for the young
man even more; nonetheless, he does explain the elementary features of the

divine lover. He does not do so plainly, but they are [deducible] from what follows on his words: for he says, 'just as difficult as it was for me to begin', and reveals from this his quality of judgement (*krisis*) – for it stems from judgement not to begin at random, or by chance.[318] And then he adds, 'it may be just as difficult for me to stop', and this clearly displays his compassion (*sumpatheia*), 20 since when [a lover] remains close to his beloved for a long time, that stems from compassion.[319]

In fact, this is just what the divine is like: it begins gradually and stops gradually, furnishing abundant goods for human beings [with a view] to the recipients' suitability (*epitêdeiotês*). For we see that those who are successful (*eutukhountas*) struggle to succeed at first, but remain successful for a long time; the same goes for those who are unfortunate (*dustukhountôn*) and those 25 who receive corrective treatment (*kolazomenôn*).[320] It should be recognised, you see, that the divine is really *always* productive of goods, and does not act intermittently, but is a constant fount of such [results]. Also, the goods that derive from it are divided, since some are primary, others secondary. Goods 48,1 produced in the *primary* sense, then, are those that the genuinely successful possess – I mean in [their] children, words, wealth, and basically everything like this; and *secondary* goods are those that [function as] corrections (*kolaseis*) of errors (*hamartêmatôn*).[321] Yes, these are also good things, for we should not 5 countenance the idea that the divine would ever do a bad deed: those who shrink from their sentences resemble children trying to escape medical incisions. Thus the divine is constantly providing goods, and the recipients, based on their suitability, have the benefit of either the primary goods or the secondary; and these both begin and stop gradually.

Speak, good man, and I will listen. Also notice how in the text he calls 10 [Socrates] 'good': he has expressed wonder at his essence as similar to the Good (*agathoeidês*) [by saying this, and] not only by [saying] 'you want'.[322]

It is difficult to play the lover with a man who doesn't give in . . . We have already observed that he neither used [the words] 'impossible' nor 'easy', and we have recognised that he was right to do this.[323] 15

All the same, I must dare . . . He speaks well when he calls the procession [from the primary] to the secondary 'daring' (*tolman*): the Pythagoreans

likewise called the Dyad 'daring', as first having dared to separate itself from the Monad.[324] It is also necessary that the soul, descending into genesis, which is a labyrinth (*laburinthos*), should make use of the monad as a thread for its
20   wandering here [on Earth], just as Theseus [made use of] the thread of Ariadne for [navigating] the Cretan labyrinth.[325]

For if I, Alcibiades, [saw that you were content with the advantages that I just mentioned]: Here is the third reason why Socrates is in love: for he says that he thinks little of [Alcibiades'] resources and does not really prize (*agapan*) the four [resources] that he listed off a little earlier [i.e. beauty, good birth, friends, and Pericles]. This will be shown, you see, from the god's subsequent
25   questions and [Alcibiades'] answers to them.

I would have set aside [my love] long ago: [The philosopher] Harpocration
49,1   got involved at this point;[326] by paying close attention to the language, he proved that the words require Socrates to be a divinely inspired lover. It is clear that he is a divinely inspired lover because he says here, 'I would have put aside [my love] long ago', but the crude lover does not set aside [his love] whenever he wishes, because he is experiencing this state [of love] due to an affection (*pathos*): and we do not set aside our affections whenever we wish, any more
5   than we begin experiencing them [whenever we wish]. Now this man [Socrates] begins when he wishes, and he wishes [to begin] when his beloved is worthy of love. So he also stops when he wishes, just as here, too, he remarks that 'had I observed you really going after *apparent* goods, I would have set aside my love long ago'.

10   **[105A] But now I'm going to show you your own, rather different plans:** He means, 'Since you do not truly desire these things, but other, greater things, and you fight over shadows because you are ignorant about the latter, I will tell you the arguments by means of which I will prove that you do not really long for these things.'[327] And he added the [phrase] 'you your own', demonstrating that he knows what belongs to [Alcibiades] better than he does himself. That's also
15   why he added, 'From that, you'll realise that I've had you constantly in mind' – meaning, '[you'll realise this] from my telling you the truth about yourself'. And the [phrase] 'I have spent all this time thinking about you' also has to do with love.

You see, as you seem to me, if one of the gods asked you . . . Here begin the questions of the god. The reason why he introduced a god to question 20 Alcibiades has been stated in the survey.

Would you rather live with what you now possess: From this one can derive the doctrine, which we have also stated, that lives are according to choice, and not according to necessity. And this is clear in the *Republic* as well.

It seems to me that you would rather die: This is the answer given by the 25 philosopher on the young man's behalf: and we should notice that, although he is just one actor 'on stage' (*en heni prosôpôi*), he preserves the form of dialogue here, himself introducing the questions as if they came from a god, and the 50,1 answers as if they came from Alcibiades. And there are two lessons to be drawn from the speech: that it is better not to exist than to exist badly, and that the body is an impediment to the acquisition of excellence.

But now I'll tell you just what your real hope in life is: From this point begins 5 the division of Alcibiades' life: for Socrates unfolds his entire chain of reasoning in the following words.

[You think that as soon as you present yourself before the Athenian people,] [105B] as indeed you expect to in just a few days . . . Proclus relates that after twenty days [Alcibiades] was to be enrolled among the Adolescents (*ephêboi*), and then was to advise the Athenians.[328] 10

That you deserve a greater reputation than Pericles himself: Another lesson emerges from this point: one should not give advice for the sake of reputation, as Alcibiades does now, but for the benefit of one's hearers. And we should recognise that [Socrates], by saying 'greater than Pericles himself', begins from the source (*hestia*) of [Alcibiades'] ambition,[329] and what is dearest to his heart (*oikeios*).

And if you're the greatest here, you'll be the greatest among the other 15 **Hellenes, and not only among the Hellenes:** [Socrates] has his speech (*logos*) proceed like a ladder: for he adds, 'you want to be famous (*eudokimein*) not only among the Hellenes, but all through Europe too, among foreigners, and across the whole totality of the Earth', and 'you think no one worth speaking of, except Cyrus and Xerxes'.

20   And I say that [Alcibiades] will not stop caring about his reputation even
        when he reaches this point, but he will want even more – as the comic poet
        puts it:[330]

        even if he achieves this, he wants forty times as much.

        For as we remarked before, it is not the case that all human beings long for just
        the same affections (for these are unlimited), but they long for more, because
        they possess a concept (*ennoia*) of certain other [sc. higher] things that they
        are unable to secure.[331]

25   We should also investigate why the affection of caring for reputation is the
        most difficult of all to wipe out (*dusekniptos*).[332] Consider: it is so [difficult]
51,1   that even those who decide *not* to care about their reputation, do *that* out of
        care for their reputation, that is, in order not to *appear* to care about their
        reputation. We assert, then, that the affection of caring for reputation is difficult
        to wipe out for the following reason: it is closer to reason (*logos*) than other
        [affections] are,[333] and is sibling to it, and reason is not something we can cast
5   aside; therefore what is close to reason is also difficult for us to cast aside.

        Or here is an alternative reason: the soul, when it descends here and flees
        slavery to its superiors, but wants to rule over its inferiors, first clothes itself in
        care for reputation from among the affections; and then, when [in ascending
        again] it casts [the affections] aside, it discards this one last of all. Since it is also
        said of [the soul],

10   Then he stripped off his rags.[334]

        And we should recognise that among our vital (*zôtikais*) capacities, the
        reputation-loving affection is difficult to cast aside, while among our cognitive
        (*gnôstikais*) capacities it is imagination (*phantasia*) that is difficult to cast aside.
        For imagination is always available to our soul, as our soul is constantly
        fashioning impressions (*tupous*) of what it does not know, and bestowing
15   shapes, sizes, and bodies on the non-bodily, and confining [even] the god in
        terms of place (*topôi*).[335]

        That selfsame (*autos*) god . . . It was fitting for him to locate 'self' (*autos*) on
        the level of the god, since the god is the unit (*henas*), and unitary in form
        (*henoeidês*).[336] But he spoke in the plural about the realities (*pragmata*) that

Alcibiades is questing after, because the [entities] that follow and extend from the divine and the monad are many, and every person quests for these.[337] That he spoke in the plural about these is clear also from his introducing [the phrase], 'to add something to the realities (*pragmata*) that are there'. And the word 'add' also suits Alcibiades.[338]

Except Cyrus and Xerxes: It has been pointed out that he made use of dissimilar examples:[339] for these [two] were not selected for the same reason, considering that one was called 'father', the other 'despot'.

I'm not guessing (*eikazô*) that this is your hope – I know it well. It was fitting that he placed the [phrase] 'I know well' after the demonstrations (*apodeixeis*), as he did at the beginning too [104C].[340] It is like the Homeric [verse] to say, as Diomedes said to Athena, 'Nor do I escape your notice when I move,'[341] but Socrates [says it] from the opposite point of view [i.e. the god's]: 'nor do you escape my notice', since he says: 'I know well, then, and am not just guessing that you have this hope.'

Lecture 6

With the god's favour

[Soc. **Since you know what I say is true, maybe you'll say,**] '**Well then, Socrates, what's this got to do with your point (*logos*)? You said you were going to tell me why you haven't abandoned me**'. [**Yes, I will tell you, my dear son of Clinias and Dinomache. It is impossible to put any of these plans of yours into effect without me – that's how much power I think I have for your practical affairs and you yourself. I think this is why the god hasn't allowed me to talk to you all this time; and I've been waiting for the day he allows me.**

Consider how you hope to demonstrate in public that you're indispensable to the city – and after that, to win unlimited power. It's just like that with me: I hope to win the greatest power over you by demonstrating that I'm worth the world to you, and that nobody has the power to give you the power you crave, neither your guardian nor your relatives, nor anybody else except me – with the god's support, of course. When you were younger,

before you were full of such ambitions, I think the god didn't let me talk to

106A   you because the conversation would have been pointless. But now he's told me to, because now you will listen to me.

Alc. Really, Socrates, now that you've started talking you seem much stranger . . . Well, on the question of whether or not these are my ambitions, you already seem to have your mind made up, and no denial of mine will do anything to convince you otherwise. Fine. But supposing I really do have these ambitions, how will they be achieved through you, and not without you? Have you got something to say?

106B   Soc. Are you asking if I can say some long speech like the ones you're used to hearing? No, that sort of thing's not for me. But I do think I'd be able to show you that what I said is true, if only you were willing to do me just one brief service.

Alc. Well, as long as the service you mean is nothing onerous, I'm willing.

Soc. Do you think it's onerous to answer questions?

Alc. No, I don't.

Soc. Then answer me.

Alc. Ask me.

Soc. Then I question you as someone who has this plan in mind?

106C   Alc. Let's say I do, if you like, so I can find out what you're going to say.]

10   Two [questions] had been advanced in the proem [103A–104E]: first, why does Socrates love [Alcibiades]? And second, why does Socrates accompany him by loving in silence (that is, why does he love him without being present with him)? In answer to the second [question], the cause has been attributed to a daimonic or divine entity. In answer to the first [question], three causes have been stated:

[1] that Alcibiades looks down on the other lovers,
[2] that he cannot be conquered by love of money, and
15   [3] that he thinks little of his resources.

Since the proem encompassed not only these two [questions], but also a third – [why is it] that Socrates does not abandon [Alcibiades] after the other lovers have ceased? – Socrates is now in position to impart the cause of this. And so he explains, 'Here is why I do not abandon you: it is because I am the only person who has the power to give you the power that all of your other 20 lovers could not give'.

[Three puzzles (aporiai)]

[1. Why does Socrates vaunt himself?]

Now first of all, we raise the puzzle (*aporoumen*), why is Socrates boastful here? – he who is everywhere ironic,[342] and about whom it is said, 'this is your habitual irony, Socrates';[343] who is always claiming that he knows 53,1 nothing, and teaches nothing, which is also why the god at Delphi said about him that

> Socrates is wisest of all men[344]

– since it was not only by striking the air, by vocal expression, that [Socrates] used to say this sort of thing, but [he also expressed himself] through his manner of living, and in his divine inspiration. We ought to investigate, then, 5 how it could be that such a person thinks [of himself] like this in the present case, announcing that he alone is able to deliver power to the youth.[345]

Well, we reply, first, that the philosopher boasts at the right moment (*kairos*): for before this, it was crucial that he *not* boast, since Alcibiades scorned him just as he scorned his other lovers. So Socrates understood the right moment for boasting. In fact, he has often done this: for example, in the *Theaetetus*, after 10 establishing himself as a judge between 'genuine' and 'wind-egg' theories (*logoi*), he says, 'For no god ever has ill-will toward a human being, nor do I do this out of any ill will, but it is never lawful (*themis*) for me either to agree to falsehood or to suppress truth.'[346] (Notice how he ranked himself with the god here, by saying, 'For 15 no god ever has ill-will . . . ') And again in the *Apology* he boasts when he says, 'It is not permissible (*themis*) for a better person to be ruled by a worse one';[347] and again in the same dialogue when he says that 'Anytus and Meletus have the power to kill me, but not to do me any harm at all' (in the first part of this sentence, he uses the word 'me' in the more ordinary way, referring to the composite 20 (*sunamphoteron*) [of soul and body]; but in the second part, he uses it in its strict sense (*kuriôs*), referring to the soul alone).

So that is one solution [to the puzzle], that he knows how to be boastful at the right moment. A second solution is that he is not [really] being boastful 54,1 (*megalorrhêmonei*) when he prefers himself to base people with a herd mentality (*agelaioi*). For it is nothing to boast about (*mega*) when the philosopher achieves what worthless people lacked the power to achieve.

And here is a third [solution]: for someone who pays precise attention (*akribôs ennoêsêi*) to the words used here, it does not seem as if Socrates is 5 boastful at all. For he says, 'with the god's support, of course' [105E], and 'It is impossible to put any of these plans (*dianoêmata*) of yours into effect without me' [105D]. (The word 'without' is a material (*hulikos*) preposition, and suitable to matter (*hulê*), since 'without' matter there is nothing here [sc. in the perceptible world] to think about).[348]

[2. Why does Socrates vaunt Alcibiades?]

Second, we raise the puzzle, why does Socrates make the young man arrogant 10 by holding out such hopes and pronouncing that he will deliver power to him?[349] Well, we say that just as the doctors do not apply themselves to the *causes* of a disease until they have made it less acute (for which reason it was well said by Hippocrates, '[One should] medicate and attack [the disease] when it is ripe, not raw nor at the beginning'),[350] likewise Socrates does not apply himself to the affections (*pathê*) before he has ameliorated 15 them, nor does he extirpate them 'by burning and incisions', as the saying goes.[351]

For we need to understand that – just as we said at the beginning[352] – there are three methods (*tropoi*) of purification, the Pythagorean, Socratic and Peripatetic or Stoic.[353] Now, the Stoic [method] heals opposites by opposites, introducing appetite (*epithumia*) to spirited emotion (*thumos*), thus softening [the former], and introducing spirited emotion to appetite and so strengthening [the latter], encouraging it to mature into manhood (*anagôn pros to* 20 *andrikôteron*). This is analogous to heated rods: if someone wants to straighten one, he bends it backwards, in order that symmetry might occur when it curves back in the opposite direction: in the case of souls, similarly, it was their custom 55,1 to foster harmony by using this method [of purification].

But the Pythagorean [method] urges us to 'concede a little' to the affections (*pathê*), and to taste them as if 'with the tip of the finger': the doctors talk about this as 'a little worse' (*smikrôi elatton*).[354] What they meant to convey was this: those who are swelling up with an affection will be unable to stay in control of 5 it, unless they act on it. For this is also what Athena did in the case of Pandarus: when he wanted to break his oath, she conceded [this] to him, which is also why he received corrective punishment (*kolazomenos*) through his tongue, since this became the instrument of his oath-breaking.[355]

But the Socratic method of purification converts likes to likes: by saying to someone who loves possessions, 'learn what true self-sufficiency is', or to 10 someone who loves pleasure, '[learn] what divine ease is', and basically everything that we stated earlier.[356] And this method is superior to the others: for the first [sc. Stoic or Peripatetic method] heals one trouble by another, since [it heals] an affection by an affection, while the second [sc. Pythagorean method] does not allow the soul to remain spotless, on account of its contact with the affections.

[3. Why does Socrates claim that he can deliver power to Alcibiades?]

Third, then, we raise the puzzle (*aporoumen*), why does Socrates claim that he 15 has the power (*dunasthai*) to provide power (*dunamis*) to Alcibiades?[357]

Well, we should reply to this[358] as follows: he means that he will provide *knowledge* (*epistêmê*) to him, and knowledge is a kind of power, since elsewhere he remarks that 'nothing is more powerful (*dunatôteron*) than demonstration existing in the soul' (and 'demonstration' is of knowledge), and that knowledge is invincible to a tyrant.[359]

Or [second, we should reply] that Socrates, who is an outstanding 20 person (*spoudaios*), is self-sufficient (*autarkês*) and is kin (*sungenês*) to the self-sufficiency of the god, and therefore here, as a lover, he applies outstanding effort (*spoudazei*) to providing this kind of self-sufficiency to his beloved, to completing him, and to guiding him upward toward the god's self-sufficiency.

Or thirdly, [one should reply] that, according to the boastful talk of the Stoics, only the 'ruler' (*arkhikos*) – that is, the person who *knows* how to rule (*arkhein*) – is in control (*arkhôn*), even if he lacks the tools to exercise the ruler's knowledge;[360] and only the wise man is wealthy, that is, the man who 56,1 knows how to make use of the wealth that is available, even if no [material] wealth is in fact available. This is the kind of 'power', then, that Socrates announces to the youth as [necessary] for his statesmanhood (*politikos*);

for it is true that [Socrates] alone, and none of the others, had the ability to
5   provide this.

Toward the end of the proem (*prooimion*) [106B], he makes the second of [the
requests] that we pointed out[361] – I mean, that [Alcibiades] answer his
questions. And here we ask again, why in the world does the philosopher ask
Alcibiades to do this?

We reply that Socrates did not want to draw dead and unbreathing words
10   (*logoi*) from him, but (so to speak) active and living [words], suitable to people
engaged in dialectic; and this is what he is hunting for in the answers.

Alternately, [we reply] that Socrates, being a lover, wants to embrace
(*periplokê*) his beloved; and the dialogue form is similar to an embrace, as the
interaction through brief exchanges becomes a process of question and answer.
15   Alternately, [our third reply is] that, as he says in the *Phaedrus*, 'it is necessary
for the speech (*logos*) to resemble a living being (*zôiôn*)';[362] and it follows that
the best-constructed speech must resemble the best of living beings. And the
best living being is the cosmos:[363] just as this [world] serves as a meadow for a
diversity (*poikilôn*) of living beings, the speech should likewise be full of all
kinds of characters (*prosôpôn*).[364] And [this is also the case] in other ways,
since, just as in this [cosmos] all things speak and act (for the activities of
20   beings are like their voices),[365] so too in the speech it is appropriate for all of its
characters to speak, just as it is for everyone to act (*energein*).

Fourth, [we answer] that the form of question and answer is stimulating
and tends to revert [the soul back upon itself] (*epistreptikos*).[366] Naturally, the
orators too, when they wish to stimulate the audience or turn their attention to
the speech, have used this [form of question and answer]: for example, 'answer
25   me, by the gods!' But a speech that drones on at length makes the audience fall
57,1   asleep: as Aischines says, for instance, 'dreaming over the pronouncement of
justice'.[367] So Socrates, who wants to revert Alcibiades [to attend to his own
soul], asks him to answer his questions.

That completes our survey (*theôria*) and [our discussion of] the proem
(*prooimion*) of the dialogue; here, then, commences the remainder of the first
5   part (*prôton meros*), which is the refutative [part].[368]

**[105C] 'Well then, Socrates, what's this got to do with your point (*logos*)?
You said you were going to tell me why you haven't abandoned me.'** Notice

that Alcibiades himself asks Socrates to explain the third point that he
mentioned in the proem, namely, why 'when the others have stopped, he alone
does not abandon him' – and, a little later, Socrates will answer this too.   10

[105D] Yes, I will tell you, my dear son of Clinias and Dinomache. It is
neither untimely nor excessive to address [Alcibiades] by his father's and
mother's names here,[369] as someone might have supposed. Rather, considering
the young man's noble birth on both sides, it is appropriate to use these words
to express the point that 'neither your relatives on your mother's side, nor those
on your father's side, can offer you the power that I can provide'.   15

**It is impossible to put any of these plans (*dianoêmata*) of yours into effect
without me.** 'This', he means, 'is the reason why I do not abandon you, since
you cannot obtain what you hope for without me.'

And he uses the word 'plans' (*dianoêmata*) about the [goals] that he
described earlier, when he said that 'you think that you will approach the
Athenians quite soon, and show them that you deserve a reputation even   20
greater than Pericles himself, and you will prove your importance among
Hellenes and foreigners',[370] and basically everything that we have discussed in
that passage.[371] And the phrase 'without me', as a preposition indicating
materiality, shows that the philosopher is not boasting, as has been stated in
the lecture (*theôria*).[372]

For your practical affairs (*pragmata*) and for you yourself . . . He says 'for
your practical affairs' meaning 'for your activities (*energeiai*)', and 'for you   25
yourself (*autos*)' meaning 'for your soul',[373] just as he used the word 'me' most
strictly of the soul in the *Apology* when he said, 'but they do not have the power
to harm *me*'.[374]

I think this is why the god hasn't allowed me to talk to you all this time,   58,1
meaning: 'if the god used to turn me away before in order that I did not speak
in vain, then now, since he does not turn me away, I will provide you with the
power that you desire by any means at my disposal'. For if the god turned him
aside then (when it was appropriate to do so), it is not in vain that the god does
not do so now. For if the good man (*spoudaios*) does nothing in vain, and   5
neither does nature (*phusis*),[375] then the god must [do nothing in vain] to an
even greater degree.[376]

For just as you hope to demonstrate in public . . . Here Socrates offers an analogy: 'for the rank that you hold in relation to the citizens, Alcibiades – surpassing them to the degree that an adviser surpasses those whom he advises

10   (for the [good] adviser must be like this) – this is [the rank] that I hold in relation to you, and the god in relation to me'.[377]

[105E] Demonstrating that I'm worth the world to you . . . We should notice that the philosopher always associates 'demonstration' (*endeixamenos*) with the dialogue form, but 'display' (*epideixamenos*) with extended speech;[378] this is also the reason why he always distinguishes these from one another. So here too, he utilises this [distinction], when [he says], 'I will prove (*deixô*) to you,

15   using question and answer, the magnitude of power that will come to you through me.'

With the god's support, of course . . . Notice, again, a sign that Socrates is not boasting; for he did not only say that he himself was able, but 'with the god'.

20   **When you were younger . . .** Here he repeats what he said above. For he
59,1   was saying then, 'I think this is also why for a long time the god has not allowed me to converse with you';[379] and that is also what he means now. He hinted riddlingly (*êinitteto*) at this remark in the beginning, as we noticed there, when he said, 'the power of which you will also learn later': here, then,

5   is the follow-up to that remark, namely, that '[the god] prevented me so that I would not converse with you in vain'. That's also why he added, 'but now he sent me [to you], for now you might listen to me', using these words to urge [Alcibiades] even more strongly to listen to him, since the god, by not turning [Socrates] aside, sent him to talk with [Alcibiades] so that the latter might be persuaded.[380]

[106A] Now you seem much more strange (*atopos*) . . . [By which he means],
10   more paradoxical and more worthy of wonder.[381] And it is appropriate that Socrates seems more wondrous to Alcibiades now, after he has conversed with him, than when he was silent. For in our case too, we wonder more at the divine when we are visibly illuminated[382] and inspired than when we are not.

Well, on the question of whether or not these are my ambitions, you already seem to have your mind made up. Since Alcibiades is naturally gifted (*euphuês*), he neither denies absolutely that he has in mind what Socrates stated, nor does he grant it, but he creates a middle ground (*khôrei*) in between 15 [these extremes] by using hypothetical language (*dia tou hupothetikou skhêmatos*).[383]

He does not grant [Socrates' claims], because in a democracy it was customary for the speaker not to appear keen on power, and so he shrank from this; but he does not deny it either, because he wished (since he wanted to become a politician) to hear from Socrates what kind of words such a person would need to use to be appointed to power over the people. Thus he says, 'Even supposing I *do* have in mind what you say, how will you provide it 20 for me?'

How will they be achieved through you . . . ? Here the philosopher Iamblichus got involved, and raised the puzzle (*aporein*) that Alcibiades appears more fulfilled (*teleioteros*)[384] than Socrates. For [Alcibiades] said '*through* you', a preposition that suits an instrumental cause, whereas [Socrates] said '*with* the 60,1 god', a preposition suitable to a productive (*poiêtikos*) cause, and he put himself on the level (*sunetaxen*) of the god; but [Alcibiades] said 'through you' as if Socrates were an *instrument* of the god.[385]

And [Iamblichus] solved this absolutely beautifully (*pankalôs*) by pointing out that Plato, in his other [works], claims that more fulfilled souls watch over 5 [works] in this world (*têide*) jointly with the god, and jointly set them in order,[386] but less fulfilled souls have the function of an instrument, and so the god uses them with a view to [works] here (*entautha*). (In fact, [the god] does not only use less complete [souls], but there are even times when [he uses] bad [souls], for instance, [using] murderers with a view to the rendering of the proper, just penalty (*dikê*) for those who owe it).[387] Thus Socrates, with reference to his own, more fulfilled capacities (*dunameis*), said '*with* the god'; but 10 Alcibiades was referring to his less complete [capacities], and so he said '*through* you' and again added 'and *without* you', the preposition suitable to matter (*hulê*).

Then are you asking if I can say some long speech, like the ones you're used to hearing? By this [remark], Socrates aims to prepare Alcibiades not to expect 15 long speeches from him.[388] For he was sure that Alcibiades, who is disposed to oratory, would expect him to converse this way, which is why he says 'such as you are accustomed to hear'. And he implants the concept (*ennoia*) that he will speak dialectically (*dialogikôs*): for he adds, 'this sort of thing is not my [habit],

20   but [rather] to demonstrate to you . . ', meaning, 'to converse by question and answer'.

If only you were willing to do just one brief service . . . Here Socrates makes a different request of Alcibiades, that is, to answer. And he says 'brief' because he practises the philosophy that does not require hypotheses, and does not

61,1   require many words.[389] We have stated in the survey (*theôria*) the reasons why he asks him to answer. At this point it should also be noted that [Alcibiades'] answers will make him appear to be set straight by his own, self-moved activity (*autokinêtôs*) – i.e. through cross-examination (*elenkhos*) by himself. For we

5   need to understand that we act in a self-moving way when we revert upon ourselves,[390] needing no one else to be set straight and to achieve relief from the affections (*pathê*) in us; but whenever we put a stop to our affections through *others'* cross-examination, then that amounts to being moved by another (*heterokinêtôs*). This is also the case in the *Gorgias* [sc. *Republic* 1][391] – for there, through Socrates' cross-examination of the spirited emotion (*thumos*) of Thrasymachus, we learn (*ennooumen*) how to put a stop to the Thrasymachus

10   in us. And likewise by [studying] Callicles' love for pleasure and Polus' love for reputation [in the *Gorgias*].[392] So too by [studying] Protagoras' [theory about] appearance (*phantasia*):[393] for Protagoras is a sophist, and appearance is quite similar to the sophist, since it misrepresents (*sophizein*) and remodels realities. And so Socrates, who wants Alcibiades to act with self-movement here,

15   prepares him to give answers: and he calls this 'doing a service', in order that the person who desires rule over all should be shown, in this case, to be Socrates' servant.[394]

Well, as long as the service you mean is nothing onerous (*khalepos*): The young man gives an appropriate answer to this sort of request from Socrates, considering that [Socrates] will provide to him a power which the others were

20   not able [to provide], and he supposed the request would be a large one.[395] This is why he replies, 'If you mean nothing onerous': for he imagined that the request would match the magnitude of the results promised. But notice, he nevertheless agrees to do the service for Socrates, on the condition that it would not be burdensome (*baru*).

And [Socrates] answers, 'If it seems onerous to give answers', in order that [Alcibiades], agreeing that it is not onerous, will readily give answers. Of course the young man replies, 'It is not onerous'; and this is well said. For if Aristotle were the questioner[396] – or some other combative [conversant] (*eristikos*) who looks just to victory and on that account delights in the speaker's mistakes in conversation – then it would be difficult and onerous to give answers;[397] but since it is Socrates, the 'midwife' who aims to benefit youths and set them straight, it is suitable [to say] 'not onerous'.[398] On the contrary, it is the [work of] questioning that is onerous, just as on a journey [it is more onerous] to lead than to follow.

Then I question you as someone who has this plan in mind? We must take this as a question, since the answer, again, makes it plain that it is [interrogative]. For [Alcibiades] answers, 'Let's say that I do.' We should recognise that in his present response, Alcibiades is again offering a hypothetical answer – with rhetorical brilliance, since he was manifestly well educated in [rhetoric] by Pericles, who was also brilliant, and his guardian. Therefore he says, 'Let's say I do, if you like, so that I can find out what you're going to say.' (The phrase 'if you like' (*ei boulei*), you see, is hypothetical.) As for the rest [of Alcibiades' statement], it suits his character (*êthikôs*) as a person who does not resist agreement.

With that, the proem (*prooimion*) of the dialogue is completed, and the beginning of the refutative [section] follows.

Here Begins the First [sc. Refutative] Section

Lecture 7

With the god's favour

Soc. Come on, then: I say that you intend to come forward and advise the Athenians [in the near future. Well, then, suppose that I caught you as you were about to mount the podium, and said, 'Alcibiades, what are the Athenians intending to deliberate about, that you should get up to advise them? Is it something that you understand better than they do?' What would be your answer?

62,1

5

10

15

20

106C

106D   ALC. Yes, I suppose I would say it was something that I know better than they do.

SOC. So it's on matters you know about that you're a good adviser.

ALC. Of course.

SOC. Now the only things you know are what you've learned from others or found out for yourself, isn't that right?

ALC. What else could I know?

SOC. Could you ever have learned or found out anything without wanting to learn it or work it out for yourself?

ALC. No, I couldn't have.

SOC. Is that right? Would you have wanted to investigate or learn something that you thought you understood?

ALC. Of course not.

106E   SOC. So there was a time when you didn't think you knew what you now understand.

ALC. There must have been.

SOC. But I've got a pretty good idea what you've learned. Tell me if I've missed anything: as far as I remember, you learned letters and lyre-playing and wrestling, but you didn't want to learn flute-playing. These are the subjects that you understand – unless perhaps you've been learning something while I wasn't looking; but I don't think you have been, either by night or by day, on your excursions from home.

ALC. No, those are the only lessons I took.

107A   SOC. Well, then, is it when the Athenians are taking counsel about how to spell a word correctly that you'll stand up to advise them?

ALC. By Zeus, I'd never do that!

SOC. Then is it when they're taking counsel about the notes on the lyre?

ALC. **No, never.**

SOC. **But surely they're not in the habit of discussing wrestling in the Assembly.**

ALC. **Certainly not.**

SOC. **Then what will they be discussing? I presume it won't be house-building.**

ALC. **Of course not.**

SOC. **Because a builder would give better advice on these matters than you.**

ALC. **Yes.**   107B

SOC. **Nor will they be taking counsel about prophecy, will they?**

ALC. **No.**

SOC. **Because then a prophet would be better at giving advice than you . . .]**

There are three basic components of being a good adviser, as follows:[399] good intentions (*prohairesis agathê*), exact knowledge (*gnôsis akribês*), and expressive ability (*dunamis apangeltikê*) (for the adviser must have goodwill for his audience, or else he is no good [for them]; and obviously he also needs exact   63,1 understanding about the subject he is going to discuss, since he is not about to give advice out of ignorance; and moreover, he also must be able to express what he had in mind and put it into words, or else the first two are useless). Given these [basics], then, Socrates demonstrates that Alcibiades is not a good adviser on the grounds of exact knowledge. He begins by using the following proof:[400]   5

1. The good adviser understands the subject of his advice, and [understands it] better than those whom he advises.
    a. For [his understanding is] not on an equal footing [with theirs] (for it would be pointless to teach people what they already know);
    b. But it is also not inferior (for it would be madness for someone who doesn't know something to explain it to people who do);
    c. It follows by necessity that the good adviser understands the subject   10 of his advice better than his audience.

2. The person with superior understanding [of something] either learned or discovered it.

   a. Because knowledge is twofold, being divided into learning and discovery. For we 'learn' when the movement comes from someone else (*heterokinêtôs*), and we 'discover' when the movement comes from ourselves (*autokinêtôs*).

      i. This is also how the poets portray Hermes, who is the overseer of knowledge, as both a messenger (*angelos*) and the son of Maia:[401] he is 'messenger' as a *learner*, because the messenger announces things he learns from others; and he is the son of Maia as a *discoverer*, because the midwife (*maia*) does not herself place infants into the women who give birth to them, but she brings into the light [the children] that are already there. In the same way, then, the discoverer brings to birth the explanations (*logoi*) that are within him.

      ii. And if learning is sometimes superior to discovery – for instance, when we learn from gods through dreams – we should recognise that in this situation, activity motivated by another is actually preferable to activity motivated by oneself: for it benefits us to be led by a god rather than by ourselves.

3. Next, the learner or discoverer either conducted an investigation or received instruction (for the ends are learning and discovery, but the means are investigation and receiving instruction); and someone who has either conducted an investigation or received instruction can tell of a time when he didn't think that he understood and so[402] either studied with teachers or toiled at [his own] investigations.

4. The good adviser, then, is able to state the time at which he thought he did not understand. But obviously Alcibiades is not able to make this statement. For when he was just a young man playing at dice with his age-mates, he swore that they were cheating him (*hup' autôn adikeisthai*), as if he had a precise fix on justice (*to dikaion*).

That is how the proof proceeded synthetically.[403] But it is also possible to present it analytically, as follows:

1. The good adviser is able to state the time at which he did not think he understood.
2. Such a person either conducted an investigation or received instruction.
3. Such a person either learned or discovered.
4. Such a person understands the subject of his advice better than those whom he advises.
5. The good adviser, then, understands the subject of his advice better than his audience.

The first proof resembles a descent of the soul that is continually assuming, or clothing itself in, affections (*pathê*), the second an ascent that is continually casting affections off. Hence one might also recite the poetic verse about this,   15

> Then he stripped off his rags . . .[404]

But Socrates tests Alcibiades not only by the proof [just] described, but by another such which goes like this:[405] 'What would you advise the Athenians   20
about? [1] About something that you know and think you understand, like wrestling or playing the cithara or writing? For these you learned. But they don't hold assemblies about these matters or debate them[406] – or if they do, not about how one should play the cithara or wrestle, but about whether they should welcome (*paralambanein*) teachers of gymnastics or of the cithara or of   25
reading and writing in their city.' (Thus, for instance, in Homer, Achilles, being   65,1
a politician, did not prophesy to the Hellenes himself, but advised them to make use of a prophet;[407] and again, Themistocles did not have the triremes built on his own initiative (*autos*), but proposed the building of a fleet after interpreting the oracle,

> [Zeus] grants to Tritogeneia [Athene] a wooden wall . . .[408] –   5

And this is appropriate. For higher-level skills don't do away with those that come under them by pre-empting what belongs to them, but, on the contrary, actually bolster them, with the consequence that philosophy can remain the 'skill of skills, and science of sciences',[409] while the skills posterior to it remain intact, and thus can provide them with their principles (*arkhai*).)

'So you wouldn't give advice about what you know and think you understand,   10
for it's not about these subjects, as we said, that they deliberate. [2] But nor

would you about subjects on which you're ignorant and which you don't suppose you understand, for simple ignorance[410] is not a cause of error. [3] And nor indeed about matters of which you're ignorant, but which you imagine you understand; for this is the characteristic of double ignorance: "advice is [the prerogative] of the person who understands a subject and not that of a wealthy person".'

15 The remaining leg [of the division], I mean [4] understanding but thinking one does not understand, or not knowing that one knows, is incoherent; for knowledge, being [a kind of] light, does not escape the notice of the person who has it. Such, then, is the division by means of which Alcibiades is once more convicted of being a poor adviser in respect of his knowledge.

20 Now these three [disciplines] were learned in Athens – reading and writing, playing the cithara,[411] and wrestling – for the organisation of the tripartition of

66,1 the soul, as we said at the beginning; the reason (*logos*) was organised by means of reading and writing, spirited emotion (*thumos*) tamed by means of playing the cithara, and desire (*epithumia*) strengthened and made tough by wrestling. And he adds that 'You refused to practice the flute.' There were a number of reasons that they did not cultivate the study of the flute: first, because this [instrument]

5 has to do with ecstasy and has more to do with inspiration and not with education.[412] For in cithara-playing, it is possible to use reasoned speech (*logos*) as well,[413] but in flute-playing that is not at all the case: not only is [the performer] himself unable to use speech or to sing, but he can't even hear someone else singing, for this is a noisy [instrument];[414] which is why we talk about 'cithara-song', but not 'flute-song'.[415] And Athena threw away her flute on this account, as

10 an impediment to reason (*logos*). (The goddess is the overseer of wisdom. [Or] as the poets say, it was because she saw that her face looked unbecoming. Or perhaps this is to be understood in the following way: that 'the face of sound is language', but the flute is hostile to it.) Also, the poet[416] is always attributing cithara-playing to the Hellenes, but nowhere portrayed them playing the flute; but to the Trojans,

15 as they are foreigners, he assigned the flute, and he also said of them that

the Trojans came on with clamour and cry like birds . . .'[417]

And it was appropriate that he assign the flute to these people, since they are

67,1 Phrygians – for reportedly the flute was invented in Phrygia, in the context of mysteries and inspirations.[418] There too [lived] Marsyas, who competed in music with Apollo and was bested, he using a flute, the other a cithara. And Alcibiades himself said about the Thebans, 'Let the children of the Thebans play the flute,[419] because they don't know how to have a conversation.'[420]

That is the content of the survey (*theôria*).

[106C] Come on, then: I say that you intend . . . We should investigate why Socrates examines the young man based on knowledge alone, and not on the other criteria [that determine a good adviser, described above].

We say, then, that he could not do so on the basis of his ability to express himself, because he knew that he had this from Pericles, with whom he had lived earlier, [and] as a consequence he was a natural (*tên phusin*) orator.[421] And [it could not be] on the basis of good intentions (*prohairesis*) either: for [Alcibiades] was good on account of his immunity to the affection of caring for money, his generosity with his possessions, and the fact that he looked down on his other lovers.[422]

Well, then, [suppose that I caught you] as you were about to mount the podium . . . Since he is addressing a person with oratorical aspirations (*rhêtorikos*), he uses rhetorical jargon throughout, as he does here.[423] He furnishes [Alcibiades] with an audience and a theatre, you see, and lays out the podium (*bêma*) with [Alcibiades] rushing toward it, and he adds himself as the bit [in his mouth], so that he can rein in the young man's affections and his passionate longing to advise [the people of Athens]: for he says, 'Supposing I took you aside and asked . . .'

Is it something that you understand better than they do? Here is the first premiss, that 'The good adviser knows the subject of his advice better than those whom he is about to advise: since his knowledge isn't worse, for that would be crazy; nor is it equal, for that would be useless.'

[106D] Now the only things you know are what you've learned from others or discovered yourself . . . [Here is] the second premiss, that 'The one who knows better either learned or discovered [his knowledge]': for understanding is twofold, as we have learned.[424]

Is that right? Would you have wanted to investigate or learn [what you thought you understood]? [Here is] the third premiss, that 'The person who has learned or discovered something, either investigated it or was taught: the latter are the means, the former the ends.' (By 'being taught' [*didakthênai*] here, one should understand 'learn' [*mathein*]).[425]

68,1 **[106E] So there was a time when you didn't think you knew . . .** [Here is] the fourth and final premiss, that 'the person who has investigated or been taught something is able to state the time when he did not think he knew it'.

We should understand that the prosyllogism[426] is in the first figure, the syllogism in the second figure.[427] For here is the prosyllogism: 'The good
5 adviser knows better about the subject of his advice than those whom he advises; such a person either learned or discovered [his knowledge]; such a person either investigated or was taught; such a person is able to state a time when he did not think he knew; therefore the good adviser is able to state the time when he did not think he knew [about the subject of his advice.]' And the syllogism, assuming the last proposition demonstrated in the prosyllogism,
10 proceeds in the second figure as follows: 'The good adviser is able to state a time when he did not think he knew; Alcibiades is not able to state the time when he did not think he knew; therefore Alcibiades is not a good adviser.' (We should understand that [Plato] himself unfolded the syllogism at greater length, but we re-organised it into syllogistic form.)

15 **Actually, I myself know just about everything that you have learned . . .** He was right to add 'just about' (*skhedon ti*): for it's likely that Alcibiades was aware of some knick-knack (*skeuarion*)[428] in his house that Socrates didn't know about!

But you didn't want to learn flute-playing . . . True enough: [Alcibiades], you see, is the one who said of the Thebans, 'let the children of the Thebans play the
20 flute, because they don't understand how to converse.'[429]

But I don't think you have been [learning something while I wasn't looking], either by night or by day, on your excursions from home . . . That is, 'You did not learn anything other than these subjects, assuming you never escaped my notice.'[430] This resembles what Diomedes[431] says to Athena, when he tells her, 'Nor do I escape your notice when I move.'[432] For Socrates was
25 always present with Alcibiades, like our conscience,[433] which attends each of our actions.

[107A] Well, then, is it when the Athenians take counsel about reading and writing . . .? Here begins the second refutation, which we reduced to a division,[434] to the effect that [Alcibiades'] advice either concerns [1] what he knows and thinks he understands, or [2] what he does not know, but thinks he understands, or [3] what he does not know and does not think he understands; and we stated that the fourth, and incoherent, leg [4] is to know, but think one 69,1 does not know. For each and every one of these alternatives, we have demonstrated that it is impossible for him to be a good adviser. But the text mentions only two, namely, [1] that he knows and thinks that he knows (and about these [objects of knowledge] the Athenians never deliberate in assembly, if in fact [Alcibiades] has only learned cithara-playing, wrestling, and reading 5 and writing), and [2] things he doesn't know about and knows he doesn't know about (for [Socrates] adds that 'you also will not advise them about house-building', and Alcibiades, who is ignorant about this, knows that he does not know).

I presume it won't be house-building . . . We should understand that it is not because advice about house-building has a low value that Socrates said 'Then 10 you will not give advice when they deliberate about house-building', but rather because Alcibiades is ignorant about house-building. (For he added that 'The house-builder will surely advise better about this than you will?', meaning he 'will give accurate advice about what pertains to house-building'.)[435] To guard against that [sort of misinterpretation], he also introduced an example from a skill with more status (with the words, 'nor surely when [they are deliberating] 15 about prophecy'), to show that it is not the status or lack of status of a subject that makes one equipped (or not equipped) to give advice, but accurate knowledge of the matters at hand. For as [Socrates] also mentions next, 'Giving advice, I think, belongs to the person who *knows* about each subject, and not to the wealthy person'. 20

[107B] Nor will they be taking counsel about prophecy . . . The prophetic skill is twofold in Plato, one kind being a kind of madness, as he says in the *Phaedrus*,[436] and this is inspired and divine; the other is, so to speak, 70,1 'investigative' and 'searching', which is indeed a 'skill' – about which he says now, that 'about this the prophet will advise better than you'. For no one will give advice about the former [kind of prophecy], since it is not teachable.[437]

5   Lecture 8

                    With the god's favour

107C   Soc. Then what will they be considering when you stand up to advise them,
        assuming you're right to do so?

        [Alc. They'll be discussing their own business, Socrates.

        Soc. You mean their shipbuilding business – what sorts of ships they should
        be building?

        Alc. No . . .

        Soc. I suppose that's because you don't understand shipbuilding . . . So
107D   what kind of 'their own business' do you think they'll be discussing?

        Alc. War, Socrates, or peace, or anything else that is the business of
        the city.

        Soc. Do you mean they'll be discussing whom they should make peace with
        and whom they should go to war with and how? . . . But shouldn't they do
107E   that with the ones with whom it's better to? . . . and when it's better . . . and
        for as long a time as it's better?

        Alc. Yes.

        Soc. Now supposing the Athenians were discussing who they should wrestle
        with and who they should spar with and how, who would be a better adviser,
        you or the trainer?

        Alc. The trainer, I guess.

108A   Soc. . . . Let's take another example: when you're singing, you should
        sometimes accompany the song with cithara-playing and dancing . . . when
        it's better to . . . as much as is better . . .

        Alc. I agree.

108B   Soc. Really? Since you used the term 'better' in both cases – in wrestling and
        in playing the cithara while singing – what do you call what's better in

cithara-playing, as I call what's better in wrestling 'athletic'? . . . Try to follow my example. My answer was, I think, 'what is correct in every case' – and what's correct, I presume, is what's done according to the rules of a skill (*tekhnê*), isn't it?

ALC. Yes.

SOC. Wasn't the skill athletics?

ALC. Of course.

SOC. I said what's better in wrestling, was 'athletic' . . . Come on then, 108C it's your turn. It's partly up to you, surely, to keep our conversation going well. Tell me what the skill is for singing and dancing and playing the cithara correctly . . . What is it called as a whole? Aren't you able to tell me yet?

ALC. No, I can't.

SOC. Well, try it this way. Who are the goddesses to whom the skill belongs?

ALC. Do you mean the Muses, Socrates?

SOC. I do indeed. Don't you see? What's the name of the skill that's named 108D after them?

ALC. I think you mean music.

SOC. Yes, I do. Now what is 'correctly' for what takes place in accordance with this skill? . . . How does it take place?

ALC. Musically, I think.]

Again Alcibiades, who is a naturally gifted individual (*euphuês*) disposed toward oratory, evades Socrates' questions [107C]. For once Socrates has demonstrated that he is not worth much as an adviser, neither about [1] subjects he really knows and imagines that he knows, such as reading and writing, cithara-playing, or wrestling (for the Athenians don't deliberate [in the 10 democratic assembly] about these [skills], that is, about how one should make use of them, but rather about whether in general one should receive teachers of reading and writing or athletes or citharists in one's own city); but it is

certainly not [2] about subjects on which he has no knowledge, nor supposes that he has knowledge (for simple ignorance [i.e. when we know that we do not know something] does not cause us to make mistakes); but again it will not be [3] about subjects that he does not know, yet supposes that he does know ('for
15   in each case it's the knowledgeable person who gives good advice, not the wealthy person' [107B–C]); and [4] the other leg [of the division] has been proven incoherent, namely, that he knows but thinks he does not (for knowledge, which has the character of light, does not escape the notice of its possessor) – so then, after it has been demonstrated that in these respects Alcibiades is not worth much as an adviser, and after he has been asked by
20   Socrates, 'what *will* they be considering when you stand up to advise them, assuming you're right to do so?', and after he has realised that the division is inescapable, he grants it, but he gives an answer from outside [the division] when he says, 'When they deliberate concerning their own affairs.'

Now if he had said 'their own' according to philosophers' principles, referring to their souls and their real essences (*ousiai*), and 'affairs' referring to their
25   activities (*energeiai*), then his answer would have been a good one, even if he was unable to give advice about these issues;[438] but in fact he gives an answer without clearly defining [his terms] (*adioristôs*). So Socrates asks him again,
71,1 'What sort of affairs? Is it about shipbuilding, then?' And his choice of example was a good one: of course shipbuilding is not appropriate to the statesman, but advising [the state] about shipbuilding is – for example, about the proper kind of ship, whether narrow and long, like triremes, or rounded and broad, like
5   merchant-ships. For this is also the kind of thing that Themistocles did: he was not himself a shipbuilder, but gave advice about naval business, when he interpreted the oracle.[439]

Now Alcibiades replies, 'When they deliberate concerning war and peace'. And it should be understood that advice is offered about five species of subject-matter, as Aristotle taught us in the *Rhetorical Arts*,[440] and these are worked out in pairs: for [political advice] concerns [1] the introduction of laws and the
10   appointment of governments (for after all the law is a sort of inanimate government, just as conversely the government is a living law), or [2] income and expenditures, or [3] imports and exports, or [4] the security of the city and country, or [5] war and peace. But [Alcibiades] himself disregards the rest and says 'Whenever [they deliberate] concerning war and peace.'

There are three reasons why he [might have] said this. [1] He may have said 'concerning war and peace' because he is a person who enjoys conflict 　15 (*philoneikos*), someone who lives according to the conflict-loving way of life. For if he had an aristocratic character,[441] he would have spoken about the introduction of laws and the appointment of governments; and if he were 　72,1 oligarchic, he would have spoken about the next two in the sequence [of five kinds of political advice listed above], about income and expenditures or imports and exports (for oligarchs think about these in particular); and if he were democratic, he would have spoken about the fourth, that is, about the security of the city and the country (for they exert themselves about this on 　5 account of their equal freedom of speech and capacity to do everything equally); but as it is, since he is a lover of conflict, he spoke about war and peace.

[2] So either it was for this reason or because, as a [natural] general, he turned his thoughts to his own proper business: for war and peace are proper to a general. [3] Or it was for a third reason, that he observed the Athenians frequently deliberating about war at this juncture, at one point against the 　10 Megarians, at another against the Aeginetans, and many others.[442]

Alcibiades, then, makes three kinds of mistakes in giving this answer. [1] First, he did not refer to the more holistic aspect of the adviser or statesman, to the shared essence of the five kinds [of political advice] that we mentioned earlier[443] – namely, what is advantageous (*sumpheron*). Instead, he referred to justice, assuming, as we will show,[444] that war always arises on account of 　15 [disputes about] what's just. [2] And second, again with a partial perspective, he did not make this claim from principle, but instead based his view on current affairs (*peristatikos*) [in Athens]: for it is [when we base our views on] current affairs that we go to war. [3] And third – again speaking from the standpoint of current affairs – he did not begin from the [condition] that is superior and natural, namely peace, but from war, which is inferior and contrary to nature. That is also why Socrates, when he sets him straight, begins 　20 from the superior [condition] when he speaks next: 'You mean about peace and war . . . .' (In fact, even our bodies make it clear that war is contrary to nature: after all, when the elements are at peace, we find ourselves in a natural condition; but whenever they conflict with each another, with any one of them taking too much, then we are in a condition contrary to nature). Thus Alcibiades 　25 makes three kinds of mistakes.

It also stands to be proven that the goal of war is justice, and that human beings go to war because they desire justice: and we demonstrate this through 73,1 three dialectical proofs.[445] [1] First, consider that the greatest wars are generally agreed to arise on account of [disputes over] what's just, such as the Trojan War and the Persian War.[446] [2] Second, consider that even in nature war arises on account of justice, since the contraries do battle with one another over the underlying place as their subject, with each one wishing to possess this as its 5 spoils.[447] [3] Third, consider that when human beings are wronged, they think themselves worthless and as good as dead, which is why they start wars. For justice is not like any of the other kinds of excellence (*aretê*), each of which attaches only to one part of the soul (for instance, self-control (*sophrosunê*) to the desiring part, practical wisdom to the rational part, and courage to the 10 spirited part),[448] since justice does not stand still,[449] but ranges through the entire tripartition of the soul, which is also why each particular part chooses to go to war on its own behalf, striving for its equal share of justice. [4] Fourth, consider that, just as the soldier, the orator, and the general all have their own respective goals, so the statesman too has another goal of his own.[450] For the soldier's goal is to grow wealthy from the spoils [of war]; and the orator's goal 15 is to persuade using words before arms, so that, if he fails to persuade, he'll prepare the general to overpower the opposing forces with arms to bring about justice (for likewise, the orators in Homer, Odysseus and Menelaus, were made ambassadors for war against the Trojans):[451] but the general's goal is victory and conquering enemies.

20 Moreover, it is clear that victory *alone* is not the goal of every one of them: for if victory belongs to the community as a whole, and the general is the leader of the community, it clearly follows that the community looks to him for its success – that is, its victory. And that is why this was well said:

But the general wins the honour.[452]

74,1 But the statesman's goal is making his citizens good and effective,[453] not gaining victory (for 'Cadmean victories' are common,[454] and defeats befall many): so, then, he makes [his people] good by keeping enemies who do injustice at bay, 5 ensuring that the victors receive their just deserts and not depriving them of what is rightly theirs, and ensuring that the defeated do not rule over what is not properly theirs: for this too is just.[455]

Thus it has been proven that justice is the goal of war. And so much [for the discussion of material] from outside [our current reading].

Socrates shows the young man that he is not a competent adviser about these matters, using his own previous words to do it [107A–C]. (There is no reason, after all, to worry that words might wear out, like old utensils given away as a hand-me-down after long use.)[456] Now he proves that Alcibiades is not a good adviser about war and peace, since he never learned nor discovered nor investigated the just, which is the goal of war. Socrates introduces two examples for this purpose, namely exercise and music, which are relevant and clear.[457] (For it is necessary that examples be both *clearer* than those things of which they are examples, and *relevant* to these. And that is the case here: these examples are clear, since Alcibiades already had an education in them, and they are relevant, since wrestling is a 'small war', while music is also itself suitable to peace, since it is pleasing to both sides.)

As for these [two fields of study], Socrates does not teach [Alcibiades] both (for he did not want to be a teacher only, but also a midwife [of Alcibiades' own ideas]); nor does he merely ask after both (for if the young man had learned nothing in advance, the midwife's skill would have yielded no child);[458] but on some points [Socrates] teaches lessons, and on others he asks questions. And he offers teaching first,[459] before he questions, not [because it has greater value] in and of itself, but in order that his midwifery, beginning from this starting-point (*enteuthen*), might bear fruit. Now, he teaches one [lesson, i.e. about physical exercise], and asks Alcibiades about two more (since he adds a third case too, namely, what is the goal of the statesman): and he does not ask about two cases for no particular reason, but rather in order that midwifery might bear more fruit than teaching.[460]

[1] Hence he teaches the first [lesson] by saying that 'as I describe "performing correctly from the athletic standpoint" or "the goal of athletics" as "performing athletically" (*gumnastikôs*), can you tell me the goal of music in the same way?' [2] After this, the youth answers that it is performing 'musically'. (And it should be understood that 'musical' performance falls into three parts, namely, song (*ôidêi*), rhythm (*rhuthmôi*), and melody (*melei*).[461] Now song is studied in metre: for song is nothing but metrical speech, and its goal is either lyrical or metrical performance. Again, 'rhythm' is observed in the rising and falling [of the beat], and its goal is rhythmical performance. And melody lies in harmony,

and its goal is melodious or harmonious performance.) [3] Again he asks what is the goal of the statesman, and likewise after much [discussion, Alcibiades] answers that it is 'the just'.

15   Now the philosopher Proclus raises a puzzle (*aporein*) here, namely, how it happens that in the other cases [Socrates] talked about the goals paronymously, e.g. performing 'athletically' from athletics, or performing 'musically' from music,[462] but in the case of the statesman, he did not do it this way: for he did not say that his goal was to perform in a 'statesmanly' (*politikôs*) way. And [Proclus] himself offers a very elegant resolution of the puzzle, arguing that here too [Socrates] spoke paronymously – not *literally* paronymously, but rather in the manner of [words] that derive from a single, focal meaning

20   (*aph' henos*):[463] in their case, the similarity or difference of the vocalisations is not relevant, but only [the similarity] or difference of the actual fact referenced (*pragma*) matters. Indeed, there is no difference between [the facts of] justice (*dikaiosunê*) and a constitution (*politeia*), whether small or large: for the constitution of a state is exactly what justice is in a soul. That is also why Plato entitled the *Constitution* [i.e. *Republic*], 'Constitution, or Concerning the Just'.[464]

25   That is the content of the survey.

76,1   **[107C] Then what will they be considering, etc.?** Since it's been shown through the previous comments that there is no aspect of the stated division in which the young man is a competent adviser, Socrates now asks him: 'What kinds of subjects, then, will *you* stand up to advise them on – since you say that it's not going to be about these subjects that we just discussed?' And

5   [Alcibiades], with his natural gift [for rhetoric], does not choose an answer from the division, knowing that it is inescapable, but he isn't at a loss for an answer, either; instead, he offers one from outside [the division], without providing a definition: 'Whenever they deliberate concerning their own [affairs]'.

        You mean their shipbuilding business? After the young man has responded

10   to the question without providing a definition, Socrates asks him this. And he chooses his example well: it is relevant, since it is perfectly conceivable that the statesman would offer advice about the construction of ships, even if he doesn't build the ships himself.

Alcibiades denies it with the words, 'By no means, Socrates!' And we should recognise that it is not because the example is off the mark that he denies that he offers such advice, but because of [his own] ignorance. In fact, he already 15 had Socrates' help, in the form of his remark that 'advice comes from the knowledgeable person, and not from the wealthy person' [107B]. It is also clear from what is added next that [ignorance] is the reason [for Alcibiades' surprised denial]: for when Socrates asked, 'Is that because you do not know how to build ships?' the young man agreed.

[107D] War, Socrates, or peace, or anything else that is the business of the 20 **city:** Notice that Alcibiades not only claims that he will offer advice about war, but also about the other four [concerns] that attach to it [in the list of five subjects of political advice cited earlier]:[465] for he adds these on when he says, 'Or anything else.' And it should be investigated why he spoke about the others 77,1 without naming them, whereas in the case of war he not only spoke of it by name, but even located it directly at the beginning of his account. Well, we say this: we utter our first words according to the kind of life that we live; for our first words disclose which kind of life belongs to us, and which things give us pleasure. Since, then, everyone has agreed that he was an undefeated military 5 general, he introduced his speech in this way. (For history has it that wherever [Alcibiades] had influence [in a battle], he was victorious; and he exercised a great deal of influence.)[466] Thus it is reasonable that he gave an answer here that referred to what was more familiar to him, to where his own strength lay.

Do you mean they'll be discussing whom they should make peace with and whom they should go to war with and how? We should understand that in 10 setting the young man straight, Socrates, as we have already commented, prioritises what's natural, by saying 'With whom they should make peace' [first, before mentioning war].[467] And he takes up all the circumstantial points here, such as the character [of the enemy], against whom one must wage war, neighbours or foreigners: and the means, by naval fighting or by infantry fighting; in and what sort of territory, our own or the enemy's; and in what sort of time, summer or winter; and the right moment, by night or day. 15

[107E] Now supposing the Athenians were discussing who they should wrestle with and who they should spar with: Socrates begins offering

examples here, and again he takes up all of the circumstantial points. And it
20   should be understood that Socrates' examples are like a spark: that is, just as the
spark that falls in a heap of chaff sets off a huge conflagration, so too the
universal formulas (*logoi*) of the soul shine forth from Socrates' examples.

**[108B] And what do you call [what's better in cithara-playing]? I don't
know:** Now that Socrates has taught the goal of athletic skill, he uses midwifery
25   on the youth to help him to state the goal of musical skill. But Alcibiades
78,1   replies that he is at a loss. And we should investigate why Alcibiades, in spite
of his natural gifts, is unable to answer the question, even with the aid of
midwifery. Now some offer the following explanation: consider that the [entire]
musical skill has a *general* goal, namely, to perform musically, but the same also
holds in *specific* cases (for instance, the goal of song is to perform in tune and
5   time, while percussion aims at a rhythmical or harmonious performance, and
lyric aims for a good melody). Alcibiades was uncertain whether Socrates
wanted the common goal or each specific goal, and that's why he replied 'I
don't know.'

But this interpretation is not in tune with the text, since a little later in
the reading, when Alcibiades is asked to state the goal of the entire musical
skill [108D], he does not answer like this.[468] So the right solution is that Socrates
10   understood the three species [of music] in a unified way, and questioned the
youth about a single thing, but Alcibiades, who had learned these species as
three different things, was uncertain about what kind of answer to give, that is,
whether to answer in terms of song or melody or rhythm. (That Socrates
understood the three in a unified way is clear from the fact that he is a statesman
(*politikos*). When the statesman encounters a person who wants to learn
courageous habits somehow, he first implants the right kinds of [courageous]
15   concepts (*ennoiai*) in him, then adds words that are useful for these, along with
the metre (for song is 'speech in metre'), and finally adds the right kinds of
melodies, and from all of this he produces courageous habits.)

**And what's correct, I presume, is what's done according to the rules of a
skill (*tekhnê*), isn't it?** We should recognise that [Socrates] does not make
'what's correct' into the more valuable subject [i.e. more valuable than beauty].
For 'what's done by the rules of the skill' is not the same as the most *beautiful*
20   thing: even when the subject is base and ugly, if it comes about according to the

skill's rules, it's 'correct'. For example, when a painter portrays Thersites, he is not painting the most *beautiful* subject, but he paints 'according to the skill's rules'; again, the painter who portrays the eye does not use the most precious colour, like azure blue.[469] But then it is fair to point out that these are 'correctly' done, since someone paints Thersites skilfully, even though he is ugly, and renders the eye using the appropriate colours, though by no means from the most precious.

Come, then, it's your turn: We find the [imperative] 'come' used frequently in Plato. This word is appropriate for a soul that thinks about different things in sequence (*metabatikôs*), rather than thinking all at once, like intellect (*nous*).[470] The [following] phrase 'it's partly up to you, surely, to keep our conversation going well', leads [Alcibiades] on: it means, 'it suits you, as a beautiful person, to speak about things beautifully'.

Tell me what the skill is for singing and dancing and playing the cithara correctly . . . What is it called as a whole? Notice here that when Socrates asks Alcibiades to articulate the common goal of the three kinds [of music], he does not say it. Now, he did say that cithara-playing is for the melody, singing for the song, and dance for the rhythm (since that is the common name for stepping up and down, when they belong to rhythm). So why is he unable to state the goal of musical skill as a whole? Perhaps this should be settled according to the second interpretation mentioned above.[471] Also, it should be recognised that the 'whole' in Plato is threefold, being either prior to the parts, or in the part, or among the parts.[472] Now, the whole *prior* to the parts is that in virtue of which a person discards his tooth then grows (*phuei*) another tooth anew, employing the natural formula (*logos*), since [his] nature (*phusis*) possesses the formulas in a universal way (*katholou*).[473] But the whole *in* the part applies when a person recognises the whole on the basis of its parts, as for instance the sons of Pelops [recognised him] from his ivory shoulder, or as in the saying 'know the lion from his claw', since each part has the patterns of the whole. And the whole *among* the parts is observed (*theôroumenon*) in the assemblage of parts and in the synthesis of them all, which would not subsist if a part were removed.

Here, then, in the case of the musical skill, Socrates speaks [of the whole] before the parts, and what is in the part as a whole, when he uses the words 'as a whole'. For certainly even in separation from one of its [particular] kinds, the remaining kinds are still called 'music'.

Who are the goddesses to whom the skill belongs? – Do you mean the Muses, Socrates? With the young man totally at a loss (*polu aporountos*), Socrates practises midwifery upon him, so that he can bring forth from himself
25 [the answer to the question] what is the goal of musical skill: he leads him to
80,1 remember the Muses, and through them Memory,[474] so that, on this basis, he might stir up the memory in the young man's soul and, leading him by the hand and using the name of the Muses, Alcibiades might express that the goal of musical skill is excellent musical performance.

Lecture 9

With the god's favour

5 Soc. Come on, now, what do you call what's better in going to war [and
108D keeping the peace? In these last two cases, you said that what was 'better'
108E was more musical and more athletic, respectively. Now try to tell me what's better in this case, too.

Alc. I really can't do it.

Soc. But surely it's shameful if when you're speaking and giving advice about food – saying that a certain kind is better than another, and better now and in a certain quantity – and someone should ask you, 'What do you mean by "better", Alcibiades?' you could tell him in that case that 'better' was 'healthier', though you don't even pretend to be a doctor; and yet in a
109A case where you do pretend to understand and are going to stand up and give advice as though you knew, if you aren't able, as seems likely, to answer the question in this case, won't you be embarrassed? Won't that seem shameful?

Alc. Yes, certainly.

Soc. Then think about it, and try to tell me what the better tends towards, in keeping the peace or in waging war with the right people.

ALC. I'm thinking, but I can't get it.

SOC. But suppose we're at war with somebody – surely you know what treatment we accuse each other of when we enter into a war, and what we call it?

ALC. I do – we say that they're playing some trick on us, or attacking us, or taking things away from us. 109B

SOC. Hold on – how do we suffer from each of these treatments? Try to tell me how one way differs from another way.

ALC. When you say 'way', Socrates, do you mean 'justly' or 'unjustly'?

SOC. Precisely . . . Who will you advise the Athenians to wage war on? Those who are treating us unjustly, or those who are treating us justly?

ALC. That's a hard question you're asking. Even if someone thought it was necessary to wage war on people who were treating us justly, he wouldn't admit it. 109C

SOC. Because I think that wouldn't be lawful (*nomimos*).

ALC. It certainly wouldn't.

SOC. Nor would it be considered a noble (*kalos*) act.

ALC. No.

SOC. So you would also frame your speech in these terms . . . Then does this 'better' I was just asking you about – when it comes to waging war or not, on whom to wage war and on whom not to, and when and when not to – does this 'better' turn out to be anything other than 'more just'?

ALC. It certainly seems like that's what it is.

SOC. But how could it be, my dear Alcibiades? Don't you realise that this is something you don't understand? Or perhaps, when I wasn't looking, you've been studying under some teacher who taught you how to tell the difference between the more just and the less just. Have you . . . Well, and who is he? Tell me who he is so that you can introduce me to him as a pupil too. 109D

ALC. Stop teasing me, Socrates.

SOC. I'm not – I'll swear by Friendship, mine and yours, whose name is the last I'd break an oath by. So tell me who he is, if you can.

109E ALC. And what if I can't? Don't you think I might know about justice and injustice in some other way?

SOC. Yes, you might – if you found it out.

ALC. Well, don't you think I might find it out?

SOC. Yes, of course – if you investigated the matter.

ALC. And don't you think I might investigate it?

SOC. Yes, I do – if you thought you didn't know.

ALC. And didn't I once think that?

SOC. A fine answer. Can you tell me when this was, when you didn't think
110A you knew about justice and injustice . . . Well, was it last year? . . . Answer me truthfully, or else our conversation will be a waste of time.

ALC. Yes, I thought I knew . . . two years ago . . . three . . . four . . .

110B SOC. But surely before that you were a boy . . . [then] I often observed you, at school and other places, and sometimes when you were playing knucklebones or some other game, you'd say to one or another of your playmates, very loudly and confidently – not at all like someone who was at a loss about justice and injustice – that he was a villain and wasn't playing fairly . . .

ALC. But what was I to do, Socrates, when somebody cheated me like that?

SOC. Do you mean, what should you have done if you didn't actually know then whether or not you were being cheated?

110C ALC. But I did know, by Zeus! . . .

SOC. So it seems that even as a child you thought you understood justice and injustice . . . At what point did you find it out? Surely it wasn't when you

thought you knew ... then when did you think you didn't know? Think about it – you won't find any such time.

Alc. By Zeus, Socrates, I really can't say.

Soc. So it isn't by finding it out that you know it ... but surely you just 110D **finished saying that it wasn't by being taught, either, that you knew it. So if you neither found it out nor were taught it, how and where did you come to know it?]**

Alcibiades has been asked to state the goal of war [108D], and he ought to answer 'justice'. We go to war for the sake of justice, just as doctors tackle illnesses for the sake of health, that is, in order to bring the elements into a blend or harmony. (After all, it is in a sense 'just' to prevent the excess of one element over another.) Alcibiades, however, doesn't give this answer; 10 instead, he says that we go to war 'because they're playing some trick on us, or attacking us, or taking things away from us' [109B]. And he makes a triple error here.[475]

First, he erred in answering one question three times.

Second, he erred because these [three actions are not unjust] unconditionally, but in a conditional way – that is, somebody could put all of these means to a good end. For example, suppose that someone handed a sword over to us on 15 deposit, and then he went mad, and when he demanded it back at the height of his insanity, we refused to hand it over,[476] and tricked and deceived him by swearing oaths. (For we should not accept the poet's view when he says

You will not utter a lie,[477]

but rather when he says 20

He excelled in the art of lies,[478]

and

He was honoured in his land as a god is.[479])

But it's also the case that we do not lie when we swear that we never received it from *him*. In reality, when he handed it over, a sane person handed it over, but 81,1 now a madman demands it back; again, what he left to us then as a deposit, he now demands to put to use (*hôs organon*): the result is that neither the giver nor the object are identical, but they are both different [from their former selves]. And when, under compulsion, we take things away from someone in this condition, we do so for a good end.

5　　Third, [Alcibiades] erred when he introduced as three distinct things 'being tricked', 'being attacked' and 'being deprived of property', although it is possible to use the common name 'injustice' for each of them. After all, when we go to war as a consequence of being tricked, we do so because we have been treated unjustly; the same holds in the cases where we are placed under compulsion or deprived of our property. Hence [Alcibiades] should not have introduced these as three distinct things, [especially] when he had already stated the common
10　name for them. Thus he erred in three ways.

But there are also two senses in which we should accept the young man's choice of answers.[480] The first is that he touched on the entire tripartition of our soul in the course of his answer: that is, when he mentioned 'being tricked', he touched on reason (*logos*) (for knowledge also belongs to this); and when he mentioned 'being attacked', he touched on spirited emotion (*thumos*) (for ruling also belongs to this); and when he mentioned 'being deprived', he
15　touched on appetite (*epithumia*) (for the love of possessions also belongs to this [part of our soul]). The second is that he is correct in his answer insofar as he preserved the necessary order of the three [parts]: since just as reason presides over spirited emotion, and spirited emotion over appetite, so too the young man mentioned being tricked before being attacked, and being attacked before being deprived.

20　　Next, Socrates proves that the young man is ignorant of justice, using his own words. (For as we remarked before,[481] there is no need to worry that words heard frequently will wear out, like old utensils.) Hence he says that 'You neither learned nor discovered', et cetera. For there are two routes to knowledge (*tropoi gnôseôs*), namely learning and discovery, as we have often remarked.[482] We 'discover' something as self-moved actors (*autokinêtôs*
25　*energountes*), but we 'learn' something when we are moved by another (*heterokinêtôs*). For we should understand that just as the soul imparts a trace of its self-movement to the body, likewise the soul takes over (*metelaben*)[483] a trace of the body's property of being moved by something else.[484] You might see this from other examples, too: for instance, time imparts to motion

something of its own property of being measurable, and [in turn] takes over from motion something of its property of extension; or again, form imparts something of its structure (*morphê*) to matter, and despite being partless, takes over something of the extension of matter – which is why we often apply the saying 'as the feet, so is the head'.[485] But the more naturally gifted (*euphuês*) souls, which are self-moving, tend more to discovery and bringing [ideas] to birth, than to learning, just as conversely the less gifted souls, which are moved by another, tend more to learning than to discovery. And these points reveal the median point of our soul's essence: for it is neither consistently incomplete, since it is in the process of discovery, nor is it consistently complete, since it is in the process of learning.

We raise two puzzles (*aporiai*) about these [passages]. First, why does Alcibiades, who is ignorant of what is just, imagine that he has that knowledge? And second, why, when Socrates asks him to state the time at which he did *not* imagine he knew justice, is he at a loss and unable to say when that was?

Now, we reply to the first puzzle[486] that he imagined he knew justice without having that knowledge because he was beguiled by the universal formulas (*logoi*) implanted in his soul[487] (and so it seems to those who are rich in their dreams and who wake up and find their hands empty).[488]

As for the second puzzle, we should reply that he is at a loss because it was with a view to *actual* knowledge that Socrates asked him to state the time when he did not imagine himself to know, but it was with a view to passively possessed (*kath' hexin*) knowledge that [Alcibiades] found himself at a loss, since he had been present with his own soul forever, and on that account he couldn't refer his ignorance back to a time.[489]

That is the content of the survey.

[108D] Come on now, what do you call what's better in both going to war [and keeping the peace]? As we also remarked in the earlier [discussion],[490] Plato has used the [imperative verb] 'come' because it is appropriate to a soul that understands facts in sequence (*metabatikôs*), and not at one grasp, as intellect (*nous*) does. Thus Socrates says here that 'Just as you articulated the goals in the two previous examples (admittedly requiring midwifery's aid in one case, and teaching in the other), now likewise state the goal of war': for this is what [the phrase] 'what you call what's better' amounts to.[491] For the goals of actions are either to be chosen or avoided, and it is for the sake of the goals that we either carry out the actions or do not.

[108E] You explained what was better in each [of the kinds of music, that it was the 'musically performed', and in the other case too, that it was the 'athletically performed'. Now try to tell me what's better in this case, too.] Understand 'in each' to refer to the kinds of music. For there were three kinds, and their goals were correspondingly three, namely, successful performances in song, melody or rhythm. Seeing that he also spoke of a single goal of musical skill,[492] namely musical performance, well then, all three kinds are embraced in this shared, general [name].[493] Here, we need to understand the word 'each' as applying to [the kinds of music], and not to the two examples [of music and athletics],[494] since the lesser [unit] in a group of three is called 'each'.[495] For it's clear that he took one of the examples, music, and said 'each' to refer to its kinds, since he adds about the other example, athletics, the following: 'and in the other case too, that it was the "athletically performed" '.

I really can't do it: The speaker is sinking and blushing to be at a loss (*aporein*) concerning the matters about which he claimed to be a counsellor. This is clear from the phrase 'really can't', which is uttered by the young man out of shame at being at a loss.[496]

But surely it's shameful if when you're speaking . . . Socrates is about to rebuke the young man (*epitiman*) for what he does not know, namely the goal of war, but he is concerned about the ill-will that could arise from the critique (*elenkhos*), so he does not come to his rebuke in a direct or obvious way, but by juxtaposing a different field where the young man *does* have knowledge, and using this to soften the sharpness of his critique.[497] So, then, he says that 'It's a shame if you know how to give advice about certain medical subjects, about which you make no pretence to be a good counsellor, nor are you a student of them; but you turn out to be ignorant about just what you suppose you know, and you're about to give advice on.' And he was right to use the word 'shameful'; for shame is the contrary to someone who is fond of his reputation and vaunts
84,1 himself for his beauty and dazzling appearance.[498]

. . . [and giving advice about food – saying that a certain kind] is better than another, and better now and in a certain quantity . . . He refers to the circumstances: by saying 'better than another', he means the kind of food, whether it is cooked rather than raw, whether it goes down easily and is easy to digest or the contrary; and by the word 'now', whether it should be eaten in the   5 evening but not at night, because of its proper time for digestion; and by saying 'in a certain quantity', he means that one should not serve a lot of it, on account of Hippocrates' saying 'hunger is the mother of health'.[499]

[109A] [But suppose we're at war with somebody –] surely you know what treatment we accuse each other of when we enter into a war, and what we call it? Since Alcibiades continues to flounder at a loss, Socrates   10 acts like a daimon (*daimôniôs*) and redirects his midwifery toward a plainer approach.[500] Because the participants are plainer than what they participate in, and composites are plainer than simple things, he says: 'Surely you know what the accusation is on each side when we enter into a war', that is, 'as behaving unjustly'. And the unjust actor participates, and hence is composite, but injustice is participated, and hence is simple.[501] For that reason   15 too, he puts [injustice] at the end, when he said 'And what do we call it?', i.e. 'injustice': and by 'it' he means the condition (*pathêma*) [of injustice]. And he also adds to this that 'These are the three accusations we make when we go to war: they're playing some trick on us, or attacking us, or taking things away from us.'

[109B] Hold on (*ekhe*) – *how* do we suffer from each of these treatments?   20 This [imperative] (*ekhe*) imitates epic style:

But hold (*ekhe*) this in your thoughts;[502]

And we should understand that he does not charge [Alcibiades] with the first [of the three errors described above, 80,12–81,10] (namely, giving three answers to one question), nor the third (for he also granted this point, namely, that we do not go to war because we suffer these injuries, but because of what they share: namely, injustice): so he charges [Alcibiades] with the second error,   25 that these things he said are not unambiguous (*hapla*), but ambiguous (*epamphoterizonta*). At any rate, he asks '*how* we suffer from each of these' – that is, unjustly or justly: then he asks him, whether these differ from each   85,1 other, for this is the force of the phrase 'Try to tell me how one way differs from another way.' And when the young man answers 'When you say "way"', Socrates,

5   do you mean "justly" or "unjustly"?', and Socrates agrees, Alcibiades adds that
     these differ 'totally, every bit' (*holon te kai pan*)[503] [in this way].

        And we should understand that the saying 'totally, every bit' assimilates two
     very different and distinct things: for the words 'whole' (*to holon*) and 'every' (*to
     pan*) are logically distinct from one another.[504] Granted that both refer to the
     universal (*katholou*), still, 'whole' refers to something continuous (*sunekhes*),
10   and 'every' to something discrete (*diôrismenon*). And someone could be
     superior in respect of the whole, but inferior in respect of every part, as for
     instance when we say of the 'whole' that the male class (*genos*) is 'as a whole'
     better than the female class, but of course not *every* individual [man] is better
     than *every* individual [woman], for neither Thersites nor Coroebus were better
     than Theano.[505]

86,1 **[109C] Even if someone believed it was necessary to wage war on people
     who were treating us justly, [he wouldn't admit it].** Callicles and Thrasymachus
     kept on maintaining in the *Gorgias* [and *Republic*, respectively][506] *both* that
     they believed it was necessary to wage war on those who treat us justly, *and*
     that they [themselves] did wage war [on such people] in practice (*en ergôi
     polemein*). Socrates, on the other hand, maintained that he believed no such
5   thing at all, and that he did not do so in practice. And Alcibiades, as the man in
     the middle, maintains that he believes it, but does not do so in practice. For he
     says 'Even if someone believed . . .' showing that he agrees, but he adds that not
     even someone who believes this agrees to it [openly].[507]

     **Because I think that wouldn't be lawful. – It certainly wouldn't. – Nor would
10   it be considered a noble act.** 'Lawful' (*nomimos*) is what is just by convention,
     but 'noble' (*kalos*) is what is just by nature. So Socrates says that it is not proper,
     either lawfully ('just' by convention), or nobly ('just' by nature), to wage war on
     those who practice justice. And the young man agrees to these points because
     he is making progress (*prokoptôn*) toward the goal.[508]

15   **Then does this 'better' that I was asking you about – when it comes to
     waging war or not, [on whom to wage war and on whom not to, and when
     and when not to] – does this 'better' turn out to be anything other than
     'more just'?** After agreement has been reached through many arguments, to
     the effect that the goal of war is the just, and that one must not make war

on those who act justly, but clearly on those who act unjustly (for obviously in that case, we would go to war for a just cause), Socrates reminds the young man of the question that he was unsure how to answer. And this was, what is the goal of war? (The phrase "this 'better' " shows that the [subject of the question] is the same, as was remarked earlier). Thus he says, 'which I was asking you about . . . turns out to be anything else?', meaning 'if not this?' For in Plato's style, 'anything else' stands by paraleipsis for 'if not this'.[509] And using the present circumstances, he reminds him of what is better in war, by saying 'on whom' and 'when'.

[109D] But how could it be, Alcibiades my friend? Don't you realise that this is something you don't understand? [Or perhaps, when I wasn't looking, you've been studying under some teacher who taught you how to tell the difference between the more just and the less just. Have you?]

The phrase 'my friend' (*ô phile*) isn't included here by accident, but because (as we have often remarked)[510] Socratic exhortations and refutations are like medicines drenched in honey.[511] But he expects to aggravate the youth on account of his ignorance about justice, and drive him to distraction, and so he conciliates him first by calling him 'friend', and again a little later by swearing 'the [god of] Friendship, mine and yours' [109D].

Now at this point, they [sc. the commentators] investigate which god he calls 'Friendship'.[512] Some of them say it's Love (*Erôs*), but this is incorrect. For 'friends are dear to their friends', but in this case Socrates is in love with the youth, while the youth does not love Socrates in return: that occurs only at the end of the dialogue, where Alcibiades' reciprocal love (*anterôs*) is given over. Whom, then, does he call [the god of] 'Friendship'? Well, we say that it is Zeus, since he befits both [Socrates and Alcibiades], on account of his function as a ruler (*arkhikos*). First, Zeus befits Socrates because Socrates is a philosopher – for philosophy is the leader of all the other skills. Also, as the Stoics have it, the person who understands how to rule is the ruler, even if he does not exercise that power,[513] and philosophers are such people: that is also why Socrates says in the *Phaedrus*, 'and I am with Zeus'.[514] Second, Zeus befits Alcibiades because he loves rule and leadership in battle. So the words '. . . mine and yours' are not trivial. Rather, it is fitting for these [words] to have been said in the sequel; for here Socrates says, 'have you failed to notice that you do not know justice' (and 'failure to notice' is kin to ignorance, for both mean the absence of understanding),[515] 'or did I fail to notice that you learned', instead of 'how were you likely to escape my notice, when I follow you around

20   like [the] conscience that is present for each of our actions?'[516]

And studying under a teacher . . . Here we should recognise that even students who learn from someone else possess some self-motivation (*ti autokinêton*), namely, choosing for themselves to learn and to study under a teacher, and not

88,1 to get hold of their studies by force or by having training imposed upon them, even if their understanding comes to them from someone else.

And who is he? Tell me who he is, so that you can introduce me to him

5   **as a pupil too.** Since a philosopher's uses of irony necessarily also carry truth, we should inquire why Socrates – who understands justice – at this point says to the youth 'Tell me from whom you learned about justice, so that I may study under him as well.'[517] Well, we reply that it is necessary for the lover both to play dumb with (*sunagnoein*) his beloved, and to play along with him (*sunagesthai*); so, insofar as Socrates is a lover, he kept pretending not know about justice, insofar as the boy was ignorant about justice; but as a teacher, he

10   understood it.

Or there is a second solution: Socrates would either have gone to a teacher than himself and been helped; or to a worse one, whom *he* would have helped; or to a teacher as good as himself – in which case 'friends share' (*koina ta philôn*).[518]

[I swear by Friendship . . .] whose name is the last I'd break an oath by: Here we should inquire what he means by the words 'I would in no way break an oath by'. Does it follow that he *would* break an oath that he took by some *other*

15   name? Instead, we respond [to this puzzle] that we need to specify in addition 'an oath *to you*' (*pros se*):[519] for it is more reasonable to break an oath made to unfamiliar people or to strangers, than to friends. Alternatively, it might be that it is more serious to swear falsely by gods who have a particular sphere [of responsibility] than by the others. For the 'spheres' and 'specific [epithets]', when *they* are transgressed, make the transgression more serious, and [in this case] the epithet 'friendship' is in question. Likewise in the *Cratylus* [sic],[520]

20   [Plato] says that one must not forswear oneself by Zeus of Strangers (*xenios*) or

Zeus of Kinship (*homognios*), and plainly this is because their specific areas [of concern] should not be transgressed. Alternatively, it may be that the word 'whom' is not being used here to set up an opposition [with other gods] (*pros antidiastolên*).[521]

[109E] And what if I can't? Don't you think I might know [about justice and injustice in some other way?] Here he presents in an analytical way the argument that he previously advanced synthetically.[522] After Socrates remarks that 'you would have known about the just, if you had studied with a teacher', and the young man replies 'don't you think I might know in some other way?', Socrates adds another premise: 'if you found out', then again 'if you looked into it: but you would only have looked into it if you thought that you didn't know. But in fact, you're not able to say when you supposed yourself to be ignorant'. And he takes full account of the young man's age, and from that he proves him ignorant about justice.

Yes, of course – if you investigated the matter. The phrase 'of course' is not merely [complimentary] here, but shows that Socrates trusts Alcibiades' natural gifts (*euphuïa*): if he had investigated it, he would by all means have found out about it.[523]

Answer me truthfully, or else our conversation will be a waste of time. Earlier, when the premises had a generic character, he did not ask the youth to answer truthfully: after all, if he had lied, he would have been refuted on the basis of other premises, thanks to their generality. But as it is here, since the premises are particular and drawn from personal history,[524] he asks him to tell the truth, since if he answers falsely, the argument will proceed in vain.[525] And one should recognise here the Platonic doctrine that nothing follows necessarily from false premises, but the argument will be empty: for he says here, 'or else ... it will be a waste of time'. For even if true conclusions sometimes follow from false premises, that does not happen because the premises *require* the conclusion by necessity, but because the material of the argument allows it.[526]

But surely before that you were a boy, weren't you? There is a difference between a boy (*pais*) and a little boy (*paidion*): one is a 'little boy' up to the age of seven, then a 'boy' from one's seventh year until the fourteenth year – then

89,1

5

10

15

20

90,1

one becomes an adolescent (*ephêbos*) in and after that year.[527] So Socrates said correctly that the boy was a 'child' five years earlier, if he was not yet twenty years old then [sc. at the time of this conversation].

[When you were a boy I often observed you at school . . . say to one of your playmates, very loudly and confidently – not at all like someone who was at
5   **a loss about justice and injustice – that] he was a villain and wasn't playing fairly.** It is a sign of the youth's magnificent and noble nature, that from boyhood he considered cheaters to be villains, and grasped this from his [innate] common concept (*apo tês koinês ennoias*) alone.[528] For at this time, he had not yet studied with teachers who had the ability to teach him the nature of the just.

What should you have done if you didn't actually know then whether or not
10   **you were being cheated?** What does he mean here? After the young man has said 'But what should I have done when I was cheated, other than *say* that I was being cheated?', Socrates replies, 'Do you mean, what should you have done if you were thoroughly ignorant of whether or not you were being cheated (since at that time you didn't know the nature of justice)? Clearly it was an option for you to take joy in learning.' When the youth responds by again swearing that
15   he was not ignorant, but knew clearly that he was being cheated, Socrates has again used the same argument, namely, the question 'at what age did you find it out? When, after admitting that you were ignorant, did you look into it? But if you neither found out by looking into it, nor learned (since you had not studied with a teacher, which you admitted above), it is clear that you do not know the nature of justice.'

20   We should understand what was said earlier [110B], that 'I often observed you with teachers', as referring only to the teacher of music, reading and writing, and exercise, since the young man was educated in these subjects alone.

[110D] How and where did you come to know it? He says 'how', meaning 'not by having looked into it and found it out', and 'where', meaning 'not by having studied with anyone else and learned it'.

Notes

1 The phrase 'from the voice' (*apo phônês*) describes notes taken by a pupil during a lecture or tutorial: see Introduction, §6.

2 Arist. *Metaph.* 1.1, 980a21–2. This preliminary reference may be viewed as a transition from the earlier, Aristotelian section of the Alexandrian curriculum, which probably ended with the *Metaphysics* (cf. Mansfeld 1994, 92) to the introductory work of Platonism (*tês tou Platônos philosophias arkhomenos*, 6). On the ancient titles of the *Metaphysics*, see Ross 1924, xxxii, and on the possibility of a 'Roman edition' by Andronicus of Rhodes, who may or may not have influenced the structure of the compilation that became our *Metaphysics*, compare Barnes 1997 and Primavesi 2007, with an excellent recent overview in Hatzimichali 2013. The modern nomenclature, *Meta ta phusika*, may date to Andronicus (first century BC). The earliest title, *On First Philosophy*, is probably reflected in Olympiodorus' title *Theology*.

 Olympiodorus offers a similar remark at the outset of his *Prolegomena to the Categories*. There, he explains that the value of studying Aristotelian philosophy, particularly at the outset of the philosophical curriculum, lies in its ability to foster precision (*akribeia*) in defining the goals of human life.

3 For the (Platonic) language and imagery, compare *Phaedrus* 235C–D, where Socrates, feeling the onset of the 'possession' remarked upon at 2,9 below, says that 'The only other possibility, I think, is that I was filled, like an empty jar, by the words of other people streaming in through my ears' (*leipetai dê oimai ex allotriôn pothen namatôn dia tês akoês peplêrôsthai me dikên angeiou*, tr. Nehamas and Woodruff in Cooper and Hutchinson 1997); see also *Phaedrus* 278B, for the 'fountain' (*nama*) of the Nymphs where the dialogue has taken place.

 Olympiodorus' emphasis on the 'Platonic inspirations' is significant, since 'inspiration' (*enthousiamos*) is the word that Olympiodorus uses to refer to the achievement of theurgic excellence, the peak of human accomplishment (see Introduction §2.1).

4 *Timaeus* 41A–D; cf. 42D6 on the 'young gods'.

5 Dillon 1973, 417 n. 1 suggests that Olympiodorus here refers not to Iamblichus' well-known *Timaeus* commentary, but to a lesser treatise *On the Speech of Zeus in the 'Timaeus'*, whose scheme Proclus would then be setting forth at *in Tim.* 1 308,18ff.

6   *Republic* 8, 546A–547C.

7   *Phaedrus* 238D–241D.

8   *Theaetetus* 173C–177B.

9   The 'coryphaeus' led the chorus in Athenian drama, and the contemplative philosopher represents the peak of philosophical excellence (see Introduction §2.1).

10 The modern reader may be surprised to learn that the value of Plato's dialogues lies in these passages of 'divine inspiration'! This claim targets Olympiodorus' (mostly Christian) audience: he suggests that Plato, like Christ, offers a kind of revelation. This is clearer in the imagery that pervades the life (*bios*) of Plato that follows, both explicit (Plato's divine conception, 2,21–4) and indirect (2,26: *Apollôni nomiôi*). In general, Olympiodorus distinguishes Platonism from Christianity even as he invests it with an equal (or greater) authority. On his attitude towards his contemporaries' religious and intellectual background, see Introduction §1, Tarrant 1997, Westerink 1990, 331–3, and on the atmosphere of the late antique Neoplatonist school, see Hoffmann 2012, 597–601.

11 Olympiodorus' *Life of Plato* provides an excellent example of late antique pagan hagiography. For Neoplatonic hagiography in general, see Edwards 2001, who discusses the biographies of Plotinus by Porphyry and of Proclus by Marinus.

12 Olympiodorus seems to use *genos* here to mean something loosely like 'ancestry and biography'. He repeats the word at 3,1 to summarise the *Life* as a whole, so it is not meant to refer only to the brief discussion of Plato's ancestry from 2,17–20.

13 'Hearing many things' or 'much-learning' (*poluêkoïa*) is contrasted with proper teaching that leads to knowledge at Plat. *Phaedr.* 275A (*poluêkooi*), and its potential dangers to children who may listen indiscriminately to the poets are noted at *Lg.* 810E–811B. In a predominately literate society like ours, calling someone 'widely read' or 'erudite' would convey the same sense as *poluêkoïa* in Plato's time.

14 Odysseus at Hom. *Od.* 9.366.

15 This phrase belongs to *Od.* 1.177, where Odysseus is the one who 'has gone to and fro among human beings' (*epistrophos ên anthrôpôn*). But while Olympiodorus' Plato is widely travelled, his service to the human soul (1,156; 166–7) is more relevant and *epistrophê* should probably be taken in its Plotinian sense: compare, for example, Plotinus *Enn.* 6.5.7 [23], 11–13, 'If a person could but be reverted [*epistraphênai*, 'turned about'] – by his own motion, or by the happy pull of Athena [cf. *Il.* 1.177] – he would see at once God and himself and the All' (tr. MacKenna 1957, lightly adapted); see also LSJ II 3b, 8. The crucial idea of 'turning back upon oneself', or 'reversion', recurs again at 9,7, etc. as the special province of the rational soul and superior levels of being, and at 10,4 as the means of self-knowledge. Plato strives to 'turn' the eye of the soul from the body to the mind (contrast Porph. *Sent.* 7, ed. Smith), and therefore he, like Athena in the Plotinian passage, is the 'turner'

or 'reverter' of many human beings. (The *Odyssey* reference may be intentionally conflated, via Plotinus, with *Il.* 1.177; see Westerink 1982, ix on blended citations of Homer in this commentary.)

Epistrophos as an agent noun might be influenced by the Christian usage of *epistrophê* to mean 'conversion' (e.g. *Act. Ap.* 15.3), and might also provide an example of Olympiodorus' effort to engage Christian students in the *Life.*

16 The manuscript ascribes '11' (*en ia'*) books to the *Republic*, but this can be explained by dittography (*en* [*hen*]*deka*), and I read '10' following Dodds 1957, 357.

It is a challenge for the editor and the translator to decide which slips of the pen (or ear) need correcting and which should be left alone (see Westerink 1982, VIII–IX). In general I agree with Dodds that obvious errors of fact should not be attributed to the lecturer, and I have erred on the side of correction, particularly where there are palaeographical grounds (cf. Westerink 1982, IX).

17 A.S. Riginos examines the sources of this and similar anecdotes in *Platonica: The Anecdotes Concerning the Life and Writings of Plato*. The story of Plato's Apollonian conception (Riginos 1976, Anecdote 1, 9–14) first appears in Plutarch, *Quaest. Conv.* 717D–E, but according to Diogenes Laertius 3.2 and others it originates with Plato's nephew and successor Speusippus, in his 'Funeral Banquet of Plato'. Speusippus, according to Diogenes Laertius, described the story as *hôs Athênêsin ên logos*, i.e. current in the Athens of his day. The narrative, especially as Olympiodorus relates it, could be profitably compared with Matthew 1:25.

18 Cicero (*De Div.* 1.36.78, 2.31.66) furnishes our earliest testimony to this episode, which does not occur in the proper biographies of Plato until Olympiodorus: previously it appears in catalogues of portents, such as Pliny's discussion of portents involving bees at *Nat. Hist.* 11.17.55. Cicero may draw on the Stoic philosopher Posidonius (135–51 BC) for this book; at any rate, he is probably indebted to an earlier source (Riginos 1976, 17–21, Anecdote 3; see esp. n. 33).

19 Of Nestor at Hom. *Il.* 1.249.

20 Cf. *Phaedo* 85B, Proclus *in Alc.* 5–6. Riginos 1976, 25 (Anecdote 6) points that that this adoption of Socrates' expression *homodoulos tois kuknois*, 'fellow-slave of the swans', and its attribution to Plato himself appears only in Olympiodorus and in the *Anonymous Prolegomena*. It clearly belongs to the tradition of later Neoplatonism.

21 Socrates recounts his visit to the school of Dionysius at ps-Plat. *Lovers* 132a. Plato's education by Dionysius the *grammatistês* is common to all the preserved biographical traditions (Riginos 1976, 39); however, the name may be suspect for the very reason that it appears in the *Amatores*, if we follow Riginos in reasoning

that some early biographer inferred the name from the dialogue, rather than the other way round (40 n. 10).

This is the first of several references (cf. 2,44; 52; 63–4) which indicate the indebtedness of Olympiodorus' biography to the text of the Dialogues.

22 Like the name of Dionysius, the name of Ariston for Plato's teacher of gymnastics recurs in all the biographical traditions. The coincidence of his name with that of Plato's father may cast suspicion on his historicity (Riginos 1976, 40), although this argument could work both ways.

23 The story of Plato's derivative 'nickname' (Riginos 1976, 35–8: Anecdote 11), and these three alternative explanations of its significance – breadth of forehead, breadth of chest, and breadth of style – first appear in the *Index Herc.* Col. II 36–42, then in Seneca (*Ep.* 58.30); for the first few lines, Olympiodorus is paraphrasing Diogenes Laertius 3.4, whose attribution of the third alternative, breadth of style, to unnamed *enioi* suggests that this was the general tradition. Some (e.g. Notopoulos 1939) have suspected the tradition. After all Plato himself refers to himself as 'Plato' (*Ap.* 34A and *Phaed.* 59B), and the notion that this name is derivative may be ascribed to the taste of the Alexandrians, who liked to see a close relationship between physical appearance and onomastic etymology. This argument certainly offers a persuasive explanation for why the commentators explained Plato's name as they did, although it does not seem to explain the introduction of a *second* name. Why would these etymologists demote *Platôn* to a nickname, unless that tradition preceded them?

24 Cf. DL 5.38.

25 Damon is mentioned at *Republic* 3, 400B–C and 4, 424C and elsewhere, including the *Alcibiades* (*Alc.* 118C, *Lach.* 180D, 200A, [*Axiochus*] 364A); the *Anonymous Prolegomena* adds, apparently in error, that he is found in the *Theaetetus*. Plutarch gives Dracon as Plato's teacher of music at *De Mus.* 1136f.

26 The following summarises Proclus *in Alc.* 193–5 on the value of 'reading and writing, lyre-playing, and wrestling'.

27 These three parts or aspects of the soul are taken from Plato's account in *Republic* 4: reason (*logos*), spirit or pride (*thumos*), and appetitive desire (*epithumia*). All three are beneficial when their relationship to one another is 'just', that is, when appetites are served only in accordance with reason, using spirit or pride to enforce its instructions.

28 *Alc.* 106E: 'You have learned, as far as I remember, reading and writing, and how to play the lyre and wrestle: but you refused to learn the pipe.'

29 *Tim.* 67C–68D. The idea that Plato studied painting occurs first in Apuleius *De Platone* 1.2. The *Timaeus* passage may be responsible for it, but the educational doctrine of the *Republic* is asserted as the more likely source (Riginos 1976, 43); it

may also be connected to the story that Socrates was a sculptor. The anecdote is not elaborated in detail in the surviving biographies. (This is Anecdote 13 in Riginos 1976, 42–3.)

30 Riginos 1976 (Anecdote 14, pp. 43–8) observes that this motivation is certainly not taken from Plato's own straightforward criticism of tragedy (cf. *Resp.* 10. 605D–607A). But Olympiodorus' account is coloured with the language of Neoplatonic educational theory, and this episode should be interpreted within that framework. The Neoplatonic education set out to scale the hierarchy of being and knowledge, ascending from the lower levels of the student's soul to the highest (see Introduction §2.1–2). Plato asserts that tragedy works on the lower part of the soul, which is freed to express the emotions of pity and fear that it has been barred from expressing in life; the best part of the soul must then undergo *paideusis* to learn the proper moderation of its inferior (*Republic* 10, 606A). For the Neoplatonist, therefore, it is natural to *begin* with the subject of study that concerns the lowest part of the soul (here, tragedy), and then to proceed to the subject of study which concerns the higher level of the soul (here, the Socratic education); it is not a question of right and wrong, but of progressive grades of being and knowledge.

Proclus elucidates this episode as follows: 'And in these words Plato seems to maintain this above all, that Socrates, meeting Plato for the first time (who was then giving serious attention to tragedy) and having demonstrated to him that tragedy offers no good to men, turned him away from imitations of this sort (*tês toiautês mimêseôs*) and, in some way, turned him to the composition of those Socratic writings in which he proved tragedy to be neither educative nor beneficial but to be at a third remove from truth, with no share of knowledge or of correct opinion about the things which it imitates and aiming not at our intelligence but at the irrational part of our soul' (*in Remp.* 1.205.4–13, tr. Riginos 1976, 222). Key words such as 'turning', 'imitation', and 'truth' make it clear that Proclus interprets this episode in the framework of the Neoplatonic philosopher's ascent; in other words, Socrates, as Plato's teacher, has turned his student's attention from a lower (and imitative) rung of the Neoplatonic hierarchy to a higher (and more real) one, and Plato has thereby progressed in the curriculum from tragedy to philosophy. Thus Olympiodorus would see no contradiction in asserting that Plato drew 'the gnomic and solemn and heroic quality' from the subjects (*hupotheseis*) of tragedy before he advanced to the higher *hupotheseis* of philosophy.

31 That is, the overseer of the world of coming-to-be and passing-away, as compared with the eternal, intelligible world of the Forms. See Proclus *in Tim.* 1.53d. Aristotle had suggested (*Poetics* 1449a10–15) that Athenian tragedy developed from the dithyramb.

32 Proclus of Athens (412–485 AD) was a prolifically productive teacher, writer, and thinker in later Neoplatonism; for a short introduction to his thought, see Helmig and Steel 2012, and for book-length surveys, Chlup 2012 and Siorvanes 1996. Proclus adopted and developed a systematic philosophy that derived from Iamblichus (*c.* 245–325 AD), Plutarch of Athens (*c.* 350–430 AD, not to be confused with the earlier Platonist and biographer), and Syrianus (born in the later fourth century, died 437 AD), with modifications at each point of the way.

33 Proclus *Hymns*, p. 156 Ludwich (1895); see van den Berg 2001, 5. Evidently 'children' are effects, and 'parents' their causes. I translate here the correct Greek from Olymp. *in Phaed.* 1.5,16 (*hoss' idon en tekeessin ephêmixanto tokeusin*); the text here at *in Alc.* 2,62 is somewhat garbled (*hoss' eidon tekeessin ephêmixanto tokeusin*). I prefer to suppose that *en* dropped out of our text in transmission or copying, and *idon* was perhaps changed to *eidon* to mend the metre, although Westerink follows Vogt in retaining the misquotation on the grounds that it may be Olympiodorus' or his redactor's.

34 Alluding to 238D, where Socrates claims to 'speak in dithyrambs' (*dithyrambôn phthengomai*), and 241E. Dicaearchus, cited in Diogenes Laertius 3.5, appears to have introduced a tradition that Plato studied the dithyramb first of all poetry (Riginos, Anecdote 14, pp. 43–8).

35 Reading *pneontos* with Casaubon for the manuscripts' *pneiôn*; more literally, the dialogue has the scent of the dithyrambic style or is 'redolent' with it. I am grateful to an anonymous reader for encouraging me to consider this reading.

36 Olympiodorus suggests that Plato composed the *Phaedrus* at this early stage of his life, when he was influenced by dithyrambic poetry. In the standard modern developmental chronology of Plato's dialogues, the *Phaedrus* is treated as a later 'middle period' or transitional dialogue.

37 This couplet is also quoted by Thomas Magister in his *Life of Aristophanes*. It is not in the Palatine and Planudean Anthologies, which preserve the other 'Epigrams of Plato'.

38 This would certainly make for an amusing situation, but it is not quite true to the story of the *Symposium*: when Aristophanes' turn comes to praise Love, he falls victim to hiccoughs and passes his turn to Eryximachus. But Aristophanes delivers a complete speech immediately after Eryximachus (189C–193E).

39 Plato adapts Hom. *Il.* 18.392. Hephaestus is the god of fire as well as craftsmen. Diogenes Laertius, Olympiodorus, the *Anonymous Prolegomena*, Eustathius, and the scholiast to Proclus all agree that Plato played on this line of Homer as he set fire to his old poetry (Riginos 1976, 47).

40 The 'Pharos' was the celebrated lighthouse that became emblematic of Alexandria, as well as the island on which it was built. Olympiodorus may have been

personally present when Alexandria welcomed its new governor, Hephaestus, to
the city in 546 AD; if so, as Watts 2006: 254 suggests, this line may be evidence for
Olympiodorus' prominent role in the city. Hephaestus was known to Procopius
(*Anecdota* 26, 35–44) as a hateful representative of Justinian, responsible for
injustices as augustalis of Egypt, and to John Lydus (*de Magistr.* III, 30) as
praefectus praetorii in Constantinople, a man born of a noble Egyptian family that
traced its descent to the first of the Pharaohs (cf. Diodorus 1,13,3). On the
chronological significance of this passage for dating Olympiodorus' lectures on the
Alcibiades, see Westerink 1990, 329–30. On the episode between Anatolius and
Hephaestus, see for example Cameron 1969: 11–12.

41 Riginos 1976, 21–4 (Anecdote 4).
42 According to Aristotle (*Metaph.* 987a32–b7) Plato followed Cratylus in his youth,
and then turned from the world without to Socrates' philosophy and the world
within. But this account would contradict the story that Socrates drew Plato from
poetry to philosophy, a problem which Olympiodorus solves by placing Plato's
association with Cratylus after his association with Socrates. On Aristotle's
testimony, see Riginos 48 n. 36 and H. Cherniss, 'Aristotle, *Metaphysics* 987a32–b7',
AJP 76 (1955): 184–6). For the development of the later Neoplatonic reading of
the *Cratylus*, see also van den Berg 2008.
43 Plato's association with Pythagoreans, in his doctrine and his life, is universally
attested in the ancient sources, including Aristotle *Metaphysics* 987b (cf. Riginos
62–3 n. 6). His journey to Magna Graecia occurs in all of the biographies.
44 There is no mention of Archytas in *Philebus*, though he appears in the seventh,
ninth, twelfth and thirteenth *Letters* as an associate of Plato in Tarentum (e.g.
338C, 350A). It is possible that *entha kai Arkhutou memnêtai* is corrupt or
intrusive; *memnêtai* is missing in the manuscript M.

　　According to a different tradition, it was Archytas who later bought the enslaved
Plato from Pollis (see below) and gave him a lesson in Pythagoran philosophy; this
story is found only in Tzetzes (*Chil.* 10.995–9 [p. 403 Kiessling]), and is patterned
on the stories about the conversion of Phaedon of Elis to philosophy (Riginos
1976, 90–1, Anecdote 35).
45 For the following, see Riginos 1976, 70–85. It seems very likely that the reports of
Plato's visits to Sicily and the Syracusan court are essentially historical. Indeed, the
seventh *Letter* among others seems designed to defend Plato against accusations
and slanders concerning this journey.
46 The 'sight-lover' (*philotheamôn*) is devoted to objects that participate in beauty, but
he does not believe in the Beautiful itself (*Republic* 5, 475D–476B). The true
philosopher, on the other hand, as one who believes in the Beautiful itself, 'can see
both it and the things that participate in it' (476C–D). Hence the philosopher is

free to take pleasure in beautiful sights, but he is also able to recognise their source and higher origin.

47 Aristides *Or.* 46.229 does not in fact accuse Plato of venturing to Sicily purely for the cuisine, but he does make the charge that Plato had leisure to acquaint himself with Sicilian food and manners, suggesting a gluttonous nature; the charge may be inspired by the *Gorgias* (463B, 465D, 518B), where Plato's Socrates claims that certain Sicilian cooks are masters of their art. The favourable biographical tradition is careful to state the real reasons (*aitiai*) why the philosopher went to Syracuse on each occasion. It was not for the 'Sicilian table', proverbial of luxury (a point elaborated in the Platonic *Seventh Letter*, 326B–D, and Plato himself scorns the *Syrakosian trapezan* at *Republic* 3, 404D). The first journey was motivated by curiosity, to see the volcano on Mount Aetna (which Plato mentions at *Phaedo* 111E). The second was motivated by a desire to be influential in practical politics and to see his theories in application (cf. the *Seventh Letter*, 328B–C). The third journey was undertaken for the sake of Plato's friend Dion.

48 Tyranny occupies the lowest rank in the hierarchy of constitutions of soul and state set out in the *Republic*; the life of the tyrannical person is described in detail in *Republic* 9. By contrast, 'aristocracy', more literally the 'rule (*kratos*) of the best (*aristoi*)' or meritocracy, occupies the highest rank.

49 This series of questions and answers was a popular element in the biographical tradition concerning Plato's stay in Sicily, and its key idea is *parrhêsia*, the freedom of speech displayed by the philosopher in the face of the tyrant. Riginos discusses this episode as her Anecdote 25 (1976, 74–9). She points out that Olympiodorus reports different questions here and in his commentary on the *Gorgias* (*in Gorg.* 41.7; here and following, in keeping with Jackson et al. 1998, I cite Olympiodorus *in Gorg.* by chapter heading. The first question in both works is 'Who is happy among men'; and the reply is 'Socrates'. In Olymp. *in Gorg.*, the second question is simpler than here. There, Dionysius simply asserts that the greatest good is judgement, and Plato replies with this same comparison of judges and weavers; the introductory question about the work of the statesman is absent. The final question differs markedly between the two commentaries. In the *in Gorg.*, Dionysius asks whether Heracles was happy (*eudaimôn*), and Plato replies that, if Heracles was as the myths portray him, he was not; but if he lived with excellence (*aretê*), he was. Riginos argues that the account of the *Alcibiades* commentary is the more structurally sophisticated of the two: the questions show an increasing boldness in Plato's answers, at first slighting the tyrant, then belittling the cornerstone of his reputation, and climaxing with a personal insult that touches Dionysius' fear of assassination. This interpretation corroborates Westerink's contention that the *Gorgias* commentary dates to a period near the beginning of

Olympiodorus' career (1990, 331). The relative simplicity of the *Gorgias* account could also point to the activity of different recorders or editors on the *Gorgias* and *Alcibiades* commentaries respectively, but this seems less likely.

50 Compare *Republic* 1, 342E on the governing statesman's responsibility to act for the good of his subjects, and not for his own good.

51 Compare *Gorgias* 520A–B on the legislator's superiority to the judge, and more generally Socrates' discussions with Polus, Callicles, and Thrasymachus (e.g. *Gorg.* 466C–E) on the status of tyrants.

52 The story of Plato's slavery (Riginos 1976, 86–92) is omitted in the report of the Platonic *Seventh Letter*, although this does not necessarily prove its falsehood; Plato, or someone writing in his name, would understandably avoid it. It is first preserved in the *Index Herculanensis*.

53 It may be significant that Aegina was not only Pollis' home, but also his destination at the time of these events: according to Aristides *Or.* 46.233, special legislation dictated that Athenians seized at Aegina be put to death.

54 Aristides *Or.* 46.234.

55 The story that Plato travelled to Egypt became very common after Cicero (*De Fin.* 5.29.87, *De Re Pub.* 1.10.16) and Diodorus Siculus (1.96.2), the earliest surviving sources for this story; see Riginos 1976, 64–5 and Moyer 2011, 58. The tale may be patterned on the reports of Pythagoras' legendary journeys to Phoenicia, Egypt, and Babylon before he settled in southern Italy. But it is certainly true, as Riginos points out (64), that the Platonic writings betray a genuine familiarity with Egyptian customs, religion and legends. Apart from the oath of Socrates, which Olympiodorus adduces below, Riginos cites *Laws* 2.656D–657A and 7.3819A–E (educational practices), *Laws* 7.799A, *Tim.* 21E, *Polit.* 290D–E (Egyptian deities and religious practices), *Resp.* 4.436A and *Laws* 5.747C (Egyptian character), *Phaedo* 80C and *Polit.* 264C (general customs), and most of all *Phaedr.* 274C–275B, *Tim.* 21E–25D, and the *Critias* (stories set in Egypt). Egyptian culture was growingly familiar in fifth- and fourth-century Athens: see for example the introduction to and commentary on Herodotus Book 2 by Lloyd 1976. Plato may well have become acquainted with Egyptian thought, regardless of whether he actually journeyed to the Nile.

56 The expertise of the Egyptian priests would include theurgy, the appropriate care for and engagement with divine images and beings, as well as theology, the systematic accounting of such beings (cf. Iamblichus *De Mysteriis* 1: 'you ... do well in laying before the priests questions about theology, such as they love to deal with, and which pertain to their expertise (*eis gnôsin*)', tr. Clarke, Dillon and Hershbell 2003).

57 482b5: *ma ton kuna ton Aiguptiôn theon*. Dodds 1959 (for instance) points out that this line does not constitute a proof that Plato visited Egypt, since Herodotus

already knew that the dog was sacred there (ad loc.) Instead, as Dodds suggests, it might be a 'jocular oath', a euphemistic distortion of the *nomen sacrum*, and at any rate not unique to Socrates (compare Aristophanes *Wasps* 83). For Olympiodorus, on the other hand, as for any Neoplatonic commentator following Proclus, the choice of words is not haphazard (*in Gorg.* 25.10, tr. Jackson et al. 1998): ' "[T]he dog" signifies the discerning faculty of the rational soul. He said "Egyptian" because the Egyptians were leaders in the use of symbols.' Earlier in the same commentary, Olympiodorus remarks, ad 461A7–B1, that 'the dog is the symbol of the life of reason . . . it is because the life of reason distinguishes what is fine from what is base, that he spoke symbolically of this life by means of the word "dog" '.

58 The story that Plato hoped to visit the Magi, and went as far as Phoenicia, also recalls the legend of Pythagoras; Cicero alludes to both philosophers reaching *ultimae terrae* (*De Fin.* 5.19.50, *Tusc. Disp.* 4.19.44). According to another tradition, Magi or Chaldaeans even came to Athens to study with Plato (*Index Herc.* Col. III 36–41, p. 13 Mekler; *Anon. Proleg.* 6.19–22, p. 15 Westerink 1962). Pliny *Nat. Hist.* 30.1.9 adds that Plato studied Zoroastrianism, and Proclus *in Remp.* 2.109.7–16, quotes Colotes as accusing Plato of borrowing from Zoroaster. At any rate, Plato's schooling in Sicily, Egypt and the East suggests his mastery of the entire *oikoumenê* of known philosophy.

59 *Tim.* 71A–72D.

60 This looks like a scholiast's observation that the second and third journeys to Sicily must postdate Plato's travels in the East. It is also possible that the interjection is Olympiodorus' own, since this is a record of spoken lectures. On the other hand, Olympiodorus might have chosen to relate all three Sicilian voyages in one place. The language of the transition at 2,134 – 'And one should know that he *also* journeyed to Egypt (*hoti kai eis Aigupton apêlthen*)' – suggests that this episode does intentionally stand after the account of the Sicilian voyages.

61 Riginos 1976, 119–21 (Anecdote 75); Diogenes Laertius 4.1 provides the earliest testimony that Plato himself established a Mouseion in the Academy, but Pausanias 1.30.2 tells of a *bômos* sacred to the Muses without giving the circumstances of its establishment.

62 Riginos (1976, 162 n. 35) suggests that this story initially conveyed Plato's preference for solitude over human company, although the anecdote seems primarily concerned with Timon's character and not with Plato's.

63 Compare Diogenes Laertius' comment that Plato taught women in his school, Lasthenea of Mantinea and Axiothea of Phlius (DL 3.46), and the latter 'even used to dress up in men's clothes, as Dicaearchus reports'.

64 If *philoponia* here echoes *Alc.* 122C, where it is characteristic of the Spartans, then this biographical detail may reflect the sentiment of *Alc.* 124A–B: Alcibiades cannot contend with the Spartans' love of hardship and self-discipline, nor with the Persians' wealth and material resources, but he can attain the *greater* goal of self-knowledge through philosophy. Alternatively, the reference might be to domestic work of the kind that ordinarily fell to women in fourth-century Athens: the pursuit of Plato's philosophy is presented as a better way of life.

65 'Himself said so' (*autos epha*) was a mark of authenticity and authority for a Pythagorean doctrine, attributing the view to Pythagoras himself. Olympiodorus is suggesting that Plato had no interest in exclusivity or the cult of leadership.

66 Cf. Aristotle, *Topics* 8.3, 158b10 on the technical division of *haplôs* and *pollakhôs*; *Metaphysics* 5 (D) is a *tour de force* of analysis of things 'said in many ways'.

67 Olympiodorus uses the metaphor of a musical mode, such as the Dorian or Ionic systems of tuning an instrument. Plato and Homer used all the different 'tunings', in the sense that their words could be interpreted symbolically or allegorically on all the levels of reality. The Neoplatonists had significant projects of allegorical exegesis; consider for example the introductions to Proclus' commentaries on the *Timaeus* or *Parmenides*, where the characters of the dialogues are carefully interpreted allegorically. See also Griffin 2014b.

68 Diogenes Laertius in 3.45 gives two of his own epigrams which compare Apollo's two sons as healers: Asclepius of the body, Plato of the soul (cf. Riginos, Anecdote 9, pp. 28–9). Olympiodorus' version is mirrored in the later *Anonymous Prolegomena*, but the author of that work seems obliged to avoid attributing an overtly miraculous birth and divine parentage to Plato, and he accordingly changes the wording to describe Plato as the son of Ariston.

69 For clarity, I have marked the beginning of the first lecture (*praxis*) on the *Alcibiades* here at 3,2, but this division is somewhat arbitrary. The manuscript (M) begins labelling Olympiodorus' 'lectures' with Lecture 2 at 9,20 (*praxis sun theôi B*). The preceding material may have been delivered as a single lecture that functioned to introduce both Platonic philosophy and the first dialogue in the Platonic curriculum, featuring a brief preamble (1,3–13), the *Life of Plato* (1,13–3,2) and Olympiodorus' initial discussion of the *Alcibiades* itself (3,2–9,19). But the *Life* has often been treated as a separate work, from its first publication in the Amsterdam edition of Diogenes Laertius in 1692 to Creuzer's edition of Olymp. *in Alc.* in 1821, and there is a clear thematic break between the introductory material on Plato (1,3–3,2), on the one hand, and Olympiodorus' commentary on the *Alcibiades* proper.

70 Proclus *in Alc.* 4–10. The *skopos* necessarily comes first in the order of seven issues which, for Iamblichus and his successors, must be dealt with 'before the reading of a text' (Mansfeld 1994, 10–11, 31, *passim*; see for example Proclus *in Remp.*

5.28–7.4): these are, in varying order and emphasis (1) the theme, target, or purpose (*skopos*) of the dialogue; (2) its position in the corpus (*taxis*); (3) its utility (*khrêsimon*); (4) the explanation of its title (*aition tês epigraphês*); (5) its authenticity (*gnêsion*); (6) its division into chapters or parts (*diairesis*); and (7) the genre or part of philosophy to which the treatise belongs (*hupo poion meros . . . anagetai*), a heading already used by Origen (Mansfeld 10–11). In the present commentary we find four of these points covered at length:

(a) *skopos*: 3,3–9,19
(b) *khrêsimon*: 9,20–10,17
(c) *taxis*: 10,18–11,6
(d) *diairesis*: 11,7–23

More briefly examined are (7) the genre, at 13,11, and (4) the title, at 3,5–8; the fifth item, authenticity, is omitted by Olympiodorus – oddly, from the perspective of modern scholarship. It is likely that the standard position of this dialogue in the Iamblichean curriculum exempted it from doubt.

71 Proclus of Athens (412–485 AD) was a prolifically productive teacher, writer, and thinker in later Neoplatonism; for a short introduction to his thought, see Helmig and Steel 2012, and for book-length surveys, Chlup 2012 and Siorvanes 1996. Proclus adopted and developed a systematic philosophy that derived from Iamblichus (*c.* 245–325 AD), Plutarch of Athens (*c.* 350–430 AD, not to be confused with the earlier Platonist and biographer), and Syrianus (born in the later fourth century, died 437 AD), with modifications at each point of the way.

Proclus' commentary on the *Alcibiades* survives in part, and it is clear that Olympiodorus is indebted to it. (An excellent text and translation are available in Segonds 1985–86, and an English translation is available in O'Neill 1965.)

72 The *Second* (or *Lesser*) *Alcibiades* is today generally regarded as spurious.

73 124A.

74 131A–C.

75 Menoeceus voluntarily gave his life to save Thebes, when it was discovered, through Tiresias' divination, that a youth must be sacrificed in order to appease Ares for the slaughter of the dragon at the foundation of the city. This story is told by Euripides at *Phoen.* 1009–14.

76 This is fragment 11 ascribed to Proclus' *Alcibiades* commentary, given at O'Neill 1965, 227–8.

77 Damascius, born around 462 AD in Damascus, became the last head of the Academy in Athens. While adopting a basically Proclan system of Neoplatonism, he also re-examined a number of Proclus' views. Olympiodorus may have had access to a commentary *On the Alcibiades* by Damascius.

78 For this and the following 'levels' of philosophical excellence or personhood (civic, purificatory, and contemplative) see the Introduction §2.1. Excellent or virtuous activity in the city or state (*polis*) – more broadly, as a member of civic society (*politikos*) – is a grade of human excellence available to the philosopher but unavailable to non-philosophers, whose virtue relies merely on natural endowment (*phusikê aretê*) and good habits (*êthikê aretê*). A 'civically' excellent person employs both the rational part of the soul (reason, *logos*) and its non-rational parts (spirited emotion, *thumos* and appetitive desire, *epithumia*) in order to operate consistently and effectively in society. One rung 'above' the civically excellent philosopher is the philosopher of 'purificatory excellence' (*kathartikê aretê*), who has made his reason (*logos*) 'separable' from the lower two parts of his soul.

Adopting the city-state analogy of *Republic* 2, 368C–369A, a Platonist could regard 'civic excellence' (*politikê aretê*) as primarily referring to the *inward* organisation of the 'civic body' (*polis*) comprising the three parts of the soul. Thus 'a good person will look to the constitution (*politeia*) within him' (*Republic* 591E), 'directing all his efforts to attaining the [best] state of his soul' (591C), not 'concerned with "doing his own work" externally, but with what is inside him, what is truly himself and his own' (443C). Just behaviour in the outward *polis* would then be of secondary concern, flowing from this inner justice.

79 Olympiodorus follows the Neoplatonic tradition in regarding emotion and appetitive desire as two faculties of the tripartite soul that require the body as an instrument: for instance, a physical process is a necessary condition for becoming angry or experiencing a strong appetitive desire. (It is not a sufficient condition, as soul [*psukhê*] is still the primary agent of these activities.) By contrast, reason (*logos*) is a faculty of the soul that does not require the body as an instrument; thus the 'reasoning' or 'rational' soul (*logikê psukhê*) can be seen as separable from the body.

80 Cleombrotus of Ambracia was said by Callimachus (*Epigram* 23) to have thrown himself from his lofty roof after reading 'that one work by Plato *On the Soul*' (sc. *Phaedo*). For the 'chains' that bind the soul to the living body, see for example *Phaedo* 67D.

81 Olympiodorus refers to the theory of a cosmic 'sympathy' between parts of the cosmos, especially (for the Neoplatonists) between ontologically 'higher' causes and the 'lower' effects which proceed from them. The lower effect can 'return' to its cause by means of their sympathy (literally 'shared experience', *sum-patheia*) or fundamental similarity: see Proclus *Elements of Theology*, props. 29, 31. As Olympiodorus suggests below, when an embodied human soul engages in contemplation (*theôria*) it becomes 'like' its higher, purely intellectual form, and thereby 'ascends' in a sense to the intelligible world.

The theory of sympathy went through several iterations in antiquity. It has an early source in a Stoic view of the cosmos as an animal whose parts are related as organic limbs: the experience of one part of the whole body can be felt in another part of the body. Plotinus' adaptation of the theory to Neoplatonism can be found, for instance, in *Enneads* 4.4.32 ('This One-All, therefore, is a sympathetic total and stands as one living being; the far is near; it happens as in one animal with its separate parts: talon, horn, finger, and any other member are not continuous and yet are effectively near', tr. MacKenna 1957). Porphyry continues to develop the idea, although his version of it is criticised by Iamblichus (see *De Mysteriis* 3.27, 5.7, etc.) In Neopythagorean circles, the acoustic principle of sympathetic resonance or vibration may also have provided a useful metaphor for 'sympathy' in the Neoplatonic sense. The Hermetic and alchemical traditions in antiquity also developed the dictum 'as above, so below' (e.g. *Emerald Tablet* 2), which reflects a similar concept of sympathy.

82 For the later Neoplatonist, the *okhêma pneumatikon* or 'pneumatic vehicle' conveys the psyche while it is 'divided in association with bodies' (Proclus *in Alc.* 4–5; in Olympiodorus' tetradic terminology, 'political'): cf. Dodds 1963, App. 2, 315–16. At its most manifest it is a 'shell-like' vehicle which conveys the irrational soul (*alogos psukhê*): cf. 203,10–11 below. The idea of this pneumatic vehicle, which serves to connect the *psukhê* to the *soma* and conveys the *alogos psukhê*, combined Aristotle's account of the *pneuma* as 'analogous to the element comprising the stars' with Plato's account of the *okhêma* or 'vehicle' onto which the Demiurge placed the soul: cf. Finamore 1985.

83 *Od.* 22.1. Following Plato, Olympiodorus elsewhere connects nakedness with freedom from body, as at *in Gorg.* 48.1.

84 The contemplative person has to work at this spiritual exercise by acting (*energousa*) 'according to what is most divine' in his soul; in other words, Olympiodorus presents us with a philosophical Odysseus whose efforts in the realm of *theôria* lead to his well-being.

85 At the beginning of Lecture 2, Olympiodorus refers to this reconciliation as the view adopted by 'the commentators' (*exêgêtai*) – that is, contemporary interpreters, presumably including himself.

86 That is, the two positions are compatible: Damascius' account of the target (*skopos*) of the text is a specific version of Proclus'. If I understand the sentence rightly, Olympiodorus is maintaining his general allegiance to Proclus while following Damascius' more particular view. Damascius may have explicitly contrasted his interpretation with Proclus', whereas Olympiodorus treats them as congruent.

87 118B.

88 *De Flat.* 1, 6 92 L.

89 See Rose 1886, frr. 80; 81. Compare *Republic* 9, 589A, where Socrates describes the rational element in the tripartite soul (the *anthrôpos*) as potentially 'familiarising or reconciling with one another' the two lower elements, rather than 'suffering them to bite and fight and devour one another'.

90 Cf. Olymp. *in Gorg.* 46.1: 'Note that aristocracy was at its height among the Pythagoreans. For aristocracy is what makes citizens upright, and people become upright by having their souls perfected. But perfection of the soul does not arise except through life and insight. Nor could insight arise unless one's life has previously been corrected, for insight does not occur in a soul that is soiled. Consequently, the Pythagoreans used first to purify their life by habituating themselves to sampling the passions with just the tips of their fingers, and so they gave insight to their successors. Hence they lived together in aristocracy' (tr. Jackson et al. 1998). As Jackson et al. 289 point out, Olympiodorus himself appears to favour the Socratic approach.

91 Hom. *Il.* 4.86–103. Athena comes among the Trojans and persuades Pandarus to fire an arrow at the Greek host. By doing so, he breaks the truce by which he swore to abide.

92 *Il.* 5.290–6: Diomedes hurls his spear at Pandarus, and Athena guides the point to his tongue.

93 Proclus describes this approach in more detail at *in Alc.* 151,16–152,20, especially 152,3–12: 'Each individual is not to be brought up in the same way, but he who has the natural aptitude to be a philosopher differently from the person inclined to love or music [cf. *Phaedrus* 248D], and he who, through the picturing of heavenly ease, is wildly excited to pleasure, must be brought up differently from one who, through the desire for self-sufficiency, yearns for the acquisition of money, and differently again from one who, because of the notion of divine power, is carried away under the influence of the mere appearances of power. For everywhere mere representations clothed in the likeness of their archetypes lead senseless souls astray; whereas they should rise up therefrom and pass over to those true and genuine realities. Such was the method of Socrates' teaching, to elevate each individual to his appropriate object of desire . . . .' Below (20,6–10) Olympiodorus adopts a similar line on the education of different types of personality.

94 *Il.* 6.138; *Od.* 4.805.

95 This paraphrase sets the text of *Alcibiades* 132D–133C into the appropriate form for the structural exegesis which follows. Compare *Phaedrus* 255C–E: 'As a gust of wind, or an echo, bounces off smooth hard surfaces and is carried back to whence it came, so too the stream of beauty goes back [from the lover] to the beautiful boy. It passes through his eyes, which are the natural route to the soul. When it arrives, . . . it fills the soul of the beloved in its turn with love. He is in love, but he does not know with what; . . . he has not realised that he has seen himself in his

lover, as if in a mirror; . . . he contains an image of love, a counterlove' (tr. Denyer 2001, ad *Alc.* 135E1).

96 I take Olympiodorus' point to be that children, and rural people, more often experience visions and inspirations from the gods than city-dwellers do. The sophistication of a cultured, urbane person might be an impediment to inspiration.

97 Olympiodorus may mean that divine inspiration is not normally consciously analysed, and thinking about it destroys the inspiration. I am grateful to an anonymous reader for this suggestion.

98 *Anth. Pal.* 14,73; see below, 31,7, with note.

99 The verb *epistrephei* again reflects the crucial idea of 'turning' or 'reversion' which Olympiodorus introduced briefly at the beginning of the biography (2,16, where Plato is *epistrophos* of many). The significance of reversion as the means of self-knowledge will be discussed below (10,4); see Lecture 2, with notes, for further details with references to Proclus' *Elements of Theology*.

100 The phrases *sun theôi* ('with the favour or help of [the] god') and *sun theois* ('with the favour or help of [the] gods') had ancient roots in Greek inscriptions and literature (see for example Pindar *Nemean* 6.24–5). It was common property of pagans and Christians in late antiquity, and the label 'lecture *sun theôi*', or something like it, occurs for example in Philoponus (e.g. *in De An.* 450,33), Elias, and David, in addition to Olympiodorus' lectures.

I have not capitalised 'God' in English, retaining some ambiguity about which 'god' is meant. Olympiodorus' comments below suggest that he would not reject this label for his lectures (cf. 39,20: 'in [the *Gorgias*], with the god's favour, we will also discover . . ', pointing forward to the next course in his own curriculum; the idea that divine support is essential in philosophical education is also familiar in later Neoplatonism).

101 Here and following, the translations of the lemmata are partially based on D.S. Hutchinson's translation of the *Alcibiades I* in Cooper and Hutchinson 1997, 557–95, with changes throughout to bring out Olympiodorus' specific points about the language. There are also some deviations from the textual tradition of Plato, some explicable by auditory error on the note-taker's part, some by mistakes in transmission, and some genuinely good readings, as at 110C6 (cf. Dodds 1957, 358).

Olympiodorus does not actually comment on this lemma (103A) in Lecture 2, but picks up the subject in Lecture 3.

102 This gloss may be unnecessary and intrusive, but the point is that Olympiodorus and his contemporaries agree upon the exegesis of the target (*skopos*) given in Lecture 1. The emphasis on 'the agreement of the exegetes' (*ton tois exêgêtais*

aresanta) reflects Olympiodorus' interest in harmonising the Proclan and Damascian views given above.

103 Olympiodorus continues through the standard list of issues to tackle at the outset of reading a new text: see again Mansfeld 1994.

104 Cf. Proclus, *El. Theol.* pr. 83: 'all that is capable of self-knowledge is capable of every form of self-reversion' (*pan to heautou gnôstikon pros heauto pantêi epistreptikon estin*). (Here and following I cite the *Elements of Theology* by proposition number and refer to the text of Dodds 1963.)

At *in Alc.* 20, Proclus explains, 'Now there are three kinds of reversion: everything that reverts either reverts to what is inferior to itself by falling away from its own perfection, or is elevated to what is superior through its own life and natural activity, or reverts upon itself according to the knowledge that is co-ordinate with itself, and the middle form of movement' (tr. O'Neill).

105 For this translation of *logos*, see note to 15,11 below.

106 Cf. Proclus *El. Theol.* p. 195: 'Every soul is all things, the things of sense after the manner of an exemplar and the intelligible things after the manner of an image' (tr. Dodds).

107 Compare Proclus *in Alc.* 1,3–9: 'If [our own being] is correctly posited, we shall in every way, I think, be able more accurately to understand both the good that is appropriate to us and the evil that fights against it.' Proclus goes on to stress that the *Alcibiades* is especially valuable for this reason.

108 The Greek noun *teleiotês*, literally 'completeness', is often translated 'perfection'. In the context of the Greek Mysteries, it can be translated as 'initiation'.

In many of Olympiodorus' uses of the words *teleios* and *teleiotês*, he has in mind a common principle that derives from Aristotle's theory of entelechy, with Neoplatonic adaptations: each body and soul is engaged in a continual process of coming-to-be from potentiality (*dunamis*) to actuality (*energeia*). I have used the English word 'fulfilment' to capture this developmental dimension of *teleios* and *teleiotês*, although I appreciate that it is not very satisfactory in other respects.

109 'Virtue' would be a more common translation for *aretê*, and 'vice' for *kakia*. But the modern language of morality can sit uneasily with the answering Greek terminology, as several of the founding figures of Anglo-American virtue ethics stressed, and I have sometimes preferred to use English terms such as 'excellence' that allow for the more basic sense of *aretê* in earlier Greek literature – in this case excellence of character.

110 Cf. *Gorg.* 523C–E, 524C–D; *Phaed.* 107C–D. See also Olymp. *in Gorg.* 48–9.

111 229E–230A.

112 Since the *Parmenides* represents the culmination of the Platonic curriculum and the perfection of understanding of the highest things (theology), as the *Alcibiades*

represents the beginning of the curriculum and the starting-points on self-knowledge. See Introduction §2.1.

113 The tripartite division of the dialogue into 'refutation' (*elenktikos*, 106C–119A), 'exhortation' (*protreptikos*, 119A–124A), and 'midwifery' (*maieutikos*, 124A–135D; on Socratic 'midwifery' see M. Burnyeat, 'Socratic Midwifery and Platonic Inspiration', *BICS* 24 [1977] 7–17) derives from Proclus *in Alc.* 13–15, who ascribes it to Iamblichus: 'First therefore comes one section that takes away ignorance from the reason . . . next after this is placed a part of the dialogue, which proves that we must not be content with physical advantages and so fall short of practices that accord with perfect excellence; and third after these is the part that provides the recollection of our true being and the discovery of the correct treatment, and brings a fitting end to the whole theme of the discussions' (tr. adapted from O'Neill 1965).

114 *Rhetoric* 1.7, 1365a29.

115 Socrates does not promote any particular doctrine, but 'elicits' wisdom from his interlocutor. Since the knowledge comes from within Socrates' interlocutor, who answers his questions, it is the answerer who 'speaks' in the dialogue, not Socrates himself.

116 The Greek word *maia* means 'midwife', as in the adjective *maieutikos* (meaning roughly 'obstetric', 'to do with assistance in childbirth').

117 For the imagery of 'pouring wisdom' into an empty vessel, cf. *Phaedr.* 235C–D and *Symp.* 175D–E (which, however, specifically denies that hearing is filling an empty vessel).

118 *Theaet.* 150C.

119 This passage, including the metaphor of the storks who nourish their parents, is drawn from *Alc.* 135D–E, where Alcibiades proposes a role-reversal (*metabolê tou skhêmatos*): 'Let us venture to reverse our arrangement, Socrates, with me taking your part and you mine: for from this day forward I must be your attendant (*paidagôgêsô*), and you must have me always in attendance on you'; to which Socrates joyfully replies, 'So my love will be just like a stork; for after hatching a winged love in you it is to be cherished in return by its nestling.' Compare *Symp.* 222B, where Alcibiades himself warns that Socrates has allegedly tricked Charmides, Euthydemus, and other youths *exapatôn hos erastês paidika mallon autos kathistatai ant' erastou*, 'by pretending to be their lover [*erastês*], but he ends up instead as the one that they love [*paidika*]'. The idea of reciprocity is clearly essential to the Platonic doctrine of *erôs*, and it is closely allied with the physics of vision; cf. the poetic metaphor of *Phaedr.* 255C–E, quoted in n. 71 above. This may be taken as a corollary of the Presocratic theory that *like perceives like* (i.e. percipient becomes like to the perceived).

120 *Phaedr.* 257A.

121 The anecdote about Alexander is puzzling. We may, as Westerink suggests (in Westerink 1982, addenda), have lost a portion of the context. Perhaps the thread of thought ran like this: Socrates, in the preceding sentence, has prayed for his erotic skill not to be disabled by the god. But his erotic skill was, it seems, disabled in Alcibiades' case, for Alcibiades 'came to a bad end' after his actions led to the ravaging of the Athenian army through the Sicilian expedition (Thucydides 6) and subsequent events. Olympiodorus then offers a parenthetical observation about Alexander the Great (he anticipated that someone who brought an army into trouble, would come to a bad end himself).

122 The following section roughly follows Proclus' distinction of the divine lover from the ordinary lover *in Alc.* 34,17–35,20. Westerink also compares Olympiodorus *in Gorg.* 25.3 (123,5–7). The Greek verb *energein* can mean sexual intercourse. But to 'act according to the body' also might be read in a Neoplatonic technical sense – as in Plotinus, *Enn.* 3.4, for instance, one might 'practise' (*energein*) the bodily and perceptible level of existence, or a series of loftier and imperceptible levels of existence, such as the daimonic.

123 Plato's 'Athenian stranger' offers a similar contrast at *Laws* 837B–D: 'The lover of the body, hungry for his partner who is ripe to be enjoyed, like a luscious fruit, tells himself to have his fill, without showing any consideration for his beloved's character and disposition. But in another case physical desire will count for very little and the lover will be content to gaze upon his beloved without lusting for him – a mature and genuine desire of soul for soul' (tr. Saunders).

124 Some Greek philosophers were committed to the idea that character could be evaluated from the signs of physical features (physiognomy); see for example Aristotle *Prior Analytics* 2.27, 70b7–31. Proclus discusses the relevance of the practice later in his commentary, ad 103B (*in Alc.* 94,2–15): 'Socrates saw in Alcibiades many remarkable natural tokens of his suitability . . . his outward beauty and height were signs of his enterprising . . . pre-eminence of soul; and to their appearance nature which creates the body attached certain tokens, which Socrates observed and judged the youth to be worthy of attention. This was originally a custom of the Pythagoreans [cf. Iamblichus *Vit. Pyth.* 17,71], to discern through bodily signs, in those that approached them, their fitness for the better life . . .'

125 *Phaedrus* 238E–240A.

126 Proclus' corresponding discussion (*in Alc.* 47,13–49,12) fills in the contrast and the solution. '[T]he end of the indulgent and the moderate person is not the same, but as their habits, so also their ends completely differ; whereas all lovers have the same end, viz. familiarisation with the beautiful, but forgetfulness and

ignorance of what is primarily beautiful make the inferior lovers rush down and concern themselves with the kind of beauty that is implicated in matter. As therefore even the lowest beauty has the same name as the primarily beautiful . . . so also the lowest of lovers claims he same name as the first . . .

'We assert that what is more divine, through abundance of power, regulates its inferior derivations and gives to them some reflected semblance of its own specific nature. Now moderation cannot do this . . . but the inspired friendship of love, since it is more divine than moderation, gives something even to its image . . . In this respect, then, it receives a share in the same name; for everywhere images desire to share the same appellation as their exemplars' (tr. O'Neill 1965, lightly adapted).

127 Literally, 'colour' (*khrôsai*).

128 This has the ring of a poetic saying, but I have not been able to locate the source. Building on Plato's *Phaedrus* and *Symposium*, Olympiodorus stresses that both inspired and vulgar love are kinds of madness with a common goal, 'birth in beauty'.

129 Cf. *Symp.* 206E.

130 I have generally elected to transliterate, rather than translate, the Greek word *daimôn*, which can refer to any divine power or apportioner (of destiny). In the later ancient technical sense relevant here, *daimôn* usually references a 'spiritual . . . being inferior to the gods' (LSJ A II 2). This technical sense owes a good deal to the speech of Diotima in Plato's *Symposium*, where *Erôs* (Love) is described as a *daimôn* 'intermediate' between gods and human beings; the Neoplatonic commentators also drew on Socrates' discussion of his 'spiritual sign' (*daimônion*).

Olympiodorus later (22,3) describes the usage from the Chaldaean Oracles that became customary after Iamblichus (cf. Saffrey 1981, and for the Oracles more generally, Majercik 1989). In the Oracles, the expanse between gods and human souls is filled by angels, daimons and heroes. The later Neoplatonic account of the 'chain of being', deriving from Iamblichus, can be outlined as follows, although the complete chain is more complex:

God (The One, *to hen*); gods (unities, *henades*)
Archangels
Angels
Daimons
Heroes
Souls

In such a scheme 'daimons' lie 'below' finer beings such as angels, archangels, and finally gods, but 'above' heroes and human souls. Olympiodorus comments shortly (21,15–22,5) on the now 'customary', Christian usage of 'angel' in a way that, in his view, best accords with the philosophers' use of *daimôn*.

It is difficult to locate an exact English equivalent for *daimôn* which is not somehow misleading. The typical connotations of 'demon' and 'spirit' are either too pejorative or too broad; 'angel' is best reserved for the Greek *angelos* and the Neoplatonic entity called by that name, and 'divinity' is best reserved for words associated with *theos*.

131 It is a general rule of Neoplatonic metaphysics that causes are 'better' than their effects, in the sense of ontological superiority and independence, and also in the sense of value (see Proclus *El. Theol.* pr. 7, and further discussion below). See also Proclus' corresponding discussion at *in Alc.* 62,8–63,11.

132 For the following account of daimons (demonology), see also Proclus *in Alc.* 73,16–75,1.

133 A diagram in the margins of the manuscript offers a helpful illustration of the three kinds of daimons discussed here. Here is a lightly augmented version (with added detail in square brackets):

Analogical daimons are so Causally (*kat' aitian*)
[These are gods]
Essential daimons are so Really (*kath' huparxin*)
[These are daimons proper]
Relational daimons are so by Participation (*kata' methexin*)
These are the souls of those who have lived well.

134 Compare Proclus *De Mal. Subst.* 17, where Proclus distinguishes entities that are daimons by nature (*phusei*) from those that are daimons by relation or disposition (*skhesei*); the latter, notably, can change. Opsomer and Steel (2003, 112) explain, 'The latter are souls that have succeeded in ascending to a demonic pattern of life. Whereas someone's nature is unalterable, one's acquired behaviour may very well change.' In addition to Proclus *in Alc.* 73,16–75,1, Opsomer and Steel point out a number of helpful comparanda: *in Tim.* 3,158,22–159,7; *in Crat.* 117, p. 68,13–19 Pasq.; 74, pp. 35,27–36,6; and *in Remp.* 1,41,11–25. They also note that Theodorus of Asine offers this distinction at *in Tim.* 3,154,19–24.

135 To follow Olympiodorus' argument here and following, it might be helpful to consider how the term 'house' could be applied to (1) the architect's blueprint for a house, (2) the completed house itself, and (3) an artist's later sketch of the same house. On the Olympiodorean scheme, the term applies properly to the middle term – (2) the built house – and only 'analogically' or 'metaphorically' to (1) the blueprint. It could also be used for (3) the later sketch, but only in a dependent way, in virtue of its 'relation' to the house itself.

Olympiodorus' hierarchy of daimons is similar: (1) 'analogical' daimons are like the blueprint, containing the formulas of (2) the essential daimons, which are in turn like the house itself; (3) 'relational' daimons are like the sketch, representations of the real thing. There is an important difference, however: here, the 'blueprint' is not merely a plan in the architect's mind, but the paradigmatic or exemplary *cause* of the next term. (Compare the notion of 'exemplary excellence' in the Introduction §2.1.)

136 For the underlying metaphysical triad, see for example Proclus *El. Theol.* pr. 65: 'All that subsists in any fashion has its being either in its cause, as an originative potency; or as a substantial predicate; or by participation, in the manner of an image.'

137 The Greek noun *logos* is notoriously difficult to translate. It can refer to language, reason or rationality, and in Neoplatonic ontology, a 'reason-principle' or 'formative principle' that conveys a timeless Platonic Form in intellect (*nous*) to soul (*psukhê*), and finally to fruition in nature (*phusis*). I have tried the English noun 'formula' here (and above, 10,8), since it imperfectly gestures toward the concepts of a verbal formula (*OED* 1c), a prescription or recipe (*OED* 2), and (through its etymology) a form.

In the Neoplatonist sense relevant in this passage, a 'superior' cause contains in a seminal way the 'reason-principles' or 'formulas' that will come to fruition in its effect. For instance, intellect (*nous*) contains the Form of a human being in a seminal way, and that Form flowers as particular human beings. Similarly here, the gods (or 'analogical' daimons) contain as if in a seed the principles of 'essential' daimons, who are manifest that seminal potential.

For the illustrative imagery of a seed, which the Neoplatonists adopted from the Stoics, see for example Plotinus *Enn.* 3.2.2,18–23: '. . . just as in the formative principle (*logos*) in a seed all the parts are together and in the same place, and none of them fights with any other . . . then something comes to be in bulk, and the different parts are in different places . . . so from intellect (*nous*) which is one, and the formative principle (*logos*) which proceeds from it, this All has arisen and separated into parts' (tr. Armstrong 1988, lightly adapted). See also Proclus *in Parm.* 754,10–14.

138 The Neoplatonic rule that 'every productive cause is superior to that which it produces', Proclus *El. Theol.* pr. 7. For the distinction between a property possessed causally (*kat' aitian*) and existentially (*kath' huparxin*), consider fire as an illustration: if I sit near a fire for an hour, the fire and I are both 'hot'. But the fire is hot *as a cause* (*kat' aitian*), and has to be present first in order for me to be heated.

139 Isocrates 1.13. Olympidorous' choice of citations is interesting. He is happy to use Isocrates (though he is hardly a Platonist) as an authority, presumably because he

testifies to classical usage and has an important place in the rhetorical curriculum. In *To Daimonikos* (1.13), Isocrates exhorts a young man, coincidentally named Daemonicus, to demonstrate devotion to the gods (*theoi*) by sacrifice and maintenance of one's vows. He goes on to advise Daemonicus to honour *to daimonion*, 'the daimonic power', at all times, but particularly in civic festivals; in context, *daimonion* seems to refer to the gods of the state, whom Olympiodorus is discussing as higher powers, or 'daimons by analogy'.

140 Throughout the translation, I have usually lightly adapted Richmond Lattimore's translation of passages from Homer's *Iliad* (Lattimore 1951) and James Huddelston's translation of passages from Homer's *Odyssey* for the Chicago Homer (Huddleston 2006), with modifications to suit Olympiodorus' use of the texts.

141 Cf. Proclus *in Alc.* 74,5–6; fr. 155 Kern; Kern cites Proclus *in Crat.* 27,21. Olympiodorus' point here is that the gods (*theoi*) are often called 'daimons' by analogy, although they are truly greater than daimons.

142 *Works and Days* 122–3.

143 This might be a subtle gesture toward the view, originating with the Stoics, that human beings share 'common concepts' (*koinai ennoiai*) that are basically true, such as the 'concept' that divine beings exist. For Olympiodorus' use of common concepts, see below, 18,3–4 ('we know certain things . . . even without demonstration' by means of common concepts), 40,20, and *in Gorg.* 44.7. See also Tarrant 1997, 189–91 and for the role of the common concepts in Neoplatonism more broadly, see van den Berg 2009; for the form of the 'argument from consensus' in antiquity and the common concepts more generally, see Obbink 1992 and Brittain 2005.

144 I have structured and numbered the following lengthy and complex sentence to show the structure of the thought more plainly in English. There are many parenthetical clauses in the Greek and the syntax is interrupted in several places (16,11; 17,4); this might reflect Olympiodorus' speech or the note-taker's process. A more direct translation would run roughly as follows.

Just as our soul, streaming with life, bubbling over with it, and unable to exist without engendering life (*zôopoiein*),
 (there are times when it is inactive with respect to the cognitive [faculties] (*kata tas gnôstikas*), for instance when it is overcome by lethargy, but with respect to the life-engendering (*zôtikos*) [part] this is never the case),
  since the shell-form body was not always attached to it, the ovoid (*ôioeidês*) vehicle, or luminous (*augoeides*) vehicle, was invented (*epenoêthê*) for it,
   (for it goes by both names:
    [it is called] 'ovoid' on account of its shape (*skhêma*),

for it is not altogether spherical like the heavenly [bodies], but less
spherical [than them], and for this reason they say that it sometimes
suffers 'distortion' (*diastrophên*), but certainly isn't destroyed, because
it is of the same essence (*ousia*) as the heavenly bodies, that is, of the
fifth body, [and] therefore also everlasting;
   and it is called 'luminous' from its essence (*ousias*),
      because it is transparent and aetherial);
   and so, just as they assigned this luminous vehicle to the soul, in order
that, being fastened all through it (*dia pantos*), it might always engender
life, in the same way, in the case of the heavenly bodies, which cannot
cease from activity (*energein*), they fastened this essentially daimonic race
to them,
   for our souls are not always fastened to them on account of our shedding our
feathers and descending into becoming.

This [daimonic race], then, being intermediary, is the interpreter for [people]
here [on earth] of [messages] from the gods.

145 The soul's capacity of generating life is fundamental, and always active: indeed,
the usual Greek word for 'alive' is *empsukhos*, literally 'having soul in it'. (As
Plato's Socrates argues in the *Phaedo* (102B–107B), one cannot imagine a soul
without life). The soul's capacities for consciousness and cognition are treated
as 'stacking' on top of elementary capacities like life, growth, and sensitivity to
the environment; the 'lower' functions can continue while the 'higher'
functions rest.

146 In later Neoplatonist thought, as a soul descends into embodied existence, it
'collects' a series of envelopes or vehicles on the way; as the soul re-ascends, these
vehicles are sequentially left behind in their natural spheres. The highest vehicles
are extremely rare and fine; in fact, the highest of all is simply pure light, a
'luminous vehicle' that Proclus identified with place (*topos*) (see Griffin 2012,
161–86). The lower vehicles are increasingly dense, and come with various
functions and limitations. For an overview of the theory of the soul's vehicle in
Neoplatonism, especially in the theory's seminal form in Iamblichus, see
Finamore 1985; for the theory in Proclus see Chlup 2012, 104–5 and Siorvanes
1996, 131–3.

147 This refers to the 'sowing' or 'implanting' of each human soul into a star at
Timaeus 41D–E. Olympiodorus' plural ('they assigned') suggests that he has the
'young gods' in mind here, although in the *Timaeus* the Demiurge himself
implants souls in stars. Later (42E–47E), the young gods develop bodies for the
souls; for the Neoplatonist, these natural bodies would be the final step after a

series of layers of denser 'vehicles', descending from the luminous vehicle (see previous note).

148 For this notion, and the discussion that follows, see Plato *Symposium* 202E, where Love is a great daimon located between (*metaxu*) the divine and the mortal.

149 Thus each heavenly being contains a more or less complete 'chain of being', reaching from the One (the peak of the Neoplatonic ontology) all the way 'down' to the pure potentiality of Matter.

150 For the following discussion, see also Proclus *in Alc.* 71,3–72,12.

151 The Neoplatonists maintained that common concepts (*koinai ennoiai*) must precede and lie beyond demonstration. This has common Platonic, Aristotelian and Stoic roots; compare for example Aristotle's position (*An. Post.* 1.2) that every process of proof must begin from the indemonstrable (*anapodeikton*).

152 *Od.* 3.27. In this passage, Athena replies to Telemachus, who wonders how he can greet Nestor, that he will find a plan in his own mind (*phrenes*) or a daimon will put it there. This Homeric passage, together with *Od.* 19.138 below, are also cited by Proclus *in Remp.* 2.298, 24–7.

153 *Od.* 19.138. Penelope describes how she came by her strategy to set up a great web and weave, to delay her suitors.

154 The source of this saying is unclear.

155 Westerink compares Orphic fr. 353 Kern and *Chaldaean Oracles* p. 10 Kroll.

156 See above, 17,12–13.

157 The reference probably points to *Iliad* 14.279, where those under Tartarus are called 'Titans', though our standard text of Homer reads slightly differently: *tous hupotartarious hoi Titênes kaleontai.*

158 Compare Proclus *in Alc.* 72,12–73,8.

159 The Neoplatonist philosopher Plotinus was represented by his pupil Porphyry as having such a divine daimon (*Life of Plotinus* 10.15–25): 'An Egyptian priest who came to Rome . . . asked Plotinus to come and see a visible manifestation of his own daimon evoked. Plotinus readily consented . . . When the daimon was summoned to appear a god came and not a being of the daimonic order, and the Egyptian said, "Blessed are you who have a god for your daimon and not a companion of the subordinate order" ' (tr. Armstrong 1966). Olympiodorus also suggests (below, 21,5) that Socrates' daimon was divine.

160 In this discussion there are aspects of various Platonic views, including the *Phaedrus* myth (246Aff.), where souls follow in the train of specific gods, and the 'chains of inspiration' in the *Ion*, where poets are inspired through chains suspended from the gods. But in the context of this discussion of our 'allotted daimon', the thought here about the possibility of ascent by following a divine example may also owe a debt to Plotinus, *Enneads* 3.4 ('On our allotted daimon').

For example, at 3.4.3, 21–4, Plotinus explains that 'if a human being is able to follow the *daimôn* which is above him, he comes to be himself above, living that *daimôn's* life, and giving the dominion to that better part of himself to which he is being led; and after that spirit he rises to another, until he reaches the heights. For soul (*psukhê*) is many things, and all things, both those above and those below [cf. Aristotle *DA* 3.6–7], down to the limit of all life, and we are each an intelligible cosmos (*kosmos noêtos*), making contact with this lower world by the powers of soul below, but with the intelligible world by its powers above, and the powers of the cosmos' (tr. Armstrong 1967, adapted).

161 The thought here draws, among other sources, on a number of Platonic dialogues: the notion that we are all linked to a certain god in our nature and for our inspiration draws on the *Ion* and the *Phaedrus*, for instance, while the insistence that each person 'does his own work' is indebted to *Republic* (see for example 435B, 443D–E).

162 See Proclus *in Alc.* 78,7–82,8.

163 Cf. 39,1–3 below.

164 As mentioned above, Plotinus was said to have a god for a daimon (*Life of Plotinus* 10.15–25), an important hagiographical point for Neoplatonists that may lie in the background in this account of Socrates. On the hagiographies of Neoplatonic philosophers, see for example M.J. Edwards, *Neoplatonic Saints: The Lives of Plotinus and Proclus by their Students* (Liverpool, 2000).

165 The 'guardian' of Alcibiades, to whom Socrates compares his divine guardian, is the celebrated Athenian statesman Pericles (124C).

166 For cases of Socrates' 'hearing' the divine voice, see for example *Phaedrus* 242C (where the voice prevents Socrates from leaving before he offers a 'palinode' to love, countering his earlier speech), and *Theages* 128D–129C (where the voice intervenes when Charmides plans to train for a race at Nemea, and again when Timarchus is about to leave a banquet, and the departure leads to his death).

167 As again below, this phrase signals the popular religion of Christianity. See Introduction §1.2.

168 Westerink (1990, 335) comments that 'the last clause is not quite clear; Olympiodorus may mean that the phrase was usually addressed to monks'. The marginal comment in the manuscript, which dates to the ninth century, paraphrases 'may your angel be disposed in such-and-such a way (toward you), if you do this'.

169 Perhaps a gentle pun on Plato's name; compare 2,35–41 above.

170 The *Chaldaean Oracles* are a collection of hexameter verses 'purported to have been "handed down by the gods" to a certain Julian the Chaldaean and/or his son, Julian the Theurgist, who flourished during the early second century AD'

(Majercik 1989, 1). They were deeply influential on later Neoplatonists from Porphyry (c. 232–303 AD) to Damascius (c. 462–537 AD); they have been called the 'Bible of the Neoplatonists' (Majercik 1989, 2–3). Especially important work on the Neoplatonists' relationship to the Oracles was done by H.-D. Saffrey; see for example Saffrey 1981.

171 Westerink compares *Chaldaean Oracles* p. 44 Kroll = frr. 88–9 Des Places, which discusses problematic, material daimons that 'draw down souls' and are 'turned toward nature' (*tên phusin epistrephomenon*); cf. Majercik 1989, 82–5.

172 Cf. *Symp.* 178A, 189C, 195A, 202D. The Greek noun *erôs* can be translated as love in the sense of passionate desire.

173 Orph. fr. 82 Kern.; cf. Proclus 65,1.

174 Epicharmus, fr. 12 Diels.

175 That is, Christianity.

176 Perhaps an oblique allusion to the risks that Olympiodorus might face for lecturing on religious matters at odds with the position of the state. See Introduction §1.

177 Olympiodorus, with his usual diplomacy, is interpreting the doctrine of daimons in ethical terms that are familiar and welcome to a Christian audience, and unlikely to provoke dissent and criticism (cf. Introduction §1). His gentle allusion to the condemnation of Socrates is a nice touch.

178 *akron aôton*: see Callimachus, *in Apoll.* 112.

179 The adjective *anamartêtos* literally means 'without (*an*) error, fault, or sin (*hamartia*)'. It might imply either infallibility or moral blamelessness; the latter is more likely here.

180 For the judgement of Minos and Rhadamanthys in Plato, see for example *Gorgias* 523Aff. and *Apology* 41A.

181 For the use of 'recoil', or 'rolling back up' (*aneillein*), compare *Symp.* 206D, where Diotima explains that '. . . whenever pregnant animals or persons draw near to beauty, they become gentle or joyfully disposed and give birth and reproduce; but near ugliness they are foul faced and draw back in pain; they turn away and coil back up (*aneilletai*) and do not reproduce . . .' (tr. Nehamas and Woodruff, lightly adapted).

182 The Greek *pros to deon* ('toward what is right or necessary to do') echoes a passage of Plutarch: worse souls are driven *pros to deon* by the *daimôn* using *metameleia* (change of purpose, repentance) and shame (*On the Daimonion* 592C). Olympiodorus nowhere else talks about turning back *pros to deon*, although he does often use the phrase *pros to theion*, that is 'to the divine' (e.g. *in Grg.* 26.18, *in Alc.* 18,1). With Plato's *Symposium* in the air, it is almost tempting to read *pros to theion* here instead of the MSS reading *deon*.

183 Pindar, fr. 214 Schroeder = *Republic* 1, 331A.

184 Supplied by Westerink 1982, v, comparing Damascius *in Phaed.* 1.271 (with his note).

185 That is, the Greek noun *suneidos* can mean (1) a genus 'consciousness', as well as (2) *cognitive* consciousness (in English, 'understanding') concerned with true and false, a species of that genus, and (3) *moral* consciousness (in English, 'conscience'), another species of the genus which has just been discussed above. One might bring this out in English by translating (1) the genus 'awareness', (2) its cognitive species 'intellectual awareness', and (3) its moral species 'moral awareness'.

186 I have added this line to mark the transition from the *theôria* (survey) to the *lexis* (line-by-line commentary), maintaining consistency with these delineations in later lectures.

187 See Proclus *in Alc.* 24,10–27,12. Proclus suggests (1) that the use of Alcibiades' father's name renders him more accommodating to Socrates, thanks to Clinias' fame; (2) that reminding Alcibiades of Clinias' excellence is a good tactic for exhorting him to excellence in his own right; and (3) in a metaphysical register, that the reminder of Alcibiades' father 'is a symbol of the reversion of souls to their invisible causes'.

188 Hom. *Il.* 10.68–9.

189 The battle of Coronea was fought in 447 BC between the Delian League led by Athens, and the Boeotian League, as part of the First Peloponnesian War. It is described by Thucydides (1.113) and Herodotus (8.17), who also notes the bravery of Alcibiades' father: Cleinias brought to the war two hundred men and a ship at his own expense. Cleinias' participation is also mentioned by Plutarch, *Life of Alcibiades* 1, who describes how Alcibiades subsequently came to be the ward of Pericles.

190 Cf. Plato *Phaedrus* 238C.

191 Hom. *Il.* 6.209. The saying occurs during Glaucus' meeting with Diomedes on the battlefield, which results in both heroes going their separate ways. Glaucus reports the instructions of his father Hippolochus, which includes this commandment alongside the famous instruction *aien aristeuein* ('always to excel').

192 Compare Socrates' suggestion at *Phaedrus* 271A–272B that the true orator must first recognise and distinguish the different types of souls of his audience, before attempting to persuade them.

193 Cf. *Theaetetus* 155D.

194 As Westerink points out, this is the first of the traditional definitions of philosophy (see Ammonius *Isagoge* 2,22–3; Elias 8,30–1; David 20,27). The

study of 'being *qua* being' is one of Aristotle's celebrated definitions of first philosophy (metaphysics) in *Metaphysics* G (4), E (6), and K (11).

195 So Hesiod *Theogony* 265–6 and 780 describes the parentage of Iris (the Rainbow).

196 This rather mystifying remark might, with Westerink, be a very liberal reminiscence of Aristotle *Metaphysics* A 2, 983a12–20 (describing the 'wonder' provoked by various real phenomena, including geometrical phenomena such as the incommensurability of the diagonal of a square).

197 Cf. Demosthenes 19.136. Philip was informed 'that a democracy is the most unstable and capricious thing in the world, like a restless wave of the sea ruffled by the breeze as chance will have it. One man comes, another goes; no one attends to, or even remembers, the common weal' (tr. Vince). Olympiodorus' compressed point is just this: if it is insulting to call the 'people' of a state a 'mob', then a mob is worse than the people.

198 So also Proclus *in Alc.* 46,13–47,12.

199 The genitive measuring *time within which* or *during which* is a classical usage that felt unfamiliar or archaic to Olympiodorus' sixth-century AD audience.

200 That is, the Greek word *kai* is not functioning here as a conjunction like 'and', and plays no role in the meaning of the clause (I have positioned the English 'too' to suggest the ambiguity). As Denyer 2001 points out ad loc. (103A6), the words (*kai husteron . . .*) are an idiomatic formula in Plato for 'dropping a subject' for the time being, for example at *Symp.* 175E, 'We'll sort this out *kai oligon husteron*.' Denyer paraphrases the Greek, 'you will have another opportunity to ask about it later, and therefore we will not discuss it now', and observes that Socrates never seems to return to the subject explicitly in *Alc.;* Olympiodorus, on the other hand, as the next paragraph shows, thinks the promise is fulfilled shortly, at *Alc.* 105E–106A.

201 On Alcibiades' advice to Sparta to fortify Deceleia in Attica, an important symbolic and strategic turning-point against his own city of Athens in the Peloponnesian War, see Plutarch *Life of Alcibiades* 23.

202 In about 432 BC (just before the Peloponnesian war broke out in 431) Athens imposed controversial economic sanctions on the city of Megara, preventing Megarians from accessing the markets of the Athenian Empire. Although the ostensible motives for the decree were not economic or military, the decree has been viewed as Pericles' deliberate provocation of Sparta (with which Megara was allied), or conversely as a pretext for Sparta to go to war (cf. Thucydides 1.139).

203 Cf. Plutarch *Life of Alcibiades* 7: Alcibiades hears that Pericles is busy considering how to render his accounts to the Athenians, and comments that it would be better if Pericles did not have to render his accounts at all. The famous statue of Athena Parthenos by Pheidias was regarded as one of the greatest images of

antiquity, and, like the rest of Pericles' building project on the Acropolis, it was not an inexpensive enterprise.

204 On the eve of the Athenian military expedition to Syracuse in Sicily (415 BC), which Alcibiades was slated to command, allegations were levelled by his political rivals that he had defaced the sacred images of Hermes (herms) and mimicked the Eleusinian mysteries (cf. Plutarch *Life of Alcibiades* 19, Thucydides 6.53). The result was that Alcibiades was recalled in mid-voyage to Sicily; but instead of returning to Athens to stand trial, he defected to Sparta. The Athenian expedition was ultimately routed and destroyed at Syracuse; whether the result would have been different under Alcibiades' military leadership has been a subject for speculation since antiquity.

205 The following explanations substantially compress Proclus' corresponding discussion at *in Alc.* 86,7–92,3. Proclus expressly sets out the constraints on a viable solution: it must vindicate both the *daimonion* and Socrates in allowing the conversation to take place, and it must show that Alcibiades benefits from the conversation. The answers in play, in brief, are: (1) Alcibiades would have done worse if he had not spent time with Socrates (attributed to unnamed parties); (2) Alcibiades was good only as long as he was with Socrates (attributed to Xenophon, and also the view expressed by Alcibiades himself in Plato's *Symposium*); but (3) the *daimonion* still allowed Socrates to converse with Alcibiades, not out of ignorance or the 'unpredictability' of human choice, but with regard to the whole cycle of multiple lives (endorsed by Proclus).

206 Platonists used solar imagery to convey the boundless compassion of the Good or the One, which can and *does* overflow throughout the entire chain of being without diminishing itself (see for example Plotinus *Enn.* 5.3.12,33–53). That imagery has roots in Plato's own analogy of the Good with the Sun (*Republic* 6, 508C).

207 There is support for this explanation in Socrates' comment that he will do philosophy with anyone he meets, 'young and old, foreigner and citizen', without discrimination (30A). But universal care does not explain why Socrates would *especially* follow Alcibiades about (e.g. *Protagoras* 309A, *Symposium* 213C), not least if Alcibiades proves to be a faulty subject of his attention. Perhaps a Neoplatonist would reply that *only* the highest principles can reach the lowest (compare Olympiodorus' remarks on the 'Proclan rule' at *in Alc.* 109,18–110,15). Thus the lower Alcibiades 'tumbles' in the hierarchy of being, the more Socrates *must* reach out to rescue him. (In a metaphysical register, Socrates represents the 'intellect of the soul', and Alcibiades represents the soul's capacity for reason, which may be confused in the sea of temporality and materiality: cf. Proclus *in Alc.* 43,7–10, and Griffin 2014b.)

208 There may be a problem with the text here; I have suggested a sentence that I think gives the right sense.

209 Olympiodorus elides two possible solutions distinguished by Proclus (whose corresponding discussion is at *in Alc.* 86,7–87,2): that Socrates actually *did* make Alcibiades better, since he would presumably have become even worse without Socrates' aid (a view attributed to unnamed sources); and that Alcibiades was good just as long as he was with Socrates, but declined when he left his company (which is Xenophon's main point at *Mem.* 1.2.24–5).

210 Ancient Platonists developed a more or less systematic picture of the transmigration of souls, in dialogue with Platonic texts such as the 'Myth of Er' (*Republic* 10, 614A–621D), the myth of the winged soul (*Phaedrus* 246A–249D), and the myth of the soul's judgement (*Gorgias* 523A–527A). Upon moving on from this embodied, human existence, the soul of Alcibiades would have proceeded to the waystation portrayed in the Myth of Er for judgement, purification if necessary, and eventually the voluntary choice of a new life.

211 Hom. *Il.* 5.201.

212 Proclus stresses that the divine remains just where it is, and it is actually we who change and approach the god, even if the god *seems* to us ('in invocations and visions', 92,8–10) to approach us. He also suggests that Socrates might treat Alcibiades as similar to a statue of the divine, approaching visible beauty as a sacred 'image' (*agalma*) of intelligible beauty (*in Alc.* 92,10–16): 'As those who are skilled in theurgy reverence even the images of the gods evident to our senses, so also the perfect lover pursues even the image of divine beauty that has proceeded to the lowest levels, as depending therefrom' (tr. O'Neill 1965). This imagery has roots in Plato's *Phaedrus*, where the lover treats his beloved like a sacred image (*agalma*) of a god (252D–E).

Olympiodorus does not mention the analogy from theurgy here, possibly because he is sensitive to the concerns of his Christian audience, although in general Olympiodorus' discussion is simply more compressed.

213 This seems slightly puzzling, but see Proclus 92,16–18, who explains that 'the term "good hope" (*euelpis*) endears (*oikeioi*) the young man to [Socrates] in an amazing way (for to call help given to Alcibiades "good hope" on his own part is surely altogether endearing)' (tr. O'Neill 1965, modified).

214 The quote appears in *Vatican Gnomology* 375, published by Leo Sternbach in *Wiener Studien* 11 (1889), 54–5 (but there attributed to Anacreon); in Stobaeus 4.47.12 (attributed to Pindar), in Diogenes Laertius 5.18 (attributed to Aristotle), in Aelian *VH* 13.29 (attributed to Plato), and in Olympiodorus *in Phaed.* 39,11–12.

215 Proclus explains: 'to allow him at all is evidence that Alcibiades was not altogether disinclined to good offices on Socrates' part. So the more the young man advanced as a result of philosophical discussion, the more Socrates considered the daimonic power would assist him toward his love' (see *in Alc.* 93,7–10).

216 The Greek is *neanikôtatos*, literally 'youngest', 'freshest', but perhaps (as with Denyer ad loc.) here 'vigorous' or 'brash'. Later, it will be the *antiquity* of Socrates' and Alcibiades' lineages that will be playfully boasted (cf. *Alc.* 121A).

217 This was Olympiodorus' focus in Lecture 2.

218 The device is called 'chiasmus' for the Greek letter *khi* (written X). It runs:

AB

BA

In the Homeric example that follows, 'Laodameia' ends the line at *Iliad* 6.197, and begins line 198. Compare Olymp. *in Meteor.* 124,5.

219 *Il.* 6.197–8.

220 Antisthenes fr. 14 Mullach.

221 *Iliad* 2.673–4.

222 Thucydides 2.65.9.

223 Eupolis fr. 94,3 Kock; cf. Westerink 1966.

224 See above, 6,6–7.

225 In the following part of the lecture, Olympiodorus argues that Socrates praises Alcibiades' natural excellence (*phusikê aretê*) in order to prepare him for a criticism of his lack of higher, philosophical grades of excellence, and to help him to advance to those grades, beginning with civic excellence (*politikê aretê*). See Introduction §2.1.

226 *Phaedo* 69B.

227 *Hippolytus* 352.

228 The text is corrupt at 31,1, but I translate Westerink's conjectural emendation of M's *protreptên* to *propetê* (from *propetês*, 'precipitate, reckless, out of control'). I am grateful to Carlos Steel for this suggestion, and for helping me through this difficult passage.

229 That is, no human being is entirely independent, and Alcibiades' vanity makes him *especially* dependent on (the evaluations of) others.

Many ancient philosophical schools regarded self-sufficiency (*autarkeia*) as a feature of the good life. Withdrawal from, or moderation of, the pleasures of the sense-sphere could be an important instrument in achieving it. For example, the Epicureans pursued self-sufficiency in moderation (Epicurus *Letter to Menoeceus* 127–32, LS 21B: 'We also regard self-sufficiency as a great good, not with the aim of always living off little, but to enable us to live off little if we do not have much'), while the Stoics argued that ethical excellence or virtue (*aretê*) alone was sufficient for the good life (Cicero *Tusc.* 5.40–1, 81–2 = LS 63 LM), allowing a good person to be wholly self-sufficient.

230 The allusion is to a verse allegedly delivered from the Oracle at Delphi (*Anth. Pal.* 14.73): when it came to determining the best people of Hellas, the Megarians were 'out of the reckoning' – we should say 'not even in the running'. The idea is an old one in the Socratic and Platonic tradition, that by obsessing over external goods we devalue our own soul. For this idea in the *Alcibiades* itself, as well as Plato and Xenophon, see Introduction §3.2–3; for its Neoplatonic adaptation, see for example Plotinus *Enn.* 5.1[10] 1–3.

231 From the Fifteenth *Epigram* ascribed to Plato (15,3–4 Diehl), *Greek Anthology* 6.1. The full epigram runs, 'I, Laïs, who laughed so disdainfully at Greece and once kept a swarm of young lovers at my door, dedicate this mirror to the Paphian – for I do not wish to see me as I am, and cannot see me as I was' (tr. Edmonds, rev. Cooper and Hutchinson 1997).

   Many of the epigrams in the collection attributed to Plato treat similar themes. For example, 'I throw the apple at you, and if you are willing to love me, take it and share your girlhood with me; but if your thoughts are what I pray they are not, even then take it, and consider how short-lived is beauty' (*Epigram* 7, *Greek Anth.* 5.79).

232 Proclus expands on the limited value of ancestry at *in Alc.* 112,19–113,1: 'Of such nobility of birth [from the divine], that according to natural succession is a mere image, concentrating whereon souls are filled with an empty arrogance, not recognising this very saying in the *Theaetetus* that there is nothing surprising if "one who prides himself on a list of twenty-five ancestors" should in the course of unlimited generations be, more remotely, descended from slaves. All such matters admit of many variations, but the stable and eternal nobility of birth in souls depends upon the gods around whom they have been sown . . .' (tr. O'Neill 1965).

   Compare *Theaetetus* 175A: '[E]very single man has countless hosts of ancestors, near and remote, among whom are to be found, in every instance, rich men and beggars, kings and slaves, Greeks and foreigners, by the thousand. When men pride themselves upon a pedigree of twenty-five ancestors, and trace their descent back to Heracles the son of Amphitryon, they seem to him to be taking a curious interest in trifles.'

233 See Iamblichus *Vit. Pyth.* 29.162. Westerink also compares Diogenes Laertius 8.10, Aristotle *Nicomachean Ethics* 8.7, 1157b36, and *Eudemian Ethics* 7.6, 1240b2 and 1241b13.

234 *Nicomachean Ethics* 9.4, 1166a31–32: 'the good person. . . is related to his friend as to himself (for his friend is another self)'. Westerink also compares *Eudemian Ethics* 7.12, 1245a30, and ps.-Aristotle *Magna Moralia* 2.15, 1213a13.

235 *Gorgias* 515C–516D.

236 Aristides was an Athenian statesman of the generation before Pericles, and he was reputed for good and just leadership; for example, Socrates remarks on his fairness at *Gorgias* 526A–B, and Plutarch wrote a *Life* about him. On the attribution of this reference to 'the comic', see Westerink 1996, 175–6.

237 On the common concepts, see above, 18,3 with note. Olympiodorus' point is that there is always some degree of truth in our conceptual framework: our 'common concepts' are never *completely* divorced from reality.

238 Throughout the following discussion, Olympiodorus argues that Alcibiades always had in mind some higher, intelligible reality (like the true Form of Beauty) even as he mistakenly took an illusory image for the reality – and so he was not entirely in error.

239 For this image of 'fighting over shadows', or 'shadow-boxing', see *Republic* 7, 520C–D, a reflection on Plato's Allegory of the Cave. Philosophers who revisit the 'cave' would find there 'cities inhabited and ruled darkly as in a dream by people who fight one another for shadows', unless philosophers who have seen the truth are able to bring about a change. See also below, 42,14–15.

240 Hom. *Il.* 5.451–3. At this point in the narrative, Aeneas has just been wounded, and Apollo whisks him to safety and replaces him in the battle with an image or phantom (*eidôlon*).

241 Cf. *Timaeus* 28A–29A: 'But whenever the Demiurge looks at what is always changeless and, using a thing of that kind as his model, reproduces its form and character, then, of necessity, all that he so completes is beautiful. But were he to look at a thing that has come to be and use as his model something that has been begotten, his work will lack beauty' (tr. Zeyl in Cooper and Hutchinson 1997).

242 Reading *hen, hênôtai* after Westerink. I understand Olympiodorus to refer here to the hypostasis 'the One', the highest grade of reality among the classical Neoplatonic hypostases 'One, Intellect, Soul'. The One, which lies properly beyond being, is the principle of the good and unification of all beings: see Proclus, *Elements of Theology* propositions 1–13, especially 11–12.

243 For this episode see Plutarch *Life of Alcibiades* 10. In terms of purchasing power, ten Athenian talents would equal roughly 200,000 dollars in early twenty-first-century American currency.

244 See *Republic* 440B–C.

245 For the following discussion, compare Proclus *in Alc.* 97,15–98,10.

246 Referring to 14,20–6 above. Taking *prôên* literally (it can mean 'the day before yesterday', LSJ A II), this might imply that Lecture 4 was delivered two days after Lecture 3. If that spacing was typical, it is tempting to speculate that Olympiodorus might have delivered the course of twenty-eight lectures at a rate of about three per week, finishing the course in about nine to ten weeks.

247 Compare Proclus *in Alc.* 100,10–22.

248 At *Theaetetus* 175B, the philosopher laughs at those persons who cannot free their mindless soul (*anoêtou psukhês*) from vanity or conceit (*khaunotês*, literally 'porousness') on account of their family lineage.

249 Compare Proclus *in Alc.* 107,19–24.

250 Above, 31,15–16.

251 See above, 7,4–8, and cf. 30,2–4.

252 If this is meant to be a direct quotation, it is hard to find anything similar in *Theaetetus*. But Olympiodorus often uses this kind of locution ('he says', *phêsin*) to refer, not to direct speech, but to his interpretation of a doctrine in a work; he might mean that the power of knowledge is a lesson that the reader can draw from the *Theaetetus* as a whole. In any case, this is certainly a view that occurs in Plato: Westerink compares *Protagoras* 352B–D, *Republic* 5.477D, and Proclus *in Alc.* 155,8–9; see also our text, 55,17–19 below.

253 Cf. Proclus *in Alc.* 199,6–7.

254 Cf. Proclus *in Alc.* 119,14–23.

255 Cf. Proclus *in Alc.* 120,1–8.

256 Here, the Greek noun *logos* means something like 'meaningful speech', as opposed to meaningless utterances. In general, *logos* can be translated by many English nouns, including 'reason', 'argument', and 'speech'. Olympiodorus' opening serves to contrast Socrates' rational arguments with Alcibiades' less rational remarks; note that we 'learn from' (*manthanein*) Socrates' words but 'examine' (*exetazein*) Alcibiades' utterances. 'Examination', of course, is crucial to the Socratic life (cf. *Apology* 38A5, where 'the unexamined life' is not worth living). I am grateful to the anonymous reader for this lecture for these points.

257 It was a commonplace of ancient class logic that human beings are distinguished from other animals by our possession of reason or language; see for example Porphyry *Isagoge* 4,21–32, with commentary by Barnes 2003, 110–11; but Porphyry also argues strongly in ch. 3 of his *On Abstinence* that animals possess reason (on this puzzle, see recently Edwards 2014).

258 That is, chiastically.

259 The account of caring for reputation here (and above and below) is indebted to Plato's imagery of the tripartite soul and state in *Republic* 4.

260 See also 135,11–13, Olymp. *in Gorg.* 2.3 (16,5–10), 12.2 (63,25–8). For the dichotomy, see for example Frede 1988.

261 *Dunamis* can mean a power, potential or capacity, while *energeia* can mean the actualisation of that potential: Aristotle works out this technical vocabulary in detail in *Metaphysics* Th. [9]. 'Potential' and 'actuality' would represent that vocabulary more clearly here than 'power' and 'activity', but it is easier to maintain the latter consistently throughout this section of the translation.

262 See Proclus *El. Theol.* pr. 77: 'All that exists potentially is advanced to actuality by the agency of something which is actually what the other is potentially' (tr. Dodds).

263 The text is uncertain here; I adopt Westerink's proposed supplement <*ei kai mê tôi khronôi*> and translate what I hope is the intended force of the sentence.

264 The intended subject of 'he says' (*phêsin*) might be Socrates (the idea could then be that Socrates, when he acknowledges Alcibiades' state of amazement, is implicitly stating and endorsing the reasons for his amazement), or Plato, or perhaps Olympiodorus' source for this explanation, such as Proclus or Damascius.

265 I take the idea to be the following: Socrates could not have approached Alcibiades just as the latter was about to approach him (with apparent clairvoyance), unless these facts were true: the leadership of the daimon, and the priority of the actual to the potential in nature; and these facts are genuinely worthy of wonder.

266 For the quotation, see Hippocrates *De Morbis* 1.5; cf. Proclus 120,14–15, Olymp. *in Phaed.* 56,7–8. The force of the saying may be that the real 'soul' of a course of treatment lies in good timing; or, read differently, it might mean that the patient must be willing, in their soul or mind (*psukhê*), to implement the doctor's instructions. The anonymous reader for this section also points out that this could allude to the first Hippocratic *Aphorism*: 'Life is short, and Art long; the crisis (*kairos*) fleeting; experience perilous, and decision difficult. The physician must not only be prepared to do what is right himself, but also to make the patient, the attendants, and externals cooperate' (tr. Adams).

267 These seem to be recollections in broad brush strokes of Aristotelian passages like *Nicomachean Ethics* 1.4 (1096a26–7), where the good in the category of When is the right moment or opportunity (*kairos*).

268 Cf. Proclus *in Alc.* 121,11–13: 'As place is determined by nature in a manner appropriate to each body, so also different portions of time are suited to different activities . . . Such time is the right moment for each activity as supplying the good and the ultimate purpose to the doers and to what is actually being done' (tr. O'Neill 1965, lightly modified).

269 That is, any being that is subject to coming-to-be, such as a plant or animal; such beings undergo a process of entelechy, beginning from their raw potential to be something (*dunamis*), to 'actualise' their natural goal or *telos*. Particularly in a Neoplatonic context, such beings require another fully actualised being to bring them to completion (cf. Proclus *El. Theol.* pr. 77, cited above); there is also a religious or initiatory sense to 'completion' or 'perfection' (*teleiôsis*).

270 As Olympiodorus discussed in the preceding survey, Socrates and Alcibiades, though not physically present together, should maintain the relationship of an actual being (Socrates) to a being with the potential to be actualised (Alcibiades). Compare Proclus *in Alc.* 122,10–15: 'On one side, the future agent must be full to overflowing and so prepared for activity that, although he destined recipient is not present, it is itself at full strength and stimulated to communication; and on the other side, the subject to be acted upon must be eager for participation and apply itself to the power of fulfilment, and if that not be present, through the greatest suitability be aroused toward participation' (tr. O'Neill 1965, lightly modified).

271 Cf. Proclus *in Alc.* 125,2–15. Proclus stresses that Plato's Demiurge desired for all things to be good (*Timaeus* 30A). It is a standard Neoplatonist view that all things 'want' the Good (see for example Proclus *El. Theol.* prr. 8–13), with roots in both Plato and Aristotle (see for example Arist. *Metaph.* 12.7, 1072a27–b4).

272 Proclus also stresses that Socrates 'has the form of the good' (is *agathoeidês*), 45,4, and that he functions as a 'good daimon' to Alcibiades (45,8).

273 *Gorgias* 467C–468D.

274 Olympiodorus anticipates studying the *Gorgias* with the class, as the second dialogue to be read in the Iamblichean curriculum following the *Alcibiades*. The same language ('with the god's favour') occurs in the heading of each lecture.

275 Compare Olympiodorus *in Gorg.* 15.4–5 (80,4–81,1).

276 For example at Hom. *Il.* 2.157; *Od.* 4.762.

277 Cf. Proclus *in Alc.* 126,22–127,4.

278 This may be a quotation, but I am not aware of the source.

279 For this label of the chief or 'chorus-leading' philosopher, see also Olympiodorus' comments on the *Theaetetus* above (Lecture 1) at 1,12 and *Theaet.* 173C–177B. Olympiodorus means the dialectician, in Plato's sense at *Republic* 7, 511B: the power of dialectic grasps 'the unhypothetical first principle of all'. Below, Olympiodorus also uses Aristotle's label of 'first philosophy' for the activity of this philosopher, namely, metaphysics. But Olympiodorus also goes on to explain this concept of the 'unhypothetical' using the post-Platonic doctrine of the common concepts (*koinai ennoiai*), for which see the following note.

280 For the role of the common concepts in Neoplatonism (also discussed above: see 18,3 with note), see for example van den Berg 2009, and on Olympiodorus,

see the Introduction and Tarrant 1997; for the form of the 'argument from consensus' in antiquity and the common concepts more generally, see Obbink 1992 and Brittain 2005.

281 Thus Aristotle argues, for example, that 'first philosophy' must concern itself with the basic axioms used in all other reasoning in the special sciences, such as the principle of non-contradiction (*Metaph.* G [4], 1005b19).

282 Cf. *Alc.* 104D, 106B, and Proclus *in Alc.* 128,2–9.

283 Cf. *Alc.* 105E.

284 See 21,4–5 above.

285 See 38,25–39,5 (with notes) for the idea that Socrates can 'bring to fulfilment' Alcibiades' potential.

286 Cf. Proclus *in Alc.* 153,10–154,2.

287 Hom. *Il.* 6.138, *Od.* 4.805.

288 See above, 32,13–19. For Olympiodorus, the divine bliss alluded to by Homer in these passages is something much greater than sensual or perceptible pleasure or experience: it is the true joy and 'ease' of the intelligible world (cf. Plotinus *Enneads* 5.8.4: 'For it is "the easy life" there [in the intelligible], and truth is their mother and nurse and being and food . . .', tr. Armstrong 1984). A person who pursues lesser goods is fighting over shadows (as discussed in the cave allegory; see note to 32,13–19 above), or reflections of this authentic comfort. 'Fighting over the image (*eidôlon*)' would also apply to the tale of the Greeks' battle over a mere phantom of Helen, for example in Herodotus 2.120 and Euripides' *Helen* (I am grateful to Carlos Steel for this point).

289 See 31,1–4, with note.

290 Cf. Proclus *in Alc.* 146,12–13. After this registration, Athenian adolescents could participate in public life. For the process and the oath sworn by ephebes, see for example Sommerstein and Bayliss 2012, 14–15.

291 Compare Proclus *in Alc.* 142,1–143,4. Proclus adds that 'we all naturally declare our thoughts to the gods, and our emotions and desires, since we are convinced by incontrovertible preconceptions (*adiastrophous prolêpseis*) that what is divine knows all things, even the invisible motions of our souls' (142,14–17, tr. O'Neill 1965).

292 The force of the verse is that god is omnipresent. Compare Philoponus *in De An.* 188,26–7. Philoponus explains that 'it is necessary for the activities [of god] to be everywhere, since it has been demonstrated that he is the cause of everything' (188,24–5).

293 The 'god from the machine' (in Latin, the 'deus ex machina') refers to the dramatic device of a divinity sweeping in from a crane (*mêkhanê*) at a tragedy's critical moment to resolve an apparently insoluble dilemma; for example, Apollo's

appearance at the end of Euripides' *Orestes* prevents apparently inevitable bloodshed. Particularly associated with Euripides, the device was sometimes criticised in antiquity; Aristotle argued that a play's solution should come from within the plot (*Poetics* 1454a33–b9), while Horace argued that the deus ex machina should only be used to resolve a challenge worthy of a god (*Ars Poetica* 191–2).

294 This refers to Euripides *Alcestis* 1–71. Apollo's appearance at the beginning of the play may be technically 'from the machine', but in a literary sense he is not there to resolve the plot; that role falls to Heracles, who rescues Alcestis from the grip of Death at the end of the play.

295 That is, on Olympiodorus' symbolic exegesis, Socrates demonstrates both compassion for Alcibiades (*sumpatheia*) and judgement on his behalf (*krisis*), and these traits belong to the divine; thus it is appropriate for Socrates to speak for the god here.

296 The idea of a complex medium between two extreme terms can be found in *Timaeus* 32A–C. The principle that extreme terms should be joined by a participating medium is a familiar commonplace of the 'triadic' Neoplatonic metaphysics elaborated by Proclus. The point here is that the god is a lofty being, Alcibiades a lower being, and Socrates himself must 'mediate' between the extreme terms by speaking for the god and answering for Alcibiades.

    See also Proclus *in Alc.* 143,14–18, who draws an analogy with the Choice of Lives in Plato's Myth of Er (see *Republic* 10, 617D–E). There, Lachesis holds lots for the order in which souls will choose their future lives; a Spokesman dispenses the lots; and souls have the freedom to select from the lives available. Proclus suggests that the god who questions Alcibiades is analogous to Lachesis; Socrates to the spokesman, and Alcibiades himself to the souls.

297 The full quotation is from *Republic* 10, 617E, which Olympiodorus will go on to cite in the next line. Westerink (IX) understandably suggests that Olympiodorus made a slip in attributing the quotation to *Timaeus*. But Olymp. may have in mind *Timaeus* 42A–D, where the Demiurge remains 'blameless' (*anaitios*, 42D) as far as the implanting of souls in bodies via Necessity is concerned (42A); then Olymp. could just mean to imply that the idea behind the *Republic* passage – *theos anaitios* – can also be found in the *Timaeus*.

298 For the Neoplatonist approach to the question of personal responsibility and 'what is up to us' (*eph' hêmin*), see Sorabji 2005.1, 14(a).

299 See also Proclus' corresponding discussion at *in Alc.* 143,4–14. Proclus argues that the Choice of Lives in the Myth of Er depicts 'autonomy embraced in the midst of providence'. Proclus' view of providence, choice, and necessity is worked out in more detail in *Ten Problems Concerning Providence* (tr. Opsomer and Steel 2012) and *On Providence* (tr. Steel 2007).

300 'Holy wanderer' (*hierophoitis*) is a variant reading for 'mist-wanderer' (*êerophoitis*) at *Il.* 19.86–7; the latter is also an epithet of Fury (*Erinus*) at *Il.* 9.571. Olympiodorus repeats the quotation at *in Alc.* 101,17–18 and *in Gorg.* 24.3,27.

301 This is also Proclus' interpretation at *in Alc.* 144,2–9; he adds that this is not a literal interpretation of the passage, but follows logically from it.

302 Reading *dia tên* for *di' autôn*, as suggested by Westerink (1982, Addenda).

303 Proclus suggests that Alcibiades' desire to 'fill all humankind with his name' indicates not only limitless desire, but also a kind of longing for likeness with god, who actually *does* 'fill the whole world'. Proclus adds that according to the theurgists, the 'secret names of the gods' do in fact 'fill the whole world': souls that yearn for likeness to god, therefore, hope to see their names do the same (150,10–19). 'So the concepts (*ennoiai*) of such [ambitious] souls are grand and admirable, but their translations into practice are petty, ignoble and illusory, pursued without true knowledge; their concepts are in character, but their actions are out of it, the former the stirrings of birth-pangs in keeping with nature, the latter the products of oblivion and unawareness' (*in Alc.* 150,19–23, tr. lightly adapted from O'Neill 1965).

304 Cyrus the Great (c. 600 or 576–530 BC), founder of the Achaemenid Empire.

305 Xerxes I (519–465 BC), who succeeded Darius I as king of the Achaemenid Empire, and undertook a second major invasion of Greece after Darius' first campaign ended in failure at the Battle of Marathon (490 BC).

306 Aristides, *Oration* 46, p. 180 Jebb. Westerink also compares Isocrates 4.89.

307 Darius I (c. 550–486 BC), king of the Achaemenid Empire and father of Xerxes, here portrayed by Olympiodorus as a 'mean' (chronologically and temperamentally) between Cyrus and Xerxes.

308 Herodotus *Hist.* 3.86.

309 See 38,22–39,7.

310 See 39,19–20.

311 See 40,6–16.

312 This is a commonplace of the relationship between Alcibiades and Socrates. Alcibiades' astonished reaction when he notices Socrates in Plato, *Symposium* 213C: 'Good lord, what's going on here? It's Socrates! You've trapped me again! You always do this to me—all of a sudden you'll turn up out of nowhere where I least expect you! Well, what do you want now?' (tr. Nehamas and Woodruff).

313 See 42,12–15.

314 That is, first philosophy or metaphysics. See above, 40,19, with note.

315 At *Alc.* 105E.

316 Proclus also remarks that this interrogative approach arouses Alcibiades' receptivity to Socrates and restrains his impulse to behave irrationally (*in Alc.* 129,10–11).

317 Discussed above at 41,8–12.

318 For the following discussion, see also Proclus *in Alc.* 130,4–131,12: Proclus also
   stresses that judgement and compassion are elementary for the divinely inspired
   lover, and explains that Socrates' judgement is the cause of his reluctance to
   begin, while his compassion explains his reluctance to stop.

319 For these two qualities of the divinely inspired lover (judgement and
   compassion), see above, 41,10–15.

320 Proclus expands: 'while many persons commit many errors, their corrective
   punishment (*kolasis*) is slow to begin, and once begun, endures for a very long
   time indeed; and while many perform good actions, their recompense from
   providence is slow to begin and extends as far as possible' (*in Alc.* 130,22–131,3).

   While *kolasis* and the verb *kolazein* can mean 'punishment', in the Platonic
   tradition they are seen as corrective and healing treatments, following Plato in
   the *Gorgias*; see following note, and Olympiodorus' following discussion.

321 That is, corrective punishments for past errors. These corrections help to purify
   and ultimately heal the soul; for the Platonic context, see for instance *Gorgias*
   525B–C.

322 See 39,17.

323 See 42,1–6.

324 See also Proclus *in Alc.* 132,11–14. In Neoplatonism and Neopythagoreanism,
   the initial separation of the Dyad from the Monad marks the beginning of
   multiplicity, and the emanation of metaphysically 'lower' principles from the One.
   The nomenclature of 'daring' for this separation was attributed to Pherecydes in
   antiquity (fr. B14 Diels). The Monad represents unification, but the Dyad
   represents separation (Iamblichus *Theology of Arithmetic* 9,5–7 De Falco). The
   Neoplatonic view of the soul's progress from higher principles is vividly
   expressed by Plotinus *Enn.* 5.1.1: 'The beginning of trouble for [souls] was daring,
   and coming to birth, and the first otherness, and wishing to be on their own . . .'
   (tr. Armstrong 1984, lightly adapted).

   Plutarch, a Platonist of the first and second centuries AD, suggests that
   Pythagoreans used names from mythology to illustrate this metaphysical
   emanation: 'The number one [the Pythagoreans] called Apollo [*a-pollôn*, using a
   folk etymology 'not-many'] because of its rejection of plurality and because of the
   singleness of unity. The number two they called "Strife," and "Daring," and three
   they called "Justice," for, although the doing of injustice and suffering from
   injustice are caused by deficiency and excess, Justice, by reason of its equality,
   intervenes between the two. The so-called sacred Tetraktys, the number thirty-six,
   was, so it is famed, the mightiest of oaths, and it has been given the name of
   "Cosmos" since it is made up of the first four even numbers and the first four

odd numbers added together' (*Isis and Osiris* §75, 381F–382A, tr. Babbitt, lightly adapted).

325 Cf. *Republic* 10, 617E.

326 This likely refers, not to Valerius Harpocration (a Greek grammarian in Alexandria and avid collector of sayings), but to the Platonist Harpocration of Argos. I am grateful to George Boys-Stones for this correction.

327 For the distinction between apparent and real goods, and Alcibiades' 'fighting over shadows', see above, 42,15 and 47,2, with notes.

328 See Proclus *in Alc.* 146,12–14.

329 In Greek, *hestia* and *oikos* can mean 'hearth and home' literally or symbolically. Olympiodorus may be playing here on the idea that ambition is at Alcibiades' 'core', but Pericles also belongs to his 'home', as his guardian. *Hestia* is here translated as 'source' in keeping with its meaning of 'beginning' (LSJ II.1).

330 Aristophanes *Plut.* 196.

331 See above, 42,7–43,8, with notes. 'Concept' is used here in the sense of a 'common concept' (*koinê ennoia*): see notes on 18,3–4.

332 Olympiodorus revisits this point later in the commentary, at 98,16–20 and 101,3–7. See also Proclus *in Alc.* 138,8–139,3 and Olympiodorus *in Phaed.* 34,10–35,7.

333 See Plato *Republic* 4, 440B.

334 Hom. *Od.* 22.1.

335 That is, even though gods are not limited by space, our imaginations formulate images of them that are spatial. For the commentators' notion of *phantasia* (appearance, imagination), see Sorabji 2005.1, section 2.

336 The quote occurs at *Il.* 10.279–80, where the speaker is Odysseus. Diomedes is, in fact, the next speaker. See also below, 68,23–4.

337 In the basic Neoplatonist ontology of three hypostases (One, Intellect, and Soul), the entities that follow from the One are the Platonic Forms, the objects of intellect, which are also 'real beings' (*onta*). Later Neoplatonism stresses the mediating role, between the One and the Forms, of individual unities (*henades*) or divinities. See for example Plotinus *Enn.* 5.1 and Proclus *El. Theol.* prr. 113–165 (divine unity), 166–182 (intellect), and 184–211 (soul).

338 Because of his ambitious temperament.

339 At 45,21–2.

340 Cf. Proclus *in Alc.* 156,17–20.

341 Hom. *Iliad* 10.279–80, where the speaker is in fact Odysseus.

342 For the portrayal of Socrates' irony or *eirôneia*, see for example Lane 2011. On the Neoplatonic portrayal of Socrates, see recently Layne and Tarrant 2014.

343 *Republic* 1, 337A.

344 *Apology* 21A–23D. Socrates explains that the Oracle must have meant that 'human wisdom is worth little or nothing, and that when he says this man, Socrates, he is using my name as an example, as if he said: "This man among you, mortals, is wisest who, like Socrates, understands that his wisdom is worthless"' (23A, tr. Grube).

345 See also Proclus' corresponding discussion at *in Alc.* 155,13–156,9.

346 *Theaetetus* 151D–E.

347 *Apology* 30C–D.

348 As Olympiodorus explains below (57,22), the use of such a 'material' preposition suggests modesty on the speaker's part: to say that 'you can't achieve this goal without me' amounts to saying that I am only the *material* cause of the goal's accomplishment (and so, in the Neoplatonic scheme of causation, a relatively low-grade contributor).

349 Cf. Proclus *in Alc.* 154,13–155,5.

350 Hippocrates *Aphorisms* 1.22, 4.468 Littré.

351 Cf. Olymp. *in Gorg.* 35.3 (164,29–30).

352 At Lecture 1, 6,6–7,8.

353 The 'Stoic' method was described as Aristotelian (Peripatetic) in Lecture 1. The present passage is included by von Arnim as *SVF* 3.489.

354 Cf. Hippocrates *Aphorisms* 2.38 Littré: 'An article of food or drink that is slightly worse (*smikrôi kheiron*), but more pleasant to the taste, is preferable to one that is better, but less pleasant.'

355 Hom. *Iliad* 4.86–103 and 5.290–3. See also above, 48,4–7.

356 See also above, 42,7–43,8.

357 Cf. Proclus *in Alc.* 155,5–12.

358 Reading *oun* for the MSS' *hous*, as suggested by Westerink in his apparatus.

359 Olympiodorus attributes this remark to Plato's *Theaetetus* at 36,14–16, but it is difficult to find any matching passage there. *Protagoras* 352B–D and *Republic* 5, 477D offer similar ideas.

360 *SVF* 3.618; cf. Diogenes Laertius 7.121–2 (LS 67M) and Proclus *in Alc.* 164,17–165,10: 'For what other conclusion may be drawn from what [Socrates] has said other than that the good man alone is ruler, he alone wields power, he alone is king, alone is leader of all, alone is free, and everything which belongs to the gods belongs to good men' (tr. O'Neill 1965).

361 See 41,5.

362 *Phaedrus* 264C.

363 Cf. *Timaeus* 92C: 'And so now we may say that our account of the universe has reached its conclusion. This world of ours has received and teems with living

things, mortal and immortal. A visible living thing containing visible ones, perceptible god, image of the intelligible Living Thing, its grandness, goodness, beauty and perfection are unexcelled. Our one universe, indeed the only one of its kind, has come to be' (tr. Zeyl).

364 For the similarity of a Platonic dialogue to the cosmos, see Proclus *in Alc.* 10,2–14.

365 I take the point to be that in the cosmic drama, the *actions* of beings are analogous to the *voices* of the actors in an earthly drama.

366 See also Proclus *in Alc.* 170,5–11. For the meaning of the soul's 'reversion' to itself, also discussed by Olympiodorus above, see for example Proclus *El. Theol.* prr. 15, 17.

367 Cf. Aeschines 3.192, describing jurors whose minds wander while the charges are read aloud. Olympiodorus returns to this point at 108,10–11. The anonymous *Prolegomena to Platonic Philosophy* expands on the example (15, 210,3–11): '[The object of the dialogue form] is to make us pay attention to the contents by the very variety of the speakers; otherwise, if it is always one and the same person teaching us, we might, so to speak, doze off and the same thing might happen that happened during an address of the orator Aeschines, because in his case it was one and the same person who spoke from the beginning to the end. Standing on the platform and making his speech, he failed to keep his audience awake because there was no discussion, no asking and answering of questions, and the jurymen fell asleep; when the orator saw this he said to them: "I hope you have had sweet dreams about the trial." ' (tr. Westerink).

368 In fact, Olympiodorus is not quite finished with the proem: what follows immediately is his discussion of the text (*lexis*). The discussion of the 'refutative' part of the dialogue begins in the following lecture.

369 Cf. Proclus *in Alc.* 157,3–9.

370 105A–B; see above, 43,9–19.

371 See above, 45,15–46,9.

372 See above, 54,3–8.

373 In the sense that, for the Neoplatonist metaphysician, the soul is the authentic being of a person, but their activities (*energeiai*), including the function of enlivening the body, emanate into the perceptible world: see Proclus *El. Theol.* pr. 9. See also Proclus *in Alc.* 157,10–13.

374 *Apology* 30B–C.

375 Cf. Aristotle *De Caelo* 1.4, 271a33.

376 See also Proclus *in Alc.* 162,15–18.

377 See also Proclus *in Alc.* 159,11–22.

378 Westerink compares Plato *Gorgias* 447A (where Gorgias has just completed a splendid 'display') and *Phaedrus* 235A (where Lysias' speech provides a similar 'display').

379 Cf. *Alc.* 103A and Olympiodorus' comments above, 26,17–21.

380 In other words, by introducing the agency of a god into the conversation, Socrates is raising the stakes and making it more likely that Alcibiades will take him seriously.

381 See also Proclus *in Alc.* 165,11–12.

382 Compare Proclus *in Alc.* 166,2–6: 'The more we become consciously aware of the influence of the superior beings, the more we stand in wonder at them. For instance, although the saviour Asclepius even now gives us health and ever preserves us and possesses in himself activities more divine than those which proceed externally, nevertheless we praise him more when we are favoured with an epiphany: for we desire our living organism to share in the perception of the god's giving' (tr. O'Neill 1965). For the notion of a visible illumination from the divine, cf. Iamblichus *De Mysteriis*, Book I.

383 See also Proclus *in Alc.* 166,18–167,10.

384 For the notion of Socrates as more 'fulfilled' or 'complete' (*teleios*) than Alcibiades – that is, a more perfect, realised being in the metaphysical hierarchy – see also above, 39,11–15, and the Introduction, §2.1 on the scale of human excellences, and §2.2 on the role of the *Alcibiades* in fostering excellence.

385 Later Neoplatonism posits six modes of causation (cf. Sorabji 2005.2, 6(d)): three true causes (*aitia*), the efficient and final and paradigmatic, and three auxiliary causes (*sunaitia*), the formal and material and the instrumental. The preposition *dia* ('through') with the genitive case can describe the instrument of an action, and is therefore appropriate to the instrumental cause; Olympiodorus asks why Alcibiades should treat the (superior) Socrates as an instrument.

(To the Neoplatonist scheme of six causes, contrast the Aristotelian framework of four causes, material, efficient, formal and final, from *Physics* 2.3. The Neoplatonists acknowledged and accepted this scheme, but argued that Plato endorsed the broader scheme of six causes, which made room especially for the 'paradigmatic' or exemplary role of the Platonic Forms.)

386 Cf. *Phaedrus* 246B–C.

387 See *Laws* 9, 870D–E. For the kind of situation that Olympiodorus envisages – where perhaps the gods might put a present-day murderer to good use in punishing a past (perhaps long past) murderer – see for example Proclus *Ten Problems Concerning Providence* §49, and Plutarch *On the Delays of God's Punishment*.

388 See also Proclus *in Alc.* 169,17–170,5.

389 See above, 40,19, with notes.

390 The capacities for self-motion, self-constitution and self-reversion are essential to the later Neoplatonist understanding of the soul (see for example Proclus *El. Theol.* prr. 40–51, 80–3). Self-movement was already essential to the Platonic soul in the *Phaedrus* (245C–246A).

391 *Republic* 1, 336B–354B. Olympiodorus (or the redactor of our text) refers to *Gorgias* here, but this appears to be a slip of the tongue or the pen in anticipation of the description of Polus and Callicles forthcoming in the next sentence (61,10–11). (Olympiodorus, who lectured on the *Gorgias*, can hardly have genuinely mistaken Thrasymachus for a character in that dialogue.) Olympiodorus tends to refer to Thrasymachus, Polus and Callicles in the same breath, as in the proem of the *in Gorg.* ('He criticises Gorgias, you see, and Polus, Callicles and Thrasymachus, too as shameless and never given to blushing . . .', tr. Tarrant et al.) On correcting 'slips' of tongue or pen in our text, see the Introduction and Westerink 1982, IX.

392 At *Gorgias* 481B–527E, 461B–481B.

393 This likely refers to the Protagorean thesis that 'every appearance (*phantasia*) is true' (Sextus Empiricus *Against the Mathematicians* 7.389–90), as Plato critiques it (*Theaetetus* 170C–171C). Compare Olympiodorus *in Gorg.* 13.2,24–6: 'Protagoras argues sophistically that nothing is false, but everything is true.'

394 Because Socrates, who possesses knowledge, represents a higher level of being than Alcibiades, who lacks knowledge (cf. Proclus *in Alc.* 172,23–173,1).

395 Cf. Proclus *in Alc.* 173,2–4.

396 Cf. Proclus *in Alc.* 171,9–18 on the challenges inherent in answering an expert sophist. The (occasional) Neoplatonist view of Aristotle as a challenging, eristic dialectician is mirrored by Syrianus in the preface to *in Metaph.* 13–14 (80,4–81,6).

397 Cf. Ammonius *in Isag.* 6,25–9,6.

398 For Socrates as a midwife, cf. *Theaetetus* 148E–151D.

399 Cf. Proclus *in Alc.* 184,11–185,4.

400 I have broken the long and periodic Greek sentences down somewhat in English, and numbered the main headings. For the proof and Olympiodorus' discussion, compare Proclus *in Alc.* 176,10–178,24 and 187,19–188,15.

401 For this portrayal, see for example Hom. *Od.* 14.435; the *Homeric Hymn to Hermes* 1.3; and Hesiod *Theogony* 938–39.

402 The Greek preposition *hina* is here used to express a consequence, which is not uncommon in later Greek; the anonymous reader for this lecture points out to me that this is rare with the infinitive.

403 For the later ancient distinction of synthetic and analytic reasoning, and its sources, see for example Menn 2002, 193–223. Analysis is reasoning *from* first principles, or from the general to the specific; synthesis is reasoning *to* first

principles. Proclus discusses the distinction between the 'apophatic' (affirmative) and 'kataphatic' (negative) syllogisms as follows: '. . . the affirmative syllogism proceeds from the more to the less fulfilled, and therefore resembles a descent, but the negative moving toward the more fulfilled resembles an ascent' (*in Alc.* 180,17–19).

404 *Od.* 22.1.

405 Cf. Proclus *in Alc.* 200,13–201,9.

406 Cf. Proclus *in Alc.* 202,1–203,13.

407 *Il.* 1.62–7.

408 Herodotus 7.141–3.

409 Cf. Ammonius *in Isag.* 6,25–9,6.

410 This goes back to the Socratic distinction between an ignorant person who fails to realise their ignorance (and so is doubly ignorant), and an ignorant person who recognises their ignorance (and so is simply ignorant). The former is better off than the latter. See the *Anonymous Prolegomena to Platonic Philosophy* §5 (16,19–27, tr. Westerink 1962): 'Simple ignorance occurs when a person does not know a particular thing and knows that he does not know; double ignorance when he does not know a thing and is not aware that he does not know . . . .'

411 The cithara was a stringed instrument similar to a lyre, which was used to accompany epic and lyric songs. For this passage, compare above, 2,44–8 and Proclus *in Alc.* 193,21–196,1.

412 For the following discussion, cf. Aristotle *Politics* 8.6, 1341a18–28; Proclus *in Alc.* 197,17–198,11; and Olympiodorus *in Phaed.* 20,25–21,5.

413 Again here the Greek *logos* is used to mean both reason and words: since one cannot speak while playing the flute, in a sense it is less compatible with 'reasoning' than a stringed instrument.

414 Cf. Aristotle *Politics* 8.6, 1341b3–8.

415 'Cithara-song' (*kitharôidia*) was a familiar Greek word, but 'flute-song' (*aulôidia*) was not. For the contrast of different kinds of music here, see also Plato *Laws* 3, e.g. 700D.

416 Cf. Hom. *Il.* 9.186, *Od.* 1.155, etc.

417 Hom. *Il.* 3.1.

418 For the association of Phrygians with orgiastic rites in Neoplatonism, and the comparison with Plato's considered views on appropriate music, see also Proclus *Essays on the Republic* 61.19, with commentary by Sheppard 1980, 113–14.

419 *Paides Thêbaiôn* may be simply periphrastic for 'the Thebans' (LSJ s.v. *pais* I.3), although in Olympiodorus' pedagogical context, 'children' may be warranted.

420 Plutarch, *Life of Alcibiades* 2: 'Flutes, then', said he, 'for the sons of Thebes; they know not how to converse. But we Athenians, as our fathers say, have Athena for

foundress and Apollo for patron, one of whom cast the flute away in disgust, and the other flayed the presumptuous flute-player'. Thus, half in jest and half in earnest, Alcibiades emancipated himself from this discipline, and the rest of the boys as well (tr. Perrin).

421 That is, Alcibiades' oratorical capacity is a matter of inborn ability and upbringing, not of human excellence (*aretê*). See Introduction §§2 and 3.2.

422 That is, Alcibiades' good behaviour arose from these factors and not from intentional, reflective action based on foresight (*prohairesis*).

423 Cf. Proclus *in Alc.* 186,4–10: 'To bring before his eyes, as if upon the stage of the assembly, the people and the actual podium with Alcibiades hastening to seize the position of adviser and himself taking hold of him and as it were applying reason as a bridle to his onrush, presents a very vivid picture, and at the same time makes it clear that one should do nothing without examination . . .' (tr. O'Neill 1965).

424 At 63,12–13.

425 As we have seen earlier (e.g. 25,24), Greek had changed sufficiently by Olympiodorus' time that some Attic words required a gloss. Here, the passive form *didaskesthai* ('to be taught') is glossed by the more familiar active form of *manthanein* ('to learn').

426 The 'prosyllogism' is a syllogism whose conclusion provides the major premiss of another syllogism. The prosyllogism that Olympiodorus describes is in the first figure (the major premiss is universal, and the minor premisses are affirmative); the syllogism is in the second figure (the major premiss is universal, and the minor premiss is negative).

427 See Proclus *in Alc.* 178,11–24.

428 Perhaps a 'gaming implement' like dice, in the sense of Aeschines 1.59.

429 See above, 67,4–5, with note.

430 Cf. Proclus *in Alc.* 198,12–199,3.

431 Cf. above, 52,3. In Homer, it is actually Odysseus who speaks these lines, with Diomedes as the next speaker.

432 Hom. *Il.* 10.279–80.

433 The Greek *suneidôs*, discussed elsewhere by Olympiodorus (see 23,2–17 and below, 87,19), also means 'witness' and can refer to a guardian angel or *daimôn* as well as personal conscience. Westerink 1962, XVIII–XIX notes that Proclus uses the word *daimôn* in places where Olympiodorus prefers 'conscience' (Proclus *in Alc.* 199,9–14 and Olympiodorus *in Alc.* 68,24; Proclus *in Alc.* 229,20–2 and Olympiodorus *in Alc.* 87,19), and speculates that Olympiodorus might avoid using the word when unnecessary (but compare 15,5–23,17, where the discussion is clearly necessary), thanks to its pejorative connotations in Jewish and Christian usage.

434 At 65,10–19.

435 Compare also *Protagoras* 319A–320B for Socrates' construction of a similar argument.

436 At *Phaedrus* 244C, Socrates suggests that prophecy (the 'mantic' art) has its roots in divine madness (*mania*), as does love.

437 The implication is that the 'investigatory', skilful mode of prophecy is properly deserving of the name 'skill' (*tekhnê*), which is not as appropriate to the loftier, inspired mode of prophecy.

438 I take the point here to be that these terms have proper *philosophical* definitions in Olympiodorus' terms: in the strictest sense, 'we' are our souls, and our 'affairs' are our bodies, possessions and actions. If Alcibiades' answer had employed these most strictly correct philosophical meanings, he would not have fallen into the error of using vague or ambiguous terminology. But in fact he was using these words according to their loose and ordinary meanings, and so he has failed to make his meaning clear.

439 That 'the wooden wall' would survive a Persian assault; Themistocles interpreted the oracle to mean a fleet of ships, and advised the Athenians to prepare for a naval battle. See Herodotus 7.140–4.

440 *Rhetoric* 1.4, 1359b19–23.

441 The allusion is to the five kinds of psychological constitutions in *Republic* Book 8: aristocracy (the best kind of rule, corresponding to a soul with reason or *logos* in charge), timocracy (rule driven by love of honour), oligarchy, democracy and tyranny.

442 For example, the Athenian sanctions against Megara (in 432 BC) contributed to the onset of the Peloponnesian War (Thucydides 1.67.4, 1.88.1, 1.139–40).

443 71,7–14.

444 At 72,26–74,7 below.

445 Three *epikheirêmata*: cf. Aristotle *Topics* 1.11, 162a12–18.

446 The introductions to Herodotus' and Thucydides' histories help to lend colour to this assertion; for instance, for the theme of justice (*dikê*) as a motivation for war in Herodotus, and the historian as 'judge', see Baragwanath 2008, 17–19.

447 Cf. Proclus *in Alc.* 222,2–7. For example, when a subject (like a human being) becomes warm and then cold, this can be understood as a struggle between contraries, the hot and the cold. This way of thinking traces its roots at least to the Presocratic philosophers. Compare the following celebrated fragment of Anaximander: 'The things that are perish into the things from which they come to be, according to necessity, for they pay penalty and retribution to each other for their injustice in accordance with the ordering of time' (Simplic. *in*

Phys. 24,13–21 = B1). The word translated here as 'penalty' (*dikê*) can also be rendered 'justice'.

448 Drawing on Plato's account of the tripartite soul – *logos* (reason), *thumos* (spirited emotion) and *epithumia* (desire, appetite) – in *Republic* 4. See also Olympiodorus' discussion of the Athenian training for the three parts of the soul in his *Life of Plato* (Lecture 1, above).

449 Reading *estê* ('stands still') with Dodds, in place of the manuscript's *esti* ('it is'). Alternatively, Westerink proposed retaining *esti* and adding *henos moriou* ('of one part'), which would give the sense 'justice does not belong to one part of the soul'.

450 Cf. Proclus *in Alc.* 213,14–214,6: the statesman 'considers only what is just and stirs up war only so far as he thinks the enemy are doing wrong. Therefore he will first resort to oratory, striving to put a stop to the wrong-doers through timely persuasion, and then to the art of generalship, inducing moderation by force of arms in those whom he has not won over by words. So in this way Nestor . . . first made representation to the Trojans . . . through the medium of speakers; but afterward . . . he attacked them. For this reason too, the Socrates of *Republic* [perhaps 5, 469D, 471B] deems that a city should possess only as much power as is sufficient to save both it and its neighbours from suffering mutual wrong.' (tr. O'Neill)

451 Hom. *Il.* 3.205–224.

452 Euripides *Andromache* 696.

453 Cf. Plato *Alc.* 134B–C, *Gorgias* 515D.

454 A victory that defeats its own purpose. Plato contrasts military victories, which can be Cadmean, with education, which is never Cadmean (*Laws* 1, 641C). The reference is to Cadmus, the legendary king of Thebes. He defeated a serpent who guarded the fresh water supply of the new foundation (e.g. Euripides *Phoen.* 1062–3), but at the cost of the lives of most of his future citizens. (The concept is similar to that of the 'Pyrrhic victory', after Pyrrhus, who defeated the Romans in battle but sustained very heavy losses in the victory.)

455 Cf. Proclus *in Alc.* 221,9–16.

456 Cf. *Alc.* 113E: 'If you say something wrong, and if there's a previous argument that can prove that it was wrong, you think you ought to be given some new and different proof, as if the previous one were a worn-out scrap of clothing that you refuse to wear again. No, you want an immaculate, brand-new proof' (tr. Hutchinson in Cooper and Hutchinson 1997).

457 Cf. Proclus *in Alc.* fr. 1: 'In correcting Alcibiades, Socrates unobserved puts forward by way of example the art of physical training, which is divided into "grappling at arm's length and close wrestling". So also war and peace are different divisions of just action. Naturally Socrates puts forward the arts of physical training and music as being familiar to Alcibiades since he was brought up on

them from childhood. And war resembles physical training, but peace resembles music' (*Schol. in Alcibiadem* 277,1–7 Hermann, tr. O'Neill 1965).

458 Some preliminary, prior knowledge is required for Socrates' method of midwifery to succeed. (For Socrates as midwife, cf. *Theaet.* 150C–D, and elsewhere in this volume, 12,10–12; 63,15–17; 74,21.)

459 By talking Alcibiades through the example of athletic activity.

460 Rather scholastically, Olympiodorus wants to explain why Socrates teaches Alcibiades directly about one point (wrestling), but asks him questions about the other two (music and statecraft). He teaches him first to ensure that the inquiry will be fruitful; and he has more questions than lessons in order to show that midwifery, which teases out Alcibiades' own innate ideas, is more productive than mere teaching.

461 Cf. Proclus *in Alc.* 208,5–8.

462 Cf. Proclus *in Alc.* 223,5–16. In the strict sense described in Aristotle's *Categories*, 'When things get their name from something, with a difference of ending, they are called paronymous. Thus, for example, the grammarian gets his name from grammar, the brave get theirs from bravery' (*Cat.* 1, 1a13–15).

463 Cf. Olympiodorus *On the Categories* 34,22–9, and for the Neoplatonic metaphysical background Proclus *Elements of Theology* prop. 110. For 'focal meaning' in Aristotle and in general, see for example Owen 1960 and Hamlyn 1977–8.

464 The Greek title of the *Republic*, *Politeia*, literally means 'constitution' or 'polity'. Olympiodorus alludes here to the city-soul analogy of *Republic* 2, in which Socrates suggests that justice within a soul might be studied by drawing an analogy with a political organisation. Westerink compares *Republic* 2, 368D–E; 4, 434C–435C; 443C–444A; and Olympiodorus *in Metaph.* 100,19–23.

465 The fivefold list developed from Aristotle *Rhetoric* 1.4 (1359b19–23), and discussed in the preceding survey, 71,7–14.

466 See for example the anecdote in Plutarch's *Life of Alcibiades* §31.4, where Alcibiades carries the right wing of an Athenian army to victory, and 173,8–9 later in this commentary.

467 Cf. 72,20–2.

468 Rather, Alcibiades at 108D arrives at the conclusion that performing 'musically' is the goal of musical skill, and does not suggest that he is confused about the kind of answer that Socrates wants.

469 Lapis lazuli. The eye is the most precious sense, but a skilful painter does not use the most precious materials to paint it.

470 Cf. Proclus *in Alc.* 208,1–4: the word 'come' is 'appropriate to our soul's knowledge, since it is in movement and does not subsist all at once and without

change, like the stable and enduring activity of the intellect (*nous*)' (tr. O'Neill 1965). Olympiodorus elaborates on the point at *in Phaed.* 7.6,10–16: 'The expressions "when I have reached" and "where I am going" are appropriate to soul, which apprehends things in time, not out of time, and fragmentarily, not undecidedly and simultaneously, as intellect (*nous*) apprehends them, without transition and eternally and simultaneously. Motion, indeed, is proper to soul, because the first of motions is locomotion and the first thing moved is the self-moved; for anything must be one of these three: unmoved, self-moved, or moved from without' (tr. Westerink 1976).

471 That is, Socrates' unified understanding of musical performance, contrasted with Alcibiades' divided understanding, at 78,9–12.

472 For the Neoplatonist view of universals as before, in, and posterior to particulars, see Sorabji 2005.3, 5(a), 5(c). But the application here is more or less common sense.

Westerink offers a number of helpful additional references, including Plato *Theaetetus* 204A–205C (on the combination of a whole out of parts, as the syllable arises from its elements); *Statesman* 262A–263B; *Timaeus* 33A; Proclus *El. Theol.* pr. 67; Proclus *Platonic Theology* 3.25; and Hermias *in Phaed.* 90,9–15.

473 Even though, say, a child loses this particular tooth, there is a universal pattern set up in her nature (*phusis*), according to which she can regrow the tooth. This Neoplatonic concept of seminal *logoi* informing nature, common already in Plotinus, can be traced to Stoicism; see for example LS 46A.

474 Memory (*Mnêmosynê*) is the mother by Zeus of the nine Muses.

475 Cf. Proclus *in Alc.* 214,13–216,9.

476 For this example, see Plato *Republic* 331C.

477 Hom. *Od.* 3.20.

478 Hom. *Od.* 19.395–6.

479 The recollection combines a portion of *Od.* 19.395–6 – describing Autolycus, Odysseus' grandfather, 'who surpassed all men in thievishness (*kleptosunêi*) and oaths' – with the familiar Homeric praise of a person 'who is honoured about his country as a god is' (e.g. *Il.* 5.78, 10.33, etc.).

480 Cf. Proclus *in Alc.* 216,12–15.

481 See 74,9–11.

482 See e.g. 63,12–13.

483 This is the technical verb in Neoplatonic metaphysics for the relationship of 'participation'. See for example Proclus *El. Theol.* pr. 65, and for the soul as 'self-constituted' and source of life and motion in bodies, *El. Theol.* prr. 40–51, 188.

484 Cf. *Phaedrus* 245C–E: 'Every soul is immortal. That is because whatever is always in motion is immortal, while what moves, and is moved by, something else stops living when it stops moving. So it is only what moves itself that never desists from motion, since it does not leave off being itself . . .'. See also Proclus *in Alc.* 225,11–226,10.

485 Olympiodorus alludes to a saying, now obscure, concerning the intelligible world – the realm of Platonic Forms. In the intelligible world, feet and the head have no distinct places of their own, since forms have no spatial differentiation. Once forms are enmattered, however, they become spatially distinct. The saying can also refer to the fertilised egg, where the seminal 'form' of the human being can be found. For a fuller explanation, see Olympiodorus *in Phaed.* 4.4,13 (24,22 Norvin), 13.2,30 (76,2–3 Norvin). Westerink also compares Plotinus *Enn.* 6.4.8 on the omnipresence of being.

486 Cf. Proclus *in Alc.* 189,4–11: '. . . although souls descend to birth filled essentially with knowledge, yet as a result of birth, they contract forgetfulness; and by possessing the innate ideas of reality as it were pulsating within them, they have concepts about them, but overcome by the draught of oblivion they are unable to articulate their own concepts and reduce them to knowledge. Therefore they carry them around as it were swooning and scarcely breathing, and for this reason they acquire twofold ignorance . . . and hence comes deceit and the illusion of knowledge' (tr. O'Neill 1965, lightly adapted).

487 For the Neoplatonist, every soul innately possesses *logoi*, formulas or 'reason-principles', of the Forms. (For the translation 'formula', see note to 15,11, above.) Learning is a process of recollecting these; for the Platonic sources of the view, see Plato *Phaedo* 73Cff. and *Meno* 80Dff.

488 Westerink compares Plato *Theaetetus* 208B (where a previously offered definition of knowledge proves to be 'a poor man's dream of gold') and *Lysis* 218C (where, similarly, a previously offered account of friendship proves to be like a dream of wealth).

489 That is, Alcibiades answered in terms of knowledge of justice that was *latent* in his mind (which had *always* been there, because the formula of justice had always been implanted in his soul), but Socrates asked for an answer in terms of *actively used* knowledge. For the distinction, see for example the 'aviary' thought-experiment in Plato *Theaetetus* 196D–200D.

See also Proclus *in Alc.* 240,10–20: 'I think this clearly shows which is the knowledge that precedes all time in us, and which is the knowledge that accrues in time. Socrates, considering only knowledge in act, enquires, what was the time before this; but Alcibiades, possessing knowledge in essence, on account of which he thinks he knows what he doesn't, cannot name a time of his participation therein, since we possess it from eternity' (tr. O'Neill 1965); see also note to 82,13 above.

490 See 78,26–79,2.

491 Cf. Proclus *in Alc.* 222,20–223,5.

492 The Greek adjective *mousikos* ('of the Muses', 'musical', 'to do with arts and letters'), when it stands alone in the feminine gender as *mousikê*, normally assumes the noun *tekhnê* (skill, art) (LSJ s.v. *mousikê*). As Olympiodorus' examples show, it has to do especially with poetry sung to music, but it can refer more broadly to literature and art.

493 Cf. Proclus *in Alc.* 208,5–8.

494 It is taken in this latter sense, for example, in the modern English translation by D.S. Hutchinson (in Cooper and Hutchinson 1997), which I have used as a reference in my rendering of the lemma (with minor divergences to reflect Olympiodorus' interpretation): 'In these last two examples you said that what was better was more musical and more athletic, respectively. Now try to tell me what's better in this case, too.'

495 Olympiodorus suggests that we use 'each' (*hekastos*) for the unit in a group of three, but a different word like 'both' or 'either' in a group of two: thus he takes *hekastos* as necessarily referring to each of the three kinds of music, not either of the two examples (the musical and athletic).

496 Cf. Proclus *in Alc.* 208,9–13.

497 Cf. Proclus *in Alc.* 209,17–210,1.

498 Cf. Proclus *in Alc.* 210,15–211,15.

499 For similar views in the Hippocratic corpus, Westerink compares *Epidemics* 6.4.18, 5.312.

500 Cf. Proclus *in Alc.* 212,18–213,1.

501 Olympiodorus' point builds on a basically Aristotelian principle – that knowledge proceeds from what is more familiar to us, to what is more truly knowable by nature (*Phys.* 1.1, 184a17–21) – and adds the Neoplatonic language of 'participant' and 'participated': the participant is the ordinary, composite entity that we encounter with sense-perception, whereas the participated is the simple, indivisible form. (See for example Proclus *El. Theol.* pr. 65.)

502 Hom. *Il.* 2.33.

503 'Totally, every bit' is a mildly awkward translation of *holon te kai pan* (wholly and totally), but helps to bring out the force of Olympiodorus' comments in the following paragraph.

504 Cf. Proclus *in Alc.* 217,9–15. See also *Theaetetus* 204A–205A.

505 Thersites was a Greek solider at Troy, notoriously deformed, weak and unlikeable (see *Il.* 2.211–77). Theano was a priestess of Athena at Troy, much respected by

the Greeks, who spared her home in the destruction of the city. Coroebus was a proverbially foolish and unhelpful ally of Priam at Troy.

See also Plato, *Republic* 5: women and men are equally qualified by nature for education, power and jobs (454B–456B), and 'women share by nature in every way of life just as men do'. And granted that 'on the whole' women are less strong than men, Glaucon notes that there are individual exceptions, where many women are better than many men at many things (455D); Plato's point there is similar to Olympiodorus' point here.

506 See *Gorgias* 483C–484C, *Republic* 1, 348B–349D. Olympiodorus, or the student redactor of these notes, has inadvertently dropped the name '*Republic*', but we should probably not conclude that Olympiodorus (who also lectured on the *Gorgias*) supposed Thrasymachus to be a character in that dialogue.

507 See also Proclus *in Alc.* 218,13–219,1.

508 To 'make progress' (from the Greek verb *prokoptô*, literally 'to cut forward') is a somewhat technical description of a disciple already along the road to moral and philosophical achievement, especially in the Stoic tradition; see for example Epictetus *Diss.* 1.4.1.

509 In the rhetorical figure of paraleipsis, the speaker intentionally omits a topic or phrase, and the omission draws attention to what is left out.

510 See 6,6–7 and 30,2–3 above.

511 Cf. Proclus *in Alc.* 228,21–4; 232,10–233,7.

512 Cf. Proclus *in Alc.* 233,7–14.

513 See above, 55,23–56,1, with note.

514 *meta men dê Dios eimi*, a loose remembering of *Phaedrus* 250B, which actually reads '*We* [i.e. philosophers] were with Zeus'.

515 Cf. Proclus *in Alc.* 229,14–17.

516 Cf. Proclus *in Alc.* 229,18–230,1.

517 Cf. Proclus *in Alc.* 230,14–15: 'the clause "that you can introduce me to him as a pupil" should not be thought of as mere irony, but also as the truth, since Socrates would not have shunned listening to a person of true knowledge' (tr. O'Neill 1965).

518 At *Phaedrus* 279C, Phaedrus shares in Socrates' prayer, commenting that friends have all things in common. At Euripides *Orestes* 735, Orestes says to his friend and collaborator Pylades that he is ruined and Pylades replies that he must himself be destroyed as well, since friends have all things in common.

519 For this and the following explanations, compare Proclus *in Alc.* 234,6–23: 'Now let us not think of Socrates as saying "whom I would be least likely to forswear" in the sense that "perhaps I might forswear myself in the case of other gods, but never in the case of the god of friendship", since we have learned in the *Gorgias*

[466E; cf. Olymp. *in Gorg.* 81,22–3] and the *Philebus* [12B–C] of Socrates' carefulness as regards both oaths and the actual orders of gods. The distinction is not in relation to other gods (for there is a single piety that unites us with them all), but to the young man who is listening; he would least of all forswear the god of friendship in his converse with Alcibiades, least of all the god of strangers in his converse with a stranger, least of all the god of suppliants in his converse with a suppliant . . . so when one's conversation is with someone loved one should least of all forswear the god of friendship' (tr. O'Neill 1965).

520 As Westerink points out, it is difficult to see where in the *Cratylus* Olympiodorus could have in mind. (Plato does elsewhere comment on the penalties that Zeus *Homognios* ('of kinship') or *Xenios* ('of strangers') might mete out upon offenders; see for example *Laws* 9, 881D, where a bystander who fails to stop an attack by a child on his parents will be liable by law to the curse of Zeus *Homognios*.) The Neoplatonists did, however, read the *Cratylus* as emphasising the sanctity and value of divine names; Westerink cites Proclus *in Crat.* 11,26 and 25,10–12 in this connection.

521 I take Olympiodorus to mean that Socrates would forswear himself least by Friendship *and all the other gods too.*

522 That is, here the argument proceeds to first principles, where previously it proceeded from first principles. See above, 64,9, and Menn 2002, 193–223.

523 Cf. Proclus *in Alc.* 235,4–5. Westerink also compares 237,15–17: Proclus argues that Socrates would not destroy Alcibiades' confidence in his good nature (*phusis*), but would cultivate it in order to encourage Alcibiades to pursue higher grades of excellence. (On the grades of excellence, see Introduction §2.1.)

524 Cf. Olymp. *in Phaed.* 2.16: 'before the judges, the point under discussion was an individual life, and particular points can be proved only by inquiry' (tr. Westerink 1976).

525 Cf. Proclus *in Alc.* 238,8–15.

526 By 'the material' Olympiodorus means the premises. (Following Aristotle, he regards the premises of a formal (syllogistic) argument as material for the conclusion: loosely, the dialectician uses premises to build the conclusion as the builder uses bricks to build the house). Consider a syllogism with false premises and a true conclusion:

'Socrates is a duck';
'all ducks are mammals';
'therefore Socrates is a mammal'.

The 'material' of the premises permits the true conclusion, but it does not follow necessarily from them.

527 'The *ephêbeia* generally described a life stage in Greece between childhood and
     manhood, more specifically puberty, and in the more narrow sense the phase at
     its conclusion . . . . At the age of eighteen the young Athenians in their respective
     demes were entered into the lists of citizens after checking their personal legal
     status, and then admitted into the *ephebeia* by *phyle*. A *kosmêtês* and ten
     sôphronistai, one per *phyle* who were chosen by the people, were responsible for
     their training. In addition, there were teachers for athletic and military training
     (two *paidotribai* as well as trainers for hoplite fighting, archery, spear throwing,
     and handling catapults); furthermore, there were military ranks (*taxiarkhoi*,
     lokhagoi)' (Gehrke 2006, I–II).

528 See Introduction §1.2 and Tarrant 1997 on Olympiodorus' use of 'common
     concepts' – building on the Stoic view that human beings share a set of essentially
     true ideas about the world that are not necessarily conscious, but can, with effort,
     be uncovered and articulated philosophically.

Bibliography

Annas, J. (1985) 'Self-knowledge in Early Plato', in D.J. O'Meara (ed.) *Platonic Investigations*, 111–38. Washington: Catholic University of America Press.

Armstrong, A.H. (1966) *Plotinus*, vol. 1: *Porphyry on Plotinus; Ennead I*. Cambridge, MA: Harvard University Press; revised 1989.

—— (1967) *Plotinus*, vol. 3: *Ennead III*. Cambridge, MA: Harvard University Press; repr. with corrections 1993.

—— (1984) *Plotinus*, vol. 5: *Ennead V*. Cambridge, MA: Harvard University Press.

—— (1988) *Plotinus*, vol. 6: *Ennead VI.1–5*. Cambridge, MA: Harvard University Press.

Assmann, J. (2008) *Of God and Gods: Egypt, Israel, and the Rise of Monotheism*. Madison: University of Wisconsin Press.

Athanassiadi, P. (ed.) (1999) *Damascius: The Philosophical History*. Athens: Apamea Cultural Association.

Aubry, G. (2004) *Plotin: Traité 53, I, 1. Introduction, traduction, commentaire et notes par Gwenaëlle Aubry*. Paris: Cerf.

Bagnall, R.S. (1996) *Egypt in Late Antiquity*. Princeton: Princeton University Press.

Baragwanath, E. (2008) *Motivation and Narrative in Herodotus*. Oxford: Clarendon Press.

Barnes, J. (1997) 'Roman Aristotle', in J. Barnes and M. Griffin (eds), *Philosophia Togata II*, pp. 1–70. Oxford: Oxford University Press.

—— (2003) *Porphyry: Introduction*. Oxford: Clarendon Press.

Barnes, J. and Griffin, M. (1997) *Philosophia Togata II: Plato and Aristotle at Rome*. Oxford: Oxford University Press.

Bénatouïl, T. and Bonazzi, M. (2012) *Theoria, Praxis, and the Contemplative Life after Plato and Aristotle*. Leiden: Brill.

Betegh, G. (2003) 'Cosmological Ethics in the *Timaeus* and Early Stoicism', *Oxford Studies in Ancient Philosophy* 24, 273–302.

Blank, D. (2012) 'Ammonius', in E. Zalta (ed.) *The Stanford Encyclopedia of Philosophy* (Winter 2012 Edition). <http://plato.stanford.edu/archives/win2012/entries/ammonius/>

Blumenthal, H.J. (1993a) 'Marinus' Life of Proclus', in Blumenthal (1993b) 469–94.

—— (1993b) *Soul and Intellect: Studies in Plotinus and later Neoplatonism*. Aldershot, Hampshire: Variorum.

Blumenthal, H.J. and Robinson, H. (eds) (1991) *Aristotle and the Later Tradition.*
Oxford Studies in Ancient Philosophy supp. 1991. Oxford: Oxford University Press.

Bonazzi, M. and Helmig, C. (2007) *Platonic Stoicism, Stoic Platonism?: The Dialogue*
Between Platonism and Stoicism in Antiquity. Leuven: Leuven University Press.

Bowersock, G. (1990) *Hellenism in Late Antiquity.* Jerome Lectures. Michigan and
Cambridge.

Brittain, C. (2005) 'Common Sense: Concepts, Definition, and Meaning in and out of
the Stoa', in Frede and Inwood (2005), 154–209.

Brown, P.R.L. (1992) *Power and Persuasion in Late Antiquity: Towards a Christian*
Empire. Madison: University of Wisconsin Press.

Burnyeat, M. (1977) 'Socratic Midwifery and Platonic Inspiration', *Bulletin of the*
Institute of Classical Studies 24, 7–17.

Busse, A. (1902) *Olympiodori prolegomena et in categorias commentarium.* Berlin:
Reimer.

Cameron, A.D. (1969) 'The Last Days of the Academy at Athens', *Proceedings of the*
Cambridge Philological Society 15, 7–29.

Carlini, A. (1964) *Platone: Alcibiade, Alcibiade secondo, Ipparco, Rivali.* Turin:
Boringhieri.

Cherniss, H. (1955) 'Aristotle, *Metaphysics* 987a32–b7', *AJP* 76, 184–6.

Chlup, R. (2012) *Proclus: An Introduction.* Cambridge: Cambridge University Press.

Clarke, E.C., Dillon, J.M. and Hershbell, J.P. (2003) *Iamblichus: On the Mysteries.*
Williston: Society of Biblical Literature.

Cooper, J.M. (2012) *Pursuits of Wisdom: Six Ways of Life in Ancient Philosophy from*
Socrates to Plotinus. Princeton: Princeton University Press.

Cooper, J.M. and Hutchinson, D.S. (eds) (1997) *Plato: Complete Works.* Indianapolis:
Hackett.

Cribiore, R. (2001) *Gymnastics of the Mind: Greek Education in Hellenistic and Roman*
Egypt. Princeton: Princeton University Press.

Denyer, N. (2001) *Plato: Alcibiades.* Cambridge: Cambridge University Press.

Derda, T., Markiewicz, T. and Wipszycka, E. (2007) *Alexandria: Auditoria of Kom*
el-Dikka and Late Antique Education. Journal of Juristic Papyrology.

Dillon, J.M. (1973) *Iamblichi Chalcidensis in Platonis Dialogos Commentariorum*
Fragmenta, Philosophia Antiqua 23. Leiden: Brill.

—— (1983) 'Plotinus, Philo and Origen on the Grades of Virtue', in H-D. Blume and
F. Mann (eds) *Platonismus und Christentum: Festschrift für Heinrich Dörrie*
(Jahrbuch für Antike und Christentum, Ergänzungsband 10), Münster:
Aschendorffsche Verlagsbuchhandlung.

—— (1996) 'An Ethic for the Late Antique Sage', in Gerson, L.P. (ed.) *The Cambridge*
Companion to Plotinus, pp. 315–35. Cambridge: Cambridge University Press.

—— (2002) 'The Platonic Philosopher at Prayer', in Kobusch and Erler (2002), 279–96.

Dodds, E.R. (1957) 'Olympiodorus: Commentary on the First Alcibiades of Plato', *Gnomon* 29.5, 356–9.

—— (1959) *Gorgias: A Revised Text with Introduction and Commentary*. Oxford: Clarendon Press.

—— (1963) *Proclus: The Elements of Theology* (2nd edn) Oxford: Clarendon Press.

Edwards, G. Fay. (2014) 'Irrational Animals in Porphyry's Logical Works: A Problem for the Consensus Interpretation of *On Abstinence*', *Phronesis* 59.1.

Edwards, M. (2000) *Neoplatonic Saints: The Lives of Plotinus and Proclus by their Students*. Liverpool: Liverpool University Press.

Festugière, A.-J. (1966) 'Proclus et la religion traditionnelle', in *Mélanges d'archéologie et d'histoire offerts à André Piganiol*, vol. 3, Paris: SEVPEN, 1581–90; repr. in A.-J. Festugière (1971) *Études de philosophie grecque*, Paris: Vrin, 575–84.

Finamore, J.F. (1985) *Iamblichus and the Theory of the Vehicle of the Soul*, Chico: Scholars Press; repr. Oxford: Oxford University Press, 2000.

Frankfurter, D. (2000) 'The Consequences of Hellenism in Late Antique Egypt: Religious Worlds and Actors', *Archiv für Religionsgeschichte* 2, 162–94.

—— (2009) 'The Interpenetration of Ritual Spaces in Late Antique Religions: An Overview', *Archiv für Religionsgeschichte* 10, 211–22.

Frede, D. and Inwood, B. (eds) (2005) *Language and Learning*. Cambridge: Cambridge University Press.

Frede, M. (1988) 'The Empiricist Attitude toward Reason and Theory', *Apeiron* 21, 79–97.

Friedländer, P. (1957) *Platon, II: Die Platonischen Schriften, Erste Periode* (2nd edn, Berlin: de Gruyter), tr. as *Plato 2: The Dialogues, First Period* (1964, London: Routledge and Kegan Paul).

Gehrke, H.-J. (2006) 'Ephebeia', *Brill's New Pauly*, antiquity volumes ed. Hubert Hancik and Helmuth Schneider; first appeared online 2006; accessed 2014. <http://referenceworks.brillonline.com/entries/brill-s-new-pauly/ephebeia-e331340>

Gerson, L.P. (2010) *The Cambridge History of Philosophy in Late Antiquity*, vol. 2. Cambridge: Cambridge University Press.

Gertz, S. (2011) *Death and Immortality in Late Neoplatonism: Studies on the Ancient Commentaries on Plato's* Phaedo. Leiden: Brill.

Gill, C. (2006) *The Structured Self in Hellenistic and Roman Thought*. Oxford: Oxford University Press.

—— (2007) 'Marcus Aurelius' *Meditations*: How Stoic and How Platonic?', in Bonazzi and Helmig (2007) 189–207.

Gribble, D. (1999) *Alcibiades and Athens: A Study in Literary Presentation*. Oxford: Clarendon Press.

Griffin, M.J. (2014a) 'Universals, Education, and Philosophical Methodology in Later Neoplatonism', in R. Chiaradonna and G. Galluzzo (eds) *Universals in Ancient Philosophy*, 353–80. Pisa: Edizioni della Scuola Normale.

—— (2014b) 'Hypostasizing Socrates', in D. Layne and H. Tarrant (eds) *The Neoplatonic Socrates*, 97–108. Pennsylvania: University of Pennsylvania Press.

—— (2014c) 'Pliable Platonism? Olympiodorus and the Profession of Philosophy in Sixth-Century Alexandria', in R.C. Fowler (ed.) *Plato in the Third Sophistic*, 73–101. Berlin: De Gruyter.

—— (2012). 'Proclus on Place as the Luminous Vehicle of the Soul'. *Dionysius* 30: 161–86.

Hadot, I. (1978) *Le problème du néoplatonisme alexandrin: Hiéroclès et Simplicius*. Paris: Études augustiniennes.

—— (1984) *Arts libéraux et philosophie dans la pensée antique*. Paris: Études augustiniennes.

—— (1987) (ed.) *Simplicius: sa vie, son oeuvre, sa survie*. Berlin: de Gruyter.

—— (1991) 'The Role of the Commentaries on Aristotle in the Teaching of Philosophy According to the Prefaces of the Neoplatonic Commentaries on the Categories', in Blumenthal and Robinson (1991) 175–89.

—— (1992) 'Aristote dans l'enseignement philosophique néoplatonicien. Les préfaces des commentaires sur les "Catégories" ', *Revue de Théologie et de Philosophie* 124, 407–25.

—— (1990) 'Les introductions aux commentaires exégétiques chez les auteurs néoplatoniciens et les auteurs chrétiens', in Hadot et al. (1990) 21–47; originally printed in M. Tardieu (ed.) *Les règles de l'interprétation*, 99–122. Paris: Cerf.

—— (1996) *Commentaire de Simplicius sur le 'Manuel' d'Épictète*. Introduction and critical edition of the Greek text. Leiden: Brill.

Hadot, I., Hoffmann, Ph., Hadot, P. and Mahé, J.-P. (1990) *Simplicius. Commentaire sur les 'Categories'*, tr. directed by I. Hadot, vol. 1: *Introduction. Première partie*. Leiden: Brill.

Hadot, P. (1995) *Philosophy as a Way of Life: Spiritual Exercises from Socrates to Foucault*, tr. Michael Chase. Oxford: Blackwell.

—— (2002) *What is Ancient Philosophy?*, tr. Michael Chase. Cambridge: Harvard University Press.

Hamlyn, D.W. (1977–78) 'Focal Meaning', *Proceedings of the Aristotelian Society* 78, 1–18.

Hatzimichali, M. (2013) 'The Texts of Plato and Aristotle in the First Century BC', in Schofield (2013), 1–27.

Hoffmann, Ph. (1987) 'Catégories et langage selon Simplicius – la question du "skopos" du traité aristotélicien des Catégories', in Hadot (1978), 61–90.

—— (2012) 'What was Commentary in Late Antiquity? The Example of the Neoplatonic Commentators', in M.L. Gill and P. Pellegrin (eds) *A Companion to Ancient Philosophy*, 597–622. Chichester: John Wiley & Sons.

Huddleston, J. 2006. *Homer: Odyssey*, in A. Kahane and M. Mueller (eds) *The Chicago Homer*. <http://digital.library.northwestern.edu/homer>

Jackson, R., Lycos, K. and Tarrant, H. (1998) *Olympiodorus: Commentary on Plato's Gorgias, Translated with Full Notes*. Leiden: Brill.

Johnson, M. and Tarrant, H. (eds) (2011) *Alcibiades and the Socratic Lover-Educator*. London: Bristol Classical Press.

Joyal, M. (2000) *The Platonic Theages: An Introduction, Commentary, and Critical Edition*. Stuttgart: Steiner Verlag.

—— (2003) Review of Denyer, *Plato: Alcibiades*. *Bryn Mawr Classical Review* 2003.01.28.

Karamanolis, G.E. (2006) *Plato And Aristotle in Agreement?: Platonists on Aristotle from Antiochus to Porphyry*. Oxford: Clarendon Press.

Kaster, R. (1988) *Guardians of Language: The Grammarian and Society in Late Antiquity*. Berkeley: University of California Press.

Kiessling, T. (1826) (ed.) *Ioannis Tzetzes Historiarum Variarum Chiliades*. Leipzig.

Kobusch, T. and Erler, M. (eds) (2002) *Metaphysik und Religion: Zur Signatur des spätantiken Denkens*. Akten des internationalen Kongresses vom 13.–17. März in Würzburg, Munich and Leipzig: Saur.

Kuisma, O. (1996) *Proclus' Defense of Homer* (Commentationes Humanarum Litterarum, 109). Helsinki: Societas Scientiarum Fennica.

Lamberton, R. (1989) *Homer the Theologian: Neoplatonist Allegorical Reading and the Growth of the Epic Tradition*. Berkeley: University of California Press.

Lane, M. (2011) 'Reconsidering Socratic Irony', in D.R. Morrison (ed.), *The Cambridge Companion to Socrates*, 237–59. Cambridge: Cambridge University Press.

Layne, D. and Tarrant, H. (eds) (2014) *The Neoplatonic Socrates*. Philadelphia: University of Pennsylvania Press.

Lattimore, R. (1951) *Homer: Iliad*. Chicago: University of Chicago Press, repr. with new introduction and notes by Richard Martin, 2011.

Lewy, H. (2011) *Chaldaean Oracles and Theurgy. Troisième édition par Michel Tardieu avec un supplément 'Les Oracles chaldaïques 1891–2001'*. Collection des Études Augustiniennes, Série Antiquité 77. Paris: Institut d'Études Augustiniennes.

Liddell, H.G. and Scott, R. (1996) *A Greek-English Lexicon*, revised and augmented throughout by Sir Henry Stuart Jones, with the assistance of Roderick McKenzie, and with the co-operation of many scholars. Supplement edited by P.G.W. Glare, 9th edn. Oxford: Clarendon Press.

Linguiti, A. (2012) 'Plotinus and Porphyry on the Contemplative Life', in Bénatouïl and Bonazzi (2012), 183–98.

Lloyd, A.B. (1976) *Herodotus Book II: Commentary 1–98*. Leiden: Brill.

Lloyd, A.C. (1967) 'The Later Neoplatonists', in A.H. Armstrong (ed.) *The Cambridge History of Later Greek and Early Medieval Philosophy*, 269–325. Cambridge: Cambridge University Press.

—— (1990) *The Anatomy of Neoplatonism*. Oxford: Clarendon Press.

Long, A.A. and Sedley, D.N. (1987) *The Hellenistic Philosophers*, 2 vols. Cambridge: Cambridge University Press.

MacKenna, S. (1957) *Plotinus: The Enneads*, tr. Stephen MacKenna; 2nd edn revised by B.S. Page, with a foreword by Professor E.R. Dodds, and an introduction by Professor Paul Henry, S.J. London: Faber and Faber.

Majcherek, G. (2010) 'The Auditoria on Kom el-Dikka: A Glimpse of Late Antique Education in Alexandria', in T. Gagos (ed.) *The Proceedings of the 25th International Congress of Papyrology*. American Studies in Papyrology, 471–84. Ann Arbor: University of Michigan Library.

Majercik, R. (1989) *The Chaldaean Oracles: Text, Translation and Commentary*. Studies in Greek and Roman Religion 5. Leiden: Brill.

Mansfeld, J. (1994) *Prolegomena: Questions to be Settled before the Study of an Author, or a Text*. Philosophia Antiqua 61. Leiden: Brill.

Menn, S. (2002) 'Plato and the Method of Analysis', *Phronesis* 47.3.

Moyer, I.S. (2011) *Egypt and the Limits of Hellenism*. Cambridge: Cambridge University Press.

Norvin, W. (ed.) (1913) *Olympiodori philosophi in Platonis Phaedonem commentaria*. Leipzig.

Notopoulos, J.A. (1939) 'The Name of Plato', *CP* 34, 135–45.

Obbink, D. (1992) ' "What all men believe – Must be true": Common Conceptions and *consensio omnium* in Aristotle and Hellenistic Philosophy', *Oxford Studies in Ancient Philosophy* 10, 193–231.

O'Meara, D.J. (2003) *Platonopolis: Platonic Political Philosophy in Late Antiquity*. Oxford: Clarendon Press.

O'Neill, W. (1965) *Proclus: Alcibiades I – A Translation and Commentary*. The Hague: Nijhoff.

Opsomer, J. (2010) 'Olympiodorus', in Gerson (2010), 697–710.

Opsomer, J. and Steel, C. (2012) *Ten Problems Concerning Providence*. London: Bristol Classical Press.

Owen, G.E.L. (1960) 'Logic and Metaphysics in Some Earlier Works of Aristotle', in I. Düring and G.E.L. Owen (eds) *Aristotle and Plato in the Mid-Fourth Century:*

Papers of the Symposium Aristotelicum held at Oxford in August, 1957, 163–90. Göteborg, repr. in J. Barnes, M. Schofield and R.R.K. Sorabji (eds) *Articles on Aristotle 1: Science* (London: Duckworth, 1975), 13–32.

Pease, A. S. (1920) (ed.) *M. Tulli Ciceronis De divinatione, liber primus*, University of Illinois Studies in Language and Literature 6.2, Urbana: University of Illinois.

Primavesi, O. (2007) 'Ein Blick in den Stollen von Skepsis: Vier Kaptiel zur frühen Überlieferung des Corpus Aristotelicum', *Philologus* 151.

Rashed, M. (1997) Textes inédits transmis par l'Ambr. Q 74 sup.: Alexandre d'Aphrodise et Olympiodore d'Alexandrie. *Revue des sciences philosophiques et théologiques*, 81.2, 219–38.

Renaud, F. (2011) 'Socrates' Divine Sign: From the Alcibiades to Olympiodorus', in Johnson and Tarrant (2011), 190–9.

Richard, M. (1950) 'Apo phones', *Byzantion* 20, 191–222.

Riginos, A. (1976) *Platonica: The Anecdotes Concerning the Life and Writings of Plato*. Leiden: Brill.

Rose, V. (1886) *Aristotelis qui ferebantur librorum fragmenta collegit*. Leipzig: Teubner.

Ross, W.D. (1924) *Aristotle's 'Metaphysics'*. Oxford: Clarendon Press.

Ruelle, C.A. (1889) (ed.) *Damascii successoris dubitationes et solutiones de primis principiis*, 2 vols. Paris: C. Klincksieck.

Saffrey, H.-D. (1981) 'Les néoplatoniciens et les Oracles Chaldaïques', *Revue des etudes augustiniennes* 27, 209–25.

—— (1984) 'Quelques aspects de la spiritualité des philosophes néoplatoniciens de Jamblique à Proclus et Damascius', in *Revue des sciences philosophiques et théologiques* 68, 169–82; repr. in H.-D. Saffrey (1990) *Recherches sur le néoplatonisme après Plotin*, 213–26. Paris: Vrin.

—— (2005) 'Olympiodore d'Alexandrie', in R. Goulet (ed.), *Dictionnaire des philosophes antiques* IV, 769–71. Paris, C.N.R.S.

Schamp, J. and Amato, E. (2006) *Approches de la troisième sophistique: hommages à Jacques Schamp* (p. 614). Editions Latomus.

Schleiermacher, F. (1836) *Schleiermacher's Introductions to the Dialogues of Plato*, tr. William Dobson. Cambridge: J. & J.J. Deighton; repr. Bristol: Thoemmes Press, 1992.

Schniewind, A. (2003) *L'Éthique du sage chez Plotin. Le paradigm du* spoudaios. Paris: Vrin.

—— (2005) 'The Social Concern of the Plotinian Sage', in Smith (2005), 51–64.

Schofield, M. (2013) *Aristotle, Plato and Pythagoreanism in the First Century BC: New Directions for Philosophy*. Cambridge: Cambridge University Press.

Sedley, D. (2012) *The Philosophy of Antiochus*. Cambridge: Cambridge University Press.

Segonds, A. (1985) *Proclus. Sur le premier Alcibiade de Platon, Tome 1*. Paris: Belles Lettres; repr. 2003.

—— (1986) *Proclus. Sur le premier Alcibiade de Platon, Tome 2*. Paris: Belles Lettres; repr. 2003.

Segonds, A. and Luna, C. (eds) (2007) *Proclus. Commentaire sur le Parménide de Platon. Tome 1, 1re partie: Introduction générale, 2e partie: Livre I, texte*. Paris: Belles Lettres.

Sheppard, A.D.R. (1980) *Studies on the 5th and 6th Essays of Proclus' Commentary on the Republic*. Göttingen: Vandenhoeck & Ruprecht.

Siorvanes, L. (1996) *Proclus: Neo-platonic Philosophy and Science*. New Haven: Yale University Press.

Slings, S.R. (1999) *Plato: Clitophon*. Cambridge: Cambridge University Press.

Smith, A. (2005) (ed.) *The Philosopher and Society in Late Antiquity*. Swansea: Classical Press of Wales.

Sommerstein, A.H. and Bayliss, A.J. (2012) *Oath and State in Ancient Greece*. Berlin: De Gruyter.

Sorabji, R. (1983) *Time, Creation, and the Continuum: Theories in Antiquity and the Middle Ages*. London: Duckworth.

—— (1990) *Aristotle Transformed: The Ancient Commentators and Their Influence*. London/Ithaca, NY: Duckworth/Cornell University Press.

—— (2005a) 'Divine Names and Sordid Deals in Ammonius' Alexandria', in Smith (2005), 203–14.

—— (2005) *The Philosophy of the Commentators 200–600 AD. A Sourcebook*, vol 1: *Psychology (With Ethics and Religion)*; vol. 2: *Physics*; vol. 3: *Logic and Metaphysics*. Ithaca: Cornell University Press [first published London: Duckworth, 2004].

—— (2006) *Self: Ancient and Modern Theories about Individuality, Life, and Death*. Oxford: Clarendon Press.

Steel, C. (2007) *Proclus: On Providence*. London: Duckworth.

Stuve, G. (1900) *Olympiodori in Aristotelis meteora commentaria*. Berlin: Reimer.

Tarrant, H. (1997) 'Olympiodorus and the Surrender of Paganism', in L. Garland (ed.) *Conformity and Non-Conformity in Byzantium. Byzantinische Forschungen* 24, 181–92. Amsterdam: Hakkert.

—— (2000) *Plato's First Interpreters*. London/Ithaca, NY: Duckworth/Cornell University Press.

—— (2007) 'Olympiodorus and Proclus on the Climax of the Alcibiades', *International Journal of the Platonic Tradition* 1.1, 3–29.

van den Berg, R.M. (2001) *Proclus' Hymns. Essays, Translations, Commentary.* Leiden: Brill.

—— (2008) *Proclus' Commentary on the Cratylus in Context: Ancient Theories of Language and Naming.* Leiden: Brill.

—— (2009) ' "As we are always speaking of them and using their names on every occasion". Plotinus, *Enn.* III.7 [45]: Language, Experience and the Philosophy of Time in Neoplatonism', in R. Chiaradonna and F. Trabattoni (eds) *Physics and Philosophy of Nature in Greek Neoplatonism: Proceedings of the European Science Foundation Exploratory Workshop, June 22–23, 2006. Philosophia Antiqua* 115. Leiden: Brill.

Van Hoof, L. (2010) 'Greek Rhetoric and the Later Roman Empire: The Bubble of the "Third Sophistic" ', *Antiquité Tardive* 18, 211–224.

Van Riel, G. (2000) *Pleasure and the Good Life: Plato, Aristotle, and the Neoplatonists. Philosophia Antiqua* 85. Leiden: Brill.

—— (2012) 'Damascius on the Contemplative Life', in Bénatouïl and Bonazzi 2012, 199–212.

Viano, C. (2006) *La matière des choses: le livre IV des Météorologiques d'Aristote et son interprétation par Olympiodore.* Paris: Vrin.

Vogt, E. (1957) (ed.) *Procli hymni accedunt hymnorum fragmenta; epigrammata, scholia, fontium et locorum similium apparatus, indices.* Wiesbaden: Harrassowitz.

von Arnim, H.F.A. (1964) *Stoicorum Veterum Fragmenta*, 4 vols. Stuttgart: Teubner.

Watts, E. (2006) *City and School in Late Antique Athens and Alexandria.* Berkeley: University of California Press.

—— (2010) *Riot in Alexandria: Tradition and Group Dynamics in Late Antique Pagan and Christian Communities.* Berkeley: University of California Press.

Westerink, L.G. (1962) *Anonymous Prolegomena to Platonic Philosophy.* Amsterdam: North-Holland Publishing Co.; repr. Westbury: Prometheus Trust, 2010.

—— (1970) *Olympiodori in Platonis Gorgiam commentaria.* Leipzig: Teubner.

—— (1976) *The Greek Commentators on Plato's Phaedo*, vol. I: *Olympiodorus.* Amsterdam: North-Holland Publishing Company.

—— (1977) *The Greek Commentators on Plato's Phaedo*, vol. II: *Damascius.* Amsterdam: North-Holland Publishing Company.

—— (1982) *Olympiodorus. Commentary on the first Alcibiades of Plato.* Amsterdam: Hakkert. 2nd printing with addenda (1st printing 1956).

—— (1990) 'The Alexandrian Commentators and the Introductions to their Commentaries', in Sorabji 1990, 325–48.

Whitmarsh, T. (2005) *The Second Sophistic.* Cambridge: Cambridge University Press.

Wildberg, C. (2005) 'Philosophy in the Age of Justinian', in M. Maas (ed.) *The Age of Justinian*, 316–40. Cambridge: Cambridge University Press.

—— (2007) 'Olympiodorus', in E. Zalta (ed.) *The Stanford Encyclopedia of Philosophy*, Fall 2007 edition. <http://plato.stanford.edu/entries/olympiodorus/>

—— (2008) 'David', in E. Zalta (ed.) *The Stanford Encyclopedia of Philosophy*, Fall 2008 edition. <http://plato.stanford.edu/entries/david>

Zintzen, C. (1967) *Damascius' Life of Isidore: Damascii vitae Isidori reliquiae.* Hildesheim: Olms.

English-Greek Glossary

abandon: *apallattesthai*
ability: *dunamis*
abundance: *periousia*
achieve: *prattein*
act out: *prattein*
action: *praxis*
activity: *energeia, energein*
adolescence: *ephêbia*
advantageous: *sumpheron*
adviser: *sumboulos*
aetherial: *aithêrios*
affair: *pragma*
affection: *pathos*
airy: *aerios*
ambiguous, to say something:
    epamphoterizein
ambivalent, to be: *amphiballein*
analogy: *analogia*
angel: *angelos*
another, moved by: *heterokinêtos*;
    heterokinêtôs
another, movement by:
    heterokinêsia
another, taught by: *heterodidaktos*
appear: *phainesthai*
appearance: *phantasia*
appetite, appetitive desire:
    epithumia
appropriate: *oikeios*
art: *tekhnê*
associate: *homilêtês*
athletically, to perform: *gumnastikôs*
awaken: *egeirein*

beautiful: *kalos*
beauty: *kallos*
becoming: *genesis*
being: *on, pragma*
beloved: *erômenos, paidika*
beneficent: *euergetikos*
beyond the cosmos: *huperkosmios*
bind: *sundein*
blameless: *anaitios*
bloom of youth: *hêlikia*
boast: *megalaukhein,*
    megalorrhêmonein
body: *sôma*
boundless deep: *abussos*
bubble over: *bluzein*

causally: *kath' aitian*
cause: *aitios, aitia*
chain: *desmos, seira*
cheat: *adikein*
chorus: *khoros*
circumstantial: *peristatikos*
civic life, civic affairs: *politika*
civic person, as: *politikôs*
civic person, person of civic excellence):
    politikos
civically: *politikôs*
class: *eidos, genos*
cognitive: *gnôstikos*
combative: *eristikos*
combination (of soul and body):
    sunamphoteron
commentator: *exêgêtês*

commentators, (the view) adopted by: *exêgêtikos*

common usage (in Christianity): *sunêtheia*

compassion: *sumpatheia*

conceit: *khaunotês*

concept: *ennoia*

conclusion, in: *teleutaios*

condition: *hexis*

conflict, enjoying: *philoneikos*

conscience: *suneidos*

conscientious: *sôphrôn*

consciousness: *suneidos*

constitution: *politeia*

contemplation: *theôria*

contemplative person, one of contemplative excellence: *theôretikos*

contemplatively, as a contemplative person: *theôretikôs*

contentious attitude, to have: *enantiousthai*

coordinate: *parametrein*

corrective treatment, to give: *kolazein*

corrective treatment: *kolasis*

cosmos, within: *enkosmios*

crowd, to: *enokhlein*

crowding: *okhlêsis*

crude: *phortikos*

current affairs, based on: *peristatikos*

daimon: *daimôn*

daimonic beings: *daimonia*

daimonic: *daimonios*

daimonically, like a daimon: *daimoniôs*

dare: *tolman*

darkening: *amaurôsis*

dear to one's heart: *oikeios*

defectiveness of character: *kakia*

demonstrate: *endeiknusthai*

demonstration, without: *anapodeiktôs*

demonstration: *apodeixis*

depend on, to: *artân*

dependently upon: *skhetikôs*

desire: *epithumein*

difference: *diaphora*

difficult: *khalepos*

discipline: *askêsis*

display: *epideiknusthai*

distinguish: *diairein*

distort: *diastrephein*

divine: *theios*

divinely inspired: *entheos*

divinity: *theotês*

division: *diairesis*

do ill: *dustunkhanein*

doctor: *iatros*

doctrine: *dogma*

drive: *ephesis*

dumb, to play alongside: *sunagnoein*

eager, be: *spoudazein*

earthly: *khthonios*

effect: *aitiaton*

effeminate: *thêluprepês*

emanation: *ellampsis*

embracing every [musical] mode: *panharmonios*

enchanted: *katokhos*

engage in acts: *energein*

engender life: *zôopoiein*

epilepsy: *selêniakos pathos* (lit. moon-disease)

error: *hamartêma*

error: *plêmmelêma*

essence, according to one's own: *kat' ousian*

essence: *ousia*

essentially: *kat' ousian*

ethics, on the (interpretive) level of: *êthikôs*

everlasting: *aïdios*

exact: *akribês*

exactly: *akribôs*

examine: *exetazein*

excellence; excellence of character: *aretê*

exchange: *metameibô*

exhort: *protrepein*

exhortation, relating to: *protreptikos*

existence, in: *kath' huparxin*

existence: *huparxis*

explanation: *logos*

eye: *ophthalmos*

faculty: *dunamis*

falling away: *apoptôsis*

familiar: *oikeios*

fasten: *exaptein*

faultless: *anamartêtos*

feathers, shedding: *pterorrhuein*

fiery: *purios*

figure (of speech): *skhêma*

finally: *teleutaios*

first principle: *arkhê*

first: *prôtos*

flux, in a state of: *rheustos*

form: *eidos*

form-like: *eidetikos*

formula: *logos*

fountain: *namata*

fulfill: *teleioun*

fulfilled: *teleios*

fulfilment: *teleiotês*

furnish abundantly: *khorêgein*

generation: *genos*

genus: *genos*

geometer: *geômetrês*; of linear shapes, *grammikos*

goal: *telos*

god: *theos*

godlike way, in: *theoeidôs*

godlike: *theoeidôs*

good: *agathos*

good birth: *eugeneia*

good hope: *euelpis*

good person: *spoudaios*

good timing: *eukairia*

great-minded: *megalophronos*

great-mindedness: *megalosôphrosunê*

grow along with: *sunauxanein*

guard: *epitropeuein*

guardian: *epitropos*

guesswork, limited to: *eikazein*

have in mind: *ennoein*

headstrong: *authadês*

heal: *epanorthoun*

heavenly: *ouranios*

herd mentality, with: *agelaios*

hero: *hêrôs*

heroic: *hêrôikos*

historian: *sungrapheus*

hold in high esteem: *eudokimein*

holy of holies: *aduton*

honour: *timan*

house-building: *oikodomia*

human being: *anthrôpos*

humour: *khumos*

hypotheses, not requiring: *anhupothetikos*

idea: *logos*

ignorance: *agnoia*

ignorant, to be: *agnoein*

ill-being: *kakodaimonia*

image: *eidôlon, indalma, phantasia*

imagination: *phantasia*; not captured by imagination, *aphantasiastos*

immortal: *athanatos*

immortality: *athanasia*

important to pick out: *exairetos*

indulgence: *akolasia*

inquire into, investigate: *zêtein*

inquiry: *zêtêsis*

inspiration: *enthousiasmos*

inspired manner, in: *enthousiastikôs*

instrument: *organon*

intellect: *nous*

intellective: *noêros*

intellectively: *noêrôs*

intellectually aware, to become: *noein*

intention: *prohairesis*

intermediary: *mesos*

interpret: *dihermeneuein*

interpreter: *dihermêneutikos*

judgement: *krisis*

judgement, to form: *krinein*

just: *dikaios*

justice: *dikaiosunê*

knick-knack: *skeuarion*

knowledge: *epistêmê, gnôsis*

knowledge, having the capacity for: *gnôstikos*

labyrinth: *laburinthos*

last: *teleutaios*

laughable: *geloion*

leader of the (philosophical) chorus: *koruphaios*

learn, to: *manthanein*

learning: *mathêsis*

lecture: *praxis*

lesson: *dogma*

life-engendering: *zôtikos*

life-style: *diatribê*

lifeless: *apsukhos*

lineage: *genos*

link: *sunaptein*

lively: *diegêgermenos* (perf. ppl. from *egeirein*)

living being: *zôion*

look down on, to: *huperphronein*

loss, being at: *aporein, aporia*

love: *erôs;* Love (the god), *Erôs*

love, to: *erasthai, erân*

love, being about: *erôtikos*

love, reciprocation of: *anterôs*

lover: *erastês*

lover's disposition, having: *erôtikos*

lowest: *eskhatos*

luminous: *augoeidês*

majority, the: *hoi polloi*

many: *polus*

master: *tithaseuein*

material: *hulôos*

matter: *hulê*

medicine: *pharmakon*

merely: *haplôs*

method: *methodos*

midwife: *maia, maieutês*

midwifery, practise: *maieuein*

midwifery, relating to: *maieutikos*

military command: *stratêgikos*

mirror: *katoptron*

misrepresent: *sophizein*

mistake, make: *hamartanein*

mob: *okhlos*

moderation: *sôphrosunê*

money, caring for, loving, or being fond of: *philokhrêmatos*

moon: *sêlênê*
moon, relating to: *sêlêniakos*
motivation: *orexis*
much: *polus*
much-learning: *poluêkoia*

natural: *phusikos*
natural gifts: *euphuïa*
natural philosophy, on the (interpretive)
   level of: *phusikôs*
naturally gifted: *euphuês*
nature: *phusis*
noble: *kalos*
non-rational, irrational: *alogos*

oath: *horkos*
oath, false: *epiorkia*
obstruct: *aporein*
obstruction: *aporia*
obtain by lot: *lankhanein*
one: *heis*
one's own: *oikeios*
onerous: *khalepos*
oneself: *heautos*
only: *monos*
open-ended: *distaktikos*
opportunity: *kairos*
opposite: *enantion*
opposition: *enantiotês*
oratorical aspirations, having: *rhêtorikos*
oratory, disposed to: *rhêtorikos*
origin: *arkhê*
outstanding effort, to apply: *spoudazein*
outstanding person: *spoudaios*
ovoid: *ôioeides*

parentage and life: *genos*
part: *meros*
passion: *pathos*

pattern: *tupos*
people: *dêmos*
perceptible: *aisthêtôs*
performing musically: *mousikôs*
person: *anthrôpos*
personality: *prosôpon*
phantasm: *phantasia*
physiognomic signs: *phusiognômonikos*
place: *topos*
pleasure, caring for, loving, or being
   fond of: *philêdonos*
point: *logos*
position: *taxis*
possession: *ktêma*
potential: *dunamis*
power: *dunamis*
praise: *epainos*
precise fix: *akriboun*
precisely, with precision: *akribôs*
presence, without: *aparousiastôs*
present with, to be: *suneinai*
preside over: *ephistasthai*
pride: *huperopsia, thumos*
primarily: *proêgoumenôs*
prize: *agapan*
process of unification: *henôsis*
proem: *prooimion*
proper: *oikeios*
prophecy, of: *mantikos*
prosyllogism: *prosullogismos*
psychic, to do with the soul: *psukhikos*
punishment, corrective: *kolasis*
pupil: *korê*
purificatory excellence, person of:
   kathartikos
purificatory person: *kathartikos*
purificatory person, acting as:
   kathartikôs
puzzle, raise: *aporein*

race: *genos*

radiance: *ellampsis*

rash: *propetês*

rational: *logikos*

reach out for: *oregesthai*

reality: *pragma*

reason: *logos*

reason, in common with: *logoeidês*

recoil: *aneillein*

reconciliation, leading to: *sumbibastikôs*

recurrent nature, having: *apokatastatikos*

refutation: *elenkhos*

refutation, relating to: *elenktikos*

relation: *skhesis*

relation, by: *kata skhesin*

release: *epilusis*

relevant: *oikeios*

remedy: *iasis*

reputation: *timê*

reputation, caring for, loving, or being
   fond of: *philotimia*

reputation, one who cares for: *philotimos*

responsible: *aitios*

revere: *semnunein*

revert: *epistrephein*

reverter: *epistrophos*

rhythm: *rhuthmos*

riddle: *ainigma*

right moment: *kairos*

roundabout way: *hupostolê*

rush, to be in: *epeigein*

sacred image: *agalma*

same; selfsame: *autos*

scientific (as opposed to empirical):
   logikos

scorn: *kataphronein*

season, of the: *opôra*

section: *kephalaion*

self: *autos*

self-movement: *autokinêsia*

self-moving: *autokinêtos, autokinêtôs*

self-originated: *autophuês*

self-sufficient: *autarkês*

sensation: *aisthêsis*

sequence, in: *metabatikôs*

servant: *hupêretês*

sexual: *aphrodisios*

shadows, fight over: *skiamakhein*

shape: *skhêma*

shell-like: *ostreïnos*

ship-building: *naupêgia*

shrink: *meiousthai*

shrink along with: *summeiousthai*

sight-lover: *philotheamôn*

similar: *homoios*

similar to the good: *agathoeidês*

simply: *haplôs*

skill: *tekhnê*

sociably: *politikôs*

Socratically: *Sôkratikôs*

song: *ôidê*

soul: *psukhê*

speech: *logos*

spirited emotion: *thumos*

standard: *gnômôn*

starry: *astrôos*

statesmanly: *politikôs*

status, with: *timios*

strange: *atopos*

stream with: *pêgazein*

strength: *rhôsis*

study with or under (a teacher):
   phoitân

succeed: *eutunkhanein*

sufficient: *hikanos*

suitable attitude, suitability: *epitêdeiotês*

superabundance: *huperbolê*

supporting: *sumphônos*
swear falsely: *epiorkein*
sympathy: *sumpatheia*
syntax, not part of: *sumplektikos*

target (of a text): *skopos*
Tartarus, under: *hupotartarios*
teachable: *didaktos*
teacher: *didaskalos*
tending to revert: *epistreptikos*
theology, on the (interpretive) level of:
   theologikôs
theory: *logos*; *theorêma*
think little of: *kataphronein*
thought: *noêma*
touch: *haphê*
touch, by means of: *haptikôs*
transparent: *diaphanês*
treat: *khrân*
true: *oikeios*
truly good: *spoudaios*
turn aside: *apotrepein*

unambiguous: *haplos*
unambiguously: *apophantikôs*
uneducated: *amathês*
unhypothetical: *anhupothetikos*
unintelligent: *anoêtos*
unitary in form: *henoeidês*

unity: *henas*, *henôsis*
universal: *katholou*
unmanly: *anandros*
unqualifiedly: *haplôs*
unstable: *astathmêtos*
up to us: *en hêmin*, *eph' hêmin*
usefulness: *khrêsimon*
utterance: *phônê*

vegetative: *phutikos*
vehicle: *okhêma*
vision: *phasma*

watch, keep: *phrourein*
watery: *enudrios*
wax: *auxanein*
well-being: *eudaimonia*
what is wanted: *boulêtos*
whole: *holos*
wisdom: *sophia*
wonder: *thauma*
wonder, causing: *thaumastos*
wonder, to: *thaumazein*
word: *logos*
words and ideas, of: *logikos*
worthy: *axios*
wrong, go: *hamartanein*

young man: *neos*

Greek-English Index

This index lists a selection of the more important words in the Greek text translated in this volume (1,3–90,24). A fuller index may be found in Westerink's word list (Westerink 1982, Index II). The translations given here may not correspond exactly to the rendering of them in a particular passage in the English text, since the demands of idiomatic translation may call for variations; but it should always be possible to work out what word is being translated. References are to the page and line numbers of the Greek text (indicated in the margins of the translation).

abussos, boundless deep, 19,7.10
adikein, cheat, 11,20
aduton, holy of holies, 11,4.5
aerios, airy, 19,15
agalma, sacred image, 2,137
agapan, prize, 48,23
agathoeidês, similar to the good, 39,17; 48,12
agathos, good, 10,11; 14,18; 23,14; 31,8; 32,3.6.12; 35,8.16.18; 38,16; 39,16; 40,1; 46,15.16; 47,22.26; 48,1.2.4.5.7.8.10.12; 49,8; 62,22.23; 63,1.5.6.10; 64,5.10.13; 65,19; 67,12.21; 68,5.7.10.12; 69,2; 74,1.3.12; 80,15; 81,4
agelaios, with a herd mentality, 53,23
agnoein, be ignorant, 10,20; 11,9.10
agnoia, ignorance, 24,13
aïdios, everlasting, 10,3.6; 17,3
ainigma, riddle, 9,15
aisthêsis, sensation, 22,9
aisthêtôs, perceptible, 27,28
aithêrios, aetherial, 17,3–4; 19,14
aitiaton, effect, 15,2
aitia, cause, 24,23; 33,20; in *kath' aitian*, causally, 15,12.13; with a cause, 34,20; 38,18; responsibility, 45,3
aitios, cause, 15,3; 26,3.5.7; responsible, 45,9
akolasia, indulgence, 14,23

akribês, exact, 62,23; 63,3.5; 69,14.18
akribôs, exactly, 4,15; 11,21; with precision, 35,9
akriboun, have a precise fix on, 64,8
alogos, non-rational, 8,2; 9,5; 17,13; 18,10
amathês, uneducated, 11,9
amaurôsis, darkening, 32,11
amphiballein, be ambivalent, 24,12
anaitios, blameless, 45,3
analogia, analogy, 15,7.8.10
anamartêtos, faultless, 23,3.5
anandros, unmanly, 14,12
anapodeiktôs, without demonstration, 18,4–5
aneillein, recoil, 23,7
angelos, angel, 21,12.19; 22,3.4
anhupothetikos, not requiring hypotheses, unhypothetical, 40,19; 41,3; 47,6; 61,1
anoêtos, unintelligent, 14,13
anterôs, reciprocation of love, 12,20; 87,8
anthrôpos, human being, person, 1,4.6; 2,17.100.135.147; 3,6; 4,3.18; 9,2.9.17.18; 10,12; 12,6; 15,1.2.5; 26,3.6; 28,7.8; 31,3; 35,3; 38,4; 39,1; 40,23; 42,10; 43,18; 45,20; 46,1; 47,22; 50,23; 53,12.16; 72,27; 73,5
apallattesthai, abandon, 13,11.18
aparousiastôs, without [physical] presence, 28,9

aphantasiastos, cannot be captured by imagination, 8,13
aphrodisios, sexual, 33,14–15
apodeixis, demonstration, 18,4
apokatastatikos, having a recurrent nature, 37,11–12
apophantikôs, unambiguously, 37,17
apoptôsis, falling away, 32,7–8
aporein, obstruct, 40,9–16; raise an [exegetical] puzzle, 52,21; 54,9; 55,15; 75,15; 82,10; be at a loss, 76,6; 78,1; 79,24; 82,12.17; 83,19; 84,10
aporia, obstruction, 40,9–16; being at a loss, 82,20
apotrepein, turn aside, 21,2.3
apsukhos, lifeless, 12,14
aretê, excellence of character, 10,15; 30,4–10; 73,6
arkhê, origin, 32,23; first principle, 40,21
artân, depend on, 32,9
askêsis, discipline, 30,6
astathmêtos, unstable, 25,13
astrôos, starry, 19,9
athanasia, immortality, 10,2
athanatos, immortal, 10,6
atopos, strange, 59,9
augoeidês, luminous, 16,12; 17,4
autarkês, self-sufficient, 7,7; 10,14; 42,15.16; 55,10.20.21.22.23
authadês, headstrong, 29,12–13
autokinêsia, self-movement, 81,26
autokinêtos, self-moving, 7,12; 8,2; 11,14; 82,4; 87,22
autokinêtôs, self-moving, 61,3.5.14; 63,13.21; 81,25
autophuês, self-originated, 11,15
autos, self, 4,8–14 *passim*; selfsame, 51,16
auxanein, wax, 18,14.15
axios, worthy, 24,11

bluzein, bubble over, 16,9
boulêtos, what is wanted, 39,19–20; 46,16–17

daimon, daimon, 14,5.6; 15,5–23,17 *passim*
daimonios, daimonic, 15,5–23,17 *passim*; 26,8; *daimonia*, daimonic beings, 22,16
daimoniôs, like a daimon, 84,10
dêmos, people, 25,10.12.13.14

desmos, chain, 5,2
diairein, distinguish, 11,8; 17,11
diairesis, division, 11,7
diaphanês, transparent, 17,3
diaphora, difference, 13,12.24; 14,9.10.20.22; 15,6; 17,14; 18.1; 39,19; 75,21.22
diastrephein, distort, 16,14
diatribê, life-style, 2,77
didaktos, teachable, 70,3
didaskalos, teacher, 11,10.17.19; 12,7
diermeneuein, interpret, 17,10
diermêneutikos, interpreter, 17,9
dikaios, just, 3,16–4,1; 11,21.22; 64,8; 72,15.16.26; 73,1.3.9.11.17; 74,5.6.7.13; 75,14.22; 80,7.9; 81,20; 82,11.12.14; 86,10.11.17.18; 87,2.17; 88,6.7.9; 89,9
dikaiosunê, justice, 73,9.11; 75,22.23
distaktikos, open-ended, 24,19
dogma, doctrine, 12,7; lesson, 43,22; 44,14; 45,15
dunamis, power, 14,24; 26,8.9.13; 32,10; 35,4, 38,22; 39,21; 46,20; faculty, 23,17; ability, 62,23
dustunkhanein, do ill, 47,25

egeirein, awaken; perf. ppl. *diegêgermenos*, lively, 24,3
eidetikos, form-like, 18,11
eidôlon, image, 32,17
eidos, form, 17,13; 18,11–12; class, 19,11
eikazein, limited to guesswork, 24,12
elenkhos, refutation, 29,18; 35,2
elenktikos, of refutation, 11,8.9.23
ellampsis, radiance, 14,1; emanation, 21,10.13
enantion, opposite, 6,8.11; 14,23
enantiotês, opposition, 14,22
enantiousthai, have a contentious attitude, 24,20
endeiknusthai, demonstrate, 58,10–11
energeia, activity, 7,15; 12,11; 22,8–9; 38,22
energein, engage in acts, 14,5; activity, 17,6
en hêmin, up to us, 45,5–6
enkosmios, within the cosmos, 19,13
ennoein, have in mind, 32,14
ennoia, concept, 16,7; 18,3–4; 33,3; 40,20; 78,14
enokhlein, crowd, 40,4.6.7.14–15; 46,19

entheos, divinely inspired, 13,13.14.18.24; 14,17.20.26; 41,11; 47,16; 49,2.5

enthousiasmos, inspiration, 1,9; 2,2–13; 18,2

enthousiastikôs, in an inspired manner, 8,10–11

enudrios, watery, 19,15

epainos, praise, 24,3; 28,23; 29,12–17; 30,5.8.9.10; 32,6; 35,1.15

epamphoterizein, to say something ambiguous, 84,26

epanorthoun, heal, 6,8; 7,4

epeigein, be in a rush, 10,19

ephêbia, adolescence (status of an ephebe), 43,11.12

ephesis, drive, 33,10

eph' hêmin, up to us, 45,7

ephistasthai, preside over, 18,2

epideiknusthai, display, 58,14

epilusis, release, 40,12

epiorkein, swear falsely, 7,1; 55,6; 88,13.14.16.17.19

epiorkia, (false) oath, 55,8

epistêmê, knowledge, 24,11.14

epistrephein, revert, 9,7; 10,4.5; 14,18; 23,7

epistreptikos, tending to revert, 56,23

epistrophos, reverter, 2,16

epitêdeiotês, suitable attitude, 39,12.15; suitability, 47,23

epithumein, desire, 45,15

epithumia, appetite, appetitive desire, 2,48; 4,20; 6,4–5; 10,13; 33,11

epitropeuein, guard, 33,3

epitropos, guardian, 21,7; 32,1; 33,3

erân, love, 12,18

erastês, lover, 2,155; 12,19; 13,10.13.14.17.18.21.24; 14,3.4.10.17.20.21; 22,9; 25,8; 34,3.5.7.10.11.21; 35,13; 36,1; 37,4; 38,11; 40,8; 41,7.11.14.15; 42,3; 47,9.16.2.3.5.6; 52,14.17.20; 53,8; 67,13

erasthai, love, 3,13–15

eristikos, combative, 62,3

erômenos, beloved, 12,18; 28,19; 29,4

erôs, Love (god), 22,6.8.12; 87,5; love, 7,6; 14,24.25; 24,5

erôtikos, having the disposition of a lover, 12,20; about love, 13,12; 27,21

eskhatos, lowest, 14,5; 19,10; 38,14

êthikôs, on the (interpretive) level of ethics, 2,161; taking character into account, 34,1

eudaimonia, well-being, 10,15

eudokimein, held in high esteem, 20,5

euelpis, good hope, 27,21

euergetikos, beneficent, 21,3

eugeneia, good birth, 28,17; 31,15; 32,20

eukairia, good timing, 38,23; 39,6.7.15

euphuês, naturally gifted, 59,14; 70,8; 76,5; 78,1; 82,4

euphuïa, natural gifts, 89,11

eutunkhanein, succeed, 47,23–4

exairetos, important to pick out, 21,2

exaptein, fasten, 16,12; 17,5.8; 19,4.13

exêgêtês, commentator, 2,159–61; 9,23; 15,5; 22,14

exêgêtikos, (the view) adopted by the commentators, 9,22

exetazein, examine, 38,2

geloion, laughable, 10,19

genesis, becoming, 17,8

genos, parentage and life, 2,14; 3,1; race, 17,7.12; 24,8; genus, 23,17; class, 85,12–13; generation, 24,8; lineage, 29,1

geômetrês, geometer, 25,6–7

gnômôn, standard, 15,8

gnôsis, knowledge, 10,7; 11,11

gnôstikos, having the capacity for knowledge, 9,3; cognitive, 16,10; 23,16

grammikos, (geometer) of linear shapes, 25,6

gumnastikôs, performing athletically, 75,6

hamartanein, go wrong, 23,16; make a mistake, 72,12

hamartêma, error, 48,4

haphê, touch, 14,5

haplos, unambiguous, 84,25

haplôs, simply, 4,10; unqualifiedly, 4,16; 26,4; merely, 89,10

haptikôs, by means of touch, 40,8

heautos, oneself, one's own self, *passim*

heis, one, 25,8; 33,2

hêlikia, bloom of youth, 13,17

henas, unity, 44,9; 51,16

henoeidês, unitary in form, 51,17

henôsis, unity, 25,15; process of unification, 33,2

hêrôikos, heroic, 24,6

hêrôs, hero, 22,3.5

heterodidaktos, taught by another, 11,15

heterokinêsia, movement by another, 81,27

heterokinêtos, moved by another, 11,14; 82,6

heterokinêtôs, moved by another, 61,8; 63,13.21; 81,25

hexis, condition, 25,19

hikanos, sufficient, 42,19

holos, whole, 79,11-22

homilêtês, associate, 2,116

homoios, similar, 7,5

horkos, oath, 80,17

hulê, matter, 17,13; 19,4

hulôos, material, 19,4

huparxis, existence; in *kath' huparxin*, in existence, 15,13

huperbolê, superabundance, 14,24

hupêretês, servant, 31,17.19

huperkosmios, beyond the cosmos, 19,12

huperopsia, pride, 29,12

huperphronein, to look down on, 28,16; 29,11; 38,10; 42,3.14; 52,13-14; 67,13

hupostolê, roundabout way, 24,17

hupotartarios, under Tartarus, 19,15.17

iasis, remedy, 40,12

iatros, doctor, 12,10; 38,17

indalma, image, 10,9

kairos, opportunity, 39,7.8.11; right moment, 53,7

kakia, defectiveness of character, 10,15

kakodaimonia, ill-being, 10,15

kallos, beauty, 28,17

kalos, beautiful, 11,23; 14,19; 28,18.24; noble, 24,10; 32,2

kataphronein, scorn, 34,4.22; 42,6.8; 53,8; think little of, 43,4; 48,23; 52,15

kathartikos, purificatory person (person of purificatory excellence), 4,21; 5,1

kathartikôs, as a purificatory person, in a purificatory sense, 7,11; 8,7

katholou, universal, 77,22; 79.14.17.21; 82,14; 85,9; 89,14.16

katokhos, enchanted, 1,8

katoptron, mirror, 9,13

kephalaion, section, 11,7

khalepos, difficult, 41,24.25; 42,1; 48,13; onerous, 61,18.21.24; 62,1.2.4.6.7.16

khaunotês, conceit, 34,21

khorêgein, furnish abundantly, 47,22

khoros, chorus, 25,11.14

khrân, treat, 38,5-6

khrêsimon, usefulness, 9,22

khthonios, earthly, 19,9

khumos, humour, 18,13

kolasis, corrective treatment, 48,4

kolazein, give corrective treatment, 47,25; 55,7

korê, pupil, 7,15

koruphaios, leader of the [philosophical] chorus, 2,12; 40,18; 41,2; 47,5

krinein, form a judgement, 25,19

krisis, judgement, 41,11.18; 44,9; 47,18

ktêma, possession, 3,14

laburinthos, labyrinth, 48,19

lankhanein, obtain by lot, 20,3.5; 21,1.6.15; 22,14

logikos, rational, 4,18; 9,7.11; 17,13; 18,5; of words and ideas, 20,8; scientific (as opposed to empirical), 38,17

logoeidês, in common with reason, 38,4

logos, reason, 2,47; 38,18; 51,3; formula, 10,8; 15,11; 77,23; 79.13.14; 82,14; idea, 12,9; theory, 15,6; 53,11; words (of reason), 38,1-3.6; point, 52,8; speech, 56,15; explanation, 63,19

maia, midwife, 12,10.12

maieuein, practise midwifery, 79,24; 83,4

maieutês, midwife, 74,21

maieutikos, of midwifery, 11,8; 12,5

manthanein, learn, 37,21

mantikos, of prophecy, 69,21-70,4

mathêsis, learning, 11,11-12

megalaukhein, boast, 32,13

megalophronos, great-minded, 34,6.12

megalorrhêmonein, boast, 52,21; 53,7.9.17.22; 54,1.4; 55,24; 57,23; 58,18

megalosophrosunê, great-mindedness, 34,10

meiousthai, shrink, 18,14

meros, part, 79,12-22

mesos, intermediary, 17,9; 22,5.8
metabatikôs, in sequence, 78,27; 83,2
metameibein, exchange, 12,17
methodos, method, 24,14
monos, only, 25,9
mousikôs, performing musically, 75,7; 80,3

nama, fountain, 1,8
naupêgia, ship-building, 70,27–71,4; 76,9
neos, young man, 24,15.19; 33,15
noein, become intellectually aware, 5,7
noêma, thought, 44,2
noêros, intellective, 18,3
noêrôs, intellectively, 22,10
nous, intellect, 8,5; 17,13; 22,12.13; 79,2

ôidê, song, 75,8
oikeios, one's own, 15,16; appropriate, 24,4; 34,12; 39,10; 71,1; 79,1; 83,1; 87,17; dear to one's own heart, 26,10, 50,14; true, 43,26; proper, 72,8; rightly one's own, 74,5; relevant, 74,15.16.18.19; familiar, 77,8
oikodomia, house-building, 69,9–20
ôioeides, ovoid, 16,12
okhêma, vehicle, 5,9; 16,12; 17,4
okhlêsis, crowding, 40,15
okhlos, mob, 25,10.12; 40,7; 46,20
on, being, 10,7–11; 25,2
ophthalmos, eye, 7,13; 12,11
opôra, of the season, 31,10
oregesthai, reach out for, 1,4.7
orexis, motivation, 33,10
organon, instrument, 4,18
ostreïnos, shell-like, 16,11
ouranios, heavenly, 2,3; 9,7; 16,14; 17,2.6.10.11.12; 18,1.10–13; 19,5.7.8.11.14; 22,1
ousia, essence, 14,2; 17,1; 22,8; 70,24; in *kat'ousian*, essentially, 15,7; according to [their own] essence, 20,3.6

paidika, beloved, 4,5; 13,14; 41,24; 44,10; 49,6
panharmonios, embracing every [musical] mode, 2,163
parametrein, coordinate, 13,17
pathos, passion, 6,12.13; 27,15; disease (epilepsy), 18,6

pêgazein, stream with, 16,8
periousia, abundance, 32,9–10; 34,8
peristatikos, based on current affairs, 72,17–18; circumstantial, 77,13.19
phainesthai, appear, 2,39.49.142; 8,1; 11.18.21; 12,9; 25,4; 29,17; 32,12.15; 35,15; 42,10; 43,3; 47,1.2; 49,8; 54,4; 59,9.23; 84,2
phantasia, imagination, 8,14; 51,12.13; image, 23,8; 32,14; phantasm, 23,8; appearance, 61,12.13
pharmakon, medicine, 6,7
phasma, vision, 2,21
philêdonos, caring for pleasure, a pleasure-lover, 7,7; 10,13; 33,9.12; 38,13.14; 42,12; 47,1.4; 55,11; 61,11
philokhrêmatos, caring for money, a money-lover, 7,6; 33,9.11; 37,3; 38,12.13; 42,11.15.17; 46,6; 52,15; 55,10; 67,12; 81,16
philoneikos, enjoying conflict, 71,15–17
philotheamôn, sight-lover, 2,94
philotimia, care for reputation, 50,20; 51,1
philotimos, one who cares for reputation, a reputation-lover, 10,13; 23,21; 24,15; 31,3; 33,5.8.10; 38,15.16; 42,11; 43,3; 45,18; 50,20.26; 51,1.2.3.7.11; 61,11; 84,1
phoitân, study with or under (a teacher), 2,32.51; 64,4; 73,7; 87,21; 88,1.4.7.10; 89,3
phônê, utterance, 38,2–3
phortikos, crude, 13,13.14.17; 14,3.10; 34,7.11
phrourein, keep watch, 19,5
phusikos, natural, 30,4
phusikôs, on the (interpretive) level of natural philosophy, 2,161
phusiognômonikos, physiognomic signs (for evaluating character), 13,19
phusis, nature, 39,10; 67,11; 79,14
phutikos, vegetative, 9,4
plêmmelêma, error, 23,9
politeia, constitution, 75,22
politika, civic life, 6,2; civic affairs, 11,9.16
politikos, a civic person (person of civic excellence), 4,19; 11,22; statesman, 2,103; 32,2; 34,17; 56,4; 73,13

Index of Passages Cited

This index includes passages cited by Olympiodorus in the Greek text of this volume (1,3–90,24), where these are reasonably secure. The reader may turn to the Index of References in Westerink (1982) for a fuller list. References in bold type are to the page and line numbers of the Greek text (indicated in the margins of the Translation).

Index of Names and Places

References are to the page and line numbers of the Greek text (indicated in the margins of the translation).

Subject Index

References in bold type are to the page and line numbers of the Greek text.
Other references are to page numbers in the Introduction to this volume.

CPSIA information can be obtained
at www.ICGtesting.com
Printed in the USA
LVHW081046201218
601201LV00009B/704/P